Military Order
of the
Stars and Bars

Sixty-fifth Anniversary Edition
2003

TURNER PUBLISHING COMPANY

MILITARY ORDER OF THE STARS AND BARS

TURNER PUBLISHING COMPANY
Publishers of America's History

Publishing Consultant: Douglas W. Sikes
Designed by: Wilson D. Sikes

Author: Military Order of the Stars and Bars, Inc.
Copyright©2004 Military Order of the Stars and Bars, Inc.
All rights reserved
Publisher: Turner Publishing Company and Military Order of the Stars and Bars, Inc.
Publishing Rights: Military Order of the Stars and Bars, Inc.

This publication was produced using available and submitted materials. The author and the publisher regret they cannot assume liability for errors or omissions.

Library of Congress Catalog No. 2004111498
ISBN: 978-1-59652-033-2
LIMITED EDITION

Cover Illustrations: top - MOS&B seal; bottom - official seal of the United Confederate Veterans

Table of Contents

CONFEDERATE COMMANDERS
WITH COMPLIMENTS OF THE TRAVELERS INSURANCE COMPANY.

Acknowledgments

The Sixty-fifth Anniversary History Book of the Military Order of Stars and Bars is now a reality. Although all Departments, Societies, and Chapters did not take part in this project, I am pleased with the response of those who did participate.

Commander-General Jeffery Massey decided that an update of the "Sixtieth Anniversary History Book" was needed. After appointing me Editor, he gave his support in the production of this "Sixty-fifth Anniversary History Book" and has provided information about the "United Confederate Veterans".

A membership roster together with a chapter roster are vital parts of this sixty-fifth year issue. This data was made available thanks to the diligent support of Executive Director Ben C. Sewell, III and staff at International Headquarters. I am grateful to them for all their work to make this book a success.

The history of the MOS&B was prepared in part from information by Past Commander-General, Col. Lindsey P. Henderson, and other contributors to the "Fiftieth Anniversary Book." Additional information was obtained from the "Sixtieth Anniversary History Book" and many contributors, too numerous to mention. To these people, I am indebted.

Information provided by several Society and Chapter Commanders, and Past Commander-General Troy Massey have allowed us to feature some Real Sons in this book. I regret that all living Real Sons are not featured. Their number is growing smaller day by day.

My personal thanks goes to Associate Editor Charles Hawks who worked many long hours on this book, and with his vast knowledge of printing techniques and editing, provided the needed assistance to get this book to the publisher. Without his help this book would not have been finished.

A special thanks goes to Darwin Roseman whose computer expertise saved the day for us when we experienced problems. To everyone else who offered advice and furnished material for this publication, I say thank you.

I'm certain that in the years to come there will be another history book project. I entreat all future Commanders at all levels to work toward the preservation of their histories, so information will be readily available when needed for the next book.

I have enjoyed my work on this History Book and have enjoyed talking to so many of you about information for this book. Thanks to everyone.

DEO VINDICE

Daniel W Jones, Editor

The Military Order of the Stars & Bars

Toll Free 1-800-380-1896
Facsimile 615-381-6712
www.mosbihq.org

MOSB International Headquarters
P. O. Box 59
Columbia, TN 38402-0059

DEO VINDICE

April 3, 2004

Commander-General
Jeffery W. Massey, Esquire

Lt. Commander-General
Collin G. Pulley, Jr.

Adjutant General
K. Patrick Sohrwide

Chief of Staff
Curtis Hopper

Communications General
Editor – Officers Call
John L. Echols, Sr.

Communications General
Internet Services
Russell Lenzini

Judge Advocate General
Richard H. Knight, Jr., Esquire

Chaplain General
Rev. John Killian, Sr.

Parliamentarian
T. Tarry Beasley, II, Esquire

Genealogist General
Rodney P. Williams

Commissary General
Baron Fain IV

Historian General
George Perry

Quartermaster General
Jack Travis

Archivist General
Lamar Roberts

Surgeon General
Dr. Neal Pitts

Inspector General
Robert O. McLendon, Jr.

Sergeant-at-Arms
C. Wayne Coleman

Comptroller General
Albert D. Jones, Jr.

Chief Of Protocol
Edward O. Cailleteau

ANV Department Commander
A. Clarke Magruder, Sr.

ANV Executive Councilman
Larry E. Beeson

ATM Commander
Michael McCullah

ATM Executive Councilman
J. David Massey

AOT Department Commander
John T. Mason

AOT Executive Councilman
Dr. C. Fred McNary

**Past Commanders-In-Chief /
Commanders-General**
Albert D. Jones, Jr.
Joe B. Gay, III
J. Troy Massey
Perry J. Outlaw
Charles H. Smith
Robert L. Hawkins, III
Edward O. Cailleteau
John L. Echols, Sr.
Mark L. Cantrell, Esquire
Ronald T. Clemmons
Ralph W. Widener, Jr.
Frank E. La Rue, Jr.

Gentlemen of *The Order*:

It is with great affection and pleasure that I bring you greetings on this the eve of our 66th Reunion Convention. When those original Confederate Veterans joined together in 1938 to found the Order, their expectations lay in the charge to perpetuate history of the Confederate Officer Corps. Not out of pride, was the Order born, but out of reverence for the unique sacrifices those officers endured during the War and during Reconstruction. I have no doubt that those founders (Atkinson, Hancock, Hopkins, Claypool, Lee, Wood, Hume, etc.) are heartened by our continued adherence to their conservative principles and cultural philosophies.

The Order continues to focus upon our academic, cultural and literary responsibilities. Over the past decade the Order has provided over $25,000 in college-level scholarships for young Southerners. The *Gen. Robert E. Lee Scholarship*; the *Gen. Patrick R. Cleburne Scholarship* and the *Gen. Nathan B. Forrest Scholarship* are presented annually to deserving students. The *Henry Timrod Southern Culture Award* recognizes outstanding Southern cultural and artistic achievements. The Order recognizes the literary field thru the *John Esten Cooke Fiction Award*; the *Douglas Southall Freeman History Award*, *Gen. Basil Duke Award*, and *John Newman Edwards Media Award*. We pay tribute to unique public defenders of *The Cause* with the *Jefferson F. Davis Southern Heritage Award*.

We have created the *Confederate Legacy Endowment Fund* for those wishing to provide life gifts to MOSB. This fund will provide needed financial assistance for monument restoration, construction and preservation. It will also fund retrieval and historical archives of Confederate artifacts, along with developing the *General William D. McCain Library* at Elm Springs.

The Books for Beauvoir Campaign is assigned with obtaining over 1,000 books for the President Jefferson Davis Library at Beauvoir in Biloxi, Mississippi. This worthy effort is being supported by our numerous compatriots and chapters across the Order. The *Genealogy Committee* has undertaken an extensive automation of our application forms and procedures. We have developed the Order's first stand alone website (www.mosbihq.org) and have boldly charged into the 21st Century by providing membership forms "on-line." We have increased the distribution and effectiveness of our printed newsletter, *The Officers Call*. The publication of the 65th Anniversary Book has been a great task by Cmdr. Dan Jones and the NC Boys. I appreciate their tireless efforts.

Additionally the Order has aided in the restoration of Hilliard's Legion flag; restoration of the cemetery wall in Fayetteville; the Jefferson Davis Memorial project in Richmond; donations to the Museum of Confederacy; the Gen. McCain Library; the Confederate Memorial Hall in Oklahoma City and other worthy efforts around our great nation. Gentlemen, these are but a few of successful and worthy projects.

Finally, I have been blessed with so many talented and dedicated men and officers. I wish to thank each member of my General Staff, especially Chief of Staff Curtis Hopper, Dr. Fred McNary, Rodney Williams, Russ Lenzini (webmaster); financial stewards Jim Barr, JEB Stuart IV and Patrick Sohrwide. My thanks to JAG Knight, Pastor Killian and Brother Troy for keeping the Main Thing, The Main Thing. To Albert, Joe B, Perry, Bob, Ed, John, Charles, Beau and RT, my special thanks for your support and guidance. My deep appreciation to Executive Director Ben Sewell and the entire SCV/MOSB Headquarters staff. I salute you all and may God continue to Bless our Great Nation.

Jeffery W. Massey
Commander General   Addresses on Reverse Side

Established 1938

Lt. Commander General's Message

Lt. Commander-General
P. O. Box 189
Courtland, Virginia 23837

Gentlemen:

It is very fitting and appropriate to recognize the 65th anniversary of the Military Order of the Stars and Bars. To be associated with such a fine group of people, and to share our common heritage, is an honor. I always have a special feeling whenever I am at an MOS&B function, for I know that all of the men in the room share a common bond. We are all descended from the leaders of the Confederate States of America: those officers and governmental officials who took it upon themselves to bear the extra duties of leadership for their country.

As MOS&B members, we also take on an extra duty to honor our ancestors. Programs such as the MOS&B scholarships, the Jackson Medal for improving grave sites, the Henry Timrod Award for artistic excellence, and projects done by local chapters all promote the understanding of our Confederate heritage.

Membership in the Order is one of the best ways to honor and remember your officer ancestor and his service to his country.

Sincerely,

Collin G. Pulley, Jr.

Collin G. Pulley, Jr.

Military Order of the Stars and Bars

General Executive Council

Commander-General
Jeffery W. Massey, Esquire

Lt. Commander-General
Collin G. Pulley, Jr.

Adjutant General
K. Patrick Sohrwide

Chief of Staff
Curtis Hopper

Communications General
Editor-*Officers Call*
John L. Echols, Sr.

Communications General
Internet Services
Russell Lenzini

Judge Advocate General
Richard H. Knight, Jr., Esquire

Chaplain General
Rev. John Killian, Sr.

Parliamentarian
T. Tarry Beasley, II, Esquire

Genealogist General
Rodney P. Williams

Commissary General
Baron Fain IV

Historian General
George Perry

Quartermaster General
Jack Travis

Archivist General
Lamar Roberts

Surgeon General
Dr. Neal Pitts

Inspector General
Robert G. McLendon, Jr.

Sergeant-at-Arms
C. Wayne Coleman

Comptroller General
Albert D. Jones, Jr.

Chief of Protocol
Edward O. Cailleteau

ANV Department Commander
A. Clarke Magruder, Sr.

ANV Executive Councilman
Larry E. Beeson

ATM Commander
Michael McCullah

ATM Executive Councilman
J. David Massey

AOT Department Commander
John T. Mason

AOT Executive Councilman
Dr. C. Fred McNary

Past Commanders-in-Chief/
Commanders-General
Albert D. Jones, Jr.
Joe B. Gay, III
J. Troy Massey
Perry J. Outlaw
Charles H. Smith
Robert L. Hawkins, III
Edward O. Cailleteau
John L. Echols, Sr.
Mark L. Cantrell, Esquire
Ronald T. Clemmons
Ralph W. Widener, Jr.
Frank E. La Rue, Jr.

Current and Past Members of
MOS&B General Executive Council

L-R, Top: Cmdr. Rick Abell, ATM Councilman David Massey, Commander-General Jeffery W. Massey, Adjutant General Patrick Sohrwide, AOT Dept. Cmdr. John T. Mason, PCG Albert Jones, Cmdr. Daniel W. Jones, Lt. Commander-General Collin Pulley, Cmdr. Charles Britton. Seated: PCIC Charles Smith, Cmdr. Lynn Shaw, PCG Troy Massey, PCG Joe B. Gay.

Chief of Staff	**Adjutant General**	*ANV Executive*	*AOT Executive*
Curtis Hopper	K. Patrick Sohrwide	Councilman	Councilman
		Larry E. Beeson	Dr. C. Fred McNary

ALBERT D. JONES, JR.

COMMANDER-GENERAL MOS&B
2000-2002

Albert Dean Jones, Jr. was born July 11, 1946 in Henderson, NC, and was raised in Oxford, NC. He attended East Carolina University and served in the US Marine Corps as a sergeant with a tour in Vietnam. After finishing Hardbarger Business College, he married Denise Owens. Together, they raised a son, Brian, and a daughter, Kelly, while owning and managing a horse business.

After joining the Col. Henry King Burgwyn SCV Camp 1485 and the Capt. James I. Waddell MOSB Chapter in 1992, he began serving both the SCV and MOSB in the capacity of MOSB adjutant and the NCSCV Division as parliamentarian.

In 1995, after serving as NC Society Chief of Staff, he was elected NC Society Commander and served four years. After revamping the NC Society, he was elected ANV Committeeman in 1996; Lt. Commander General in 1998; and served as Commander-General in the years of 2000-2002.

Many new programs were started during his tenure, but the complete revamping of the scholarship program and the MOSB endowment fund were his favorite programs.

His MOSB awards include the Robert E. Lee Chalice, the Gold Star Award, the Distinguished Service Award, and the Meritorious Service Award. He also holds the title of Distinguished Commander. His SCV awards include the Distinguished Service Medal and the Commander-in-Chief's Award.

Past Commander-General Jones' current interests include restoration of an 1894 home, traveling, and local town politics.

JOE B. GAY, III

COMMANDER-GENERAL MOS&B
1998-2000

Joe B. Gay, III was born on August 13, 1929 in Franklin, Virginia and was educated at Virginia Polytechnic Institute (Business Administration) and Richmond Professional Institute (Business). He is married to Anne Pearson Franklin of Albertville, Alabama. They have one daughter, Ferreby Anne Sinclair, one son, Ashby Lee Gay, and one granddaughter, Sarah Ansley Sinclair.

Joe is retired from Union Camp Corporation and is president and owner of Franklin Lumber Sales Corporation in Franklin, Virginia.

He has been a member of the SCV since 1979 and is a Life Member. He is the Past Commander of both the Lee-Jackson Camp #1 in Richmond and the Urquhart-Gillette Camp #1471 in Franklin.

He has been a member of the MOSB since 1980 and is a Life Member. He is the Past Commander of the George E. Pickett Chapter in Richmond and the Virginia Society. He has served as the ANV Committeeman, Lt. Commander-General, and Commander-General.

He is also active in other organizations including: Sons of the American Revolution, Franklin Lodge #151 AF&AM, A&A Scottish Rite of Freemasonry, Nobles of Mystic Shrine, Franklin Shrine Club, Henry Lee Society, Stuart Mosby Society, Southampton Historical Society, Order of the Southern Cross, and the National Gavel Society.

JAMES TROY MASSEY
COMMANDER-IN-CHIEF, MOS&B
1996-1998

James Troy Massey was born March 27, 1955, at Harrison, AR, the son of Samuel A. Massey Jr. and Jo Ann O'Neal Massey. Graduated in 1973 from Marshall (AR) High School. In 1973 enrolled at the University of Arkansas. Later transferred and graduated from Arkansas Tech University in Russellville, AR, with a bachelor of science in parks and recreation administration, in 1977.

Joined SCV on Oct. 7, 1982, Headquarters Camp 584, in Hattiesburg, MS. Chartered General Jo Shelby Camp 1414, in Harrison, AR, on June 7, 1983. Joined MOS&B on July 7, 1983, in Headquarters Camp. Chartered Abner-Cone-Langston-Shaver-Wright Chapter in 1984 and renamed chapter in 1994 to Captain James Tyrie Wright Chapter.

Served SCV as charterer and first commander of General Jo Shelby Camp 1414, 1984; adjutant of camp since 1987; becoming a life member on July 8, 1985. Reactivated Arkansas Div. in 1983 and was commander from 1983-86. Has held the positions of adjutant, editor and Heritage Violations chairman on division level. Served as department adjutant, 1992-94; chief of protocol, 1994-96. Served as national historian-in-chief, 1992-96; and aide-de-camp; as well as committees on grave marking procedures and the 100th reunion.

Served MOS&B as charterer and first commander of Abner-Cone-Langston Shaver-Wright Chapter, 1984; adjutant since 1988; becoming a life member on July 8, 1985. Established the Arkansas Society in 1984 and became first commander; adjutant since 1986. Served the department as commander of Trans-Mississippi, 1994-96. Also served at the national level as historian-general, 1986-88; quartermaster-general, 1992-94; and aide-de-camp twice.

Recipient of SCV's national Commander-in-Chief's Award, 1983; Citation for Distinguished Service, 1984; Dixie Club (3), Citation for Meritorious Service, 1985; Citation for Meritorious Service, 1989; Gold Medal Award, 1986; Citation for Distinguished Service, 1996. On the division level he received the Thomas C. Hindman Award, 1984, and the Patrick C. Cleburne Award, 1984.

Recipient of MOS&B's National Rebel Club (3); Gold Star Award, 1984; Merit Award 1985 and 1986; Commander-in-Chief's Award, 1986 and 1988; Lt. Charles S. Read Merit Award, 1987; Colonel John Pelham Legion of Merit Award, 1989 and 1995; and the society Certificate of Commendation, 1995. He first joined Wiggin's Btry., Arkansas Horse Arty., Reenacting Unit and was elected 1st sergeant. Presently a captain in Hughey's Btry., 8th Arkansas Field Arty., CSA.

Married Beverly Jean Campbell, daughter of N.F. Campbell Jr. and Virginia Williams Campbell, on Dec. 20, 1975, at Marshall, AR. They have one child, Whitney Brooke Massey, born Oct. 4, 1979, in Harrison, AR. After graduation from college in 1977, Troy worked for the summer as a seasonal park ranger at Pea Ridge National Military Park in Pea Ridge, AR. His first and only full-time job since graduation has been as a claims representative for Arkansas Farm Bureau Insurance Co. in Harrison, AR. He is a member of the following: Kiwanis Club of Harrison since 1978, elected as president in 1987-88, lieutenant governor in 1993 and various committee chairmanships; Boone County Historical Society; Consolidated Youth of Harrison, president in 1981-87 and board of directors; SAR, president 1995-present; Boone County United Way Fund; Boone County Lodge F&AM 314, in Harrison, AR, and Campbell Lodge F&AM 115, in Marshall, AR; Scimitar Shrine Temple, Little Rock, AR; Ozark Shrine Club, Harrison, AR, president 1987, secretary/treasurer, 1996; Scottish Rite Temple, Little Rock, AR; and York Rite, Huntsville, AR.

PERRY J. OUTLAW

COMMANDER-IN-CHIEF, MOS&B
1994-1996

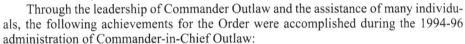

Perry James Outlaw was born August 19, 1941 in Jackson, Alabama. He received his BS degree in 1963 and his MA in 1965 from Auburn University. He joined the Raphael Semmes Camp II SCV, Mobile, Alabama in 1972 and joined the Franklin Buchanan Chapter 2297 MOSB, Mobile, Alabama in 1983.

Offices held include: Chapter-Editor, Adjutant, Commander, Society-Editor, Adjutant, Lt. Commander, Commander, Army-Lt. Commander, Commander, National-Lt. Commander-in-Chief, Commander-in-Chief

Awards include the Distinguished Commander Status, AOT Gold Star Award, 1994 and Robert E. Lee Chalice, 1996.

Through the leadership of Commander Outlaw and the assistance of many individuals, the following achievements for the Order were accomplished during the 1994-96 administration of Commander-in-Chief Outlaw:

1. Establishment of MOS&B Rituals, i.e., Pledge of the MOS&B, MOS&B Benediction, MOS&B Roll of Honor, MOS&B Memorial Service, MOS&B Graveside Service for Departed Members.

2. Billfold size copies of Pledge and Benediction for distribution to renewal and new members.

3. Establishment of Basil W. Duke Literary Award for republished books.

4. Small size Membership Certificates distributed free to new members.

5. Publication of Volume I of The Papers of the MOS&B

6. Creation of special neck ribbon for Society Commanders.

7. Placement of framed exhibit of MOS&B medals for display at MOS&B HQ.

8. Bar added to MOS&B Membership Medal designating years of service.

9. Bar added to MOS&B War Service Medal to indicate specific war service.

10. Establish annual placement of MOS&B wreath at grave of President Jefferson Davis.

11. Approval for following new awards: Lt. Simeon W. Cummings Award (for grave marking of Confederate officers), Lt. Gen. Simon Bolivar Buckner Chapter Retention Award, Gen. William D. McCain Society Recruiting Award, Lt. Homer Atkinson Award (Army Department with most new chapters) and the MOS&B Military Service Medal (military service without a combat roll).

12. Reorganization of MOS&B records and placement in filing cabinets.

13. Re-establish funding for MOS&B scholarship program.

14. Establish separate account for life membership dues.

15. Providing chapters-societies with opportunity to be placed under the IRS tax umbrella coverage of the General Society.

16. Secure deed for the MOS&B 1/10 ownership of "Elm Springs" and the original property purchase.

17. Re-establish the registration of the MOS&B service mark with the US Patent Office.

18. Secure set of the Confederate Military History for MOS&B HQ.

19. Preparation of extended listing of suggested activities for chapter-society activities.

20. Grant money provided to Army Department Commanders to assist in funding department activities.

Married to Harriet B. Outlaw, Commander Outlaw and his wife have six children and six grandchildren. He has been a teacher, coach and school administrator and retired in 1992 with 29 years of service. He has also retired from the Alabama National Guard with 21 years of service. He is a member of the United Methodist Church.

CHARLES HERBERT SMITH

COMMANDER-IN-CHIEF, MOS&B
1992-1994

Charles Herbert Smith was born Oct. 12, 1934, in Sabetha, KS. He grew up in central Oklahoma where his grandfather had homesteaded in 1889. Graduated from Oklahoma State University, 1958, with a bachelor of fine arts. He was head of Graphics Dept. for the FAA and retired in October 1988. He formed and currently operates his own company, CSA Graphic Communicators, Yukon, OK. Military service with 13th Cav., 1st Armored Div., US Army.

He married Carolyn Holliman in 1967. He has two children, Charles Michael Burton (a 1994 graduate of OSU) and Michelle Elizabeth Susan (a sophomore at OSU). He enjoys firearms, hunting, re-enactment and speaking.

Smith became a charter member of Brigadier General Stand Watie Camp 1303 in February 1970 and was later elected to two terms as Oklahoma Div. commander, 1989 and 1990. Other offices include commander, Trans-Mississippi Dept.; SCV chief of staff; and commander-in-chief. In 1978 he organized Brigadier General Douglas H. Cooper Chapter for MOS&B and was elected first chapter commander. He was elected lieutenant commander-in-chief and commander-in-chief in 1990. His MOS&B awards include the Robert E. Lee Chalice, Gold Award, Distinguished Service Medal and Meritorious Service Medal. He established the *Rebel Yell,* monthly newsletter of Camp 1303. It is currently the oldest camp newsletter in the SCV and has won nine First Place awards. As department commander, he assisted Col. Joseph B. Mitchell in re-writing SCV Constitution and again later for the MOS&B; as commander-in-chief, he led an aggressive campaign to establish a national headquarters and directed re-establishment of the *Confederate Veteran* publication for the membership. He designed the General Staff Medal for SCV.

Past CIC Smith currently serves as the Executive Director of the Oklahoma Rifle Association of the Oklahoma NRA.

ROBERT L. HAWKINS, III

COMMANDER-IN-CHIEF, MOS&B
1990-1992

Robert L. Hawkins, III, was born Randolph County, MO, April 7, 1951, educated Westminster College, Central Missouri State University, University of Missouri School of Law. Member of M.M. Parsons Camp 718; J.S. Marmaduke Chapter, MOS&B; life member, SCV and MOS&B; commander-in-chief, SCV (1992-94), MOS&B (1990-92); Society of the Order of the Southern Cross; Forrest Cavalry Corps; Morgan's Men Assoc.; Confederate Historical Assoc. of Belgium. Awards: O'Connor Missouri Silver Star (1995), Robert E. Lee Chalice (1993), Jefferson Davis Chalice (1994), George Graham Vest Oratorical (1995), John Randolph of Roanoke Oratorical (1995). Directed funerals of W.C. Quantrill (1992) and Jesse James (1995).

EDWARD OVERTON CAILLETEAU
Commander-in-Chief, MOS&B
1988-1990

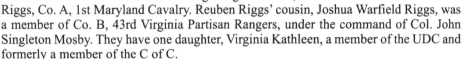

Edward Overton Cailleteau was born on December 15, 1945 in Baton Rouge, Louisiana. He is the son of the late Dr. and Mrs. Edward Grant Cailleteau and grandson of the late Dr. and Mrs. Ralph C. Cailleteau and the late U.S. Senator and Mrs. John Holmes Overton, all of Alexandria, Louisiana.

He was educated in the public schools of East Baton Rouge Parish with the exception of one year at Jefferson Military College, Washington, MS. He graduated from Louisiana State University with a B.S. degree in 1970. He majored in History.

In 1974 he married the former Virginia Riggs of Mobile, a member of UDC on the Record of her great-grandfather, Reuben Riggs, Co. A, 1st Maryland Cavalry. Reuben Riggs' cousin, Joshua Warfield Riggs, was a member of Co. B, 43rd Virginia Partisan Rangers, under the command of Col. John Singleton Mosby. They have one daughter, Virginia Kathleen, a member of the UDC and formerly a member of the C of C.

Cailleteau joined SCV and MOS&B in 1979. Originally a member of Headquarters Camp 584 and the General Society, MOS&B, he assisted in the organization of the Louisiana Society, MOS&B and affiliated with the Francis T. Nicholls Camp No. 1362 in Baton Rouge. Cailleteau was instrumental in the organization of SCV Camps in New Orleans, Lafayette and Monroe, and MOS&B Chapters in New Orleans, Baton Rouge and Lafayette. He transferred his SCV membership to the Colonel Charles D. Dreux Camp No. 110 in New Orleans in 1986. He is a member of the Maj. Gen. Earl Van Dorn Chapter, MOS&B, also in New Orleans.

In MOS&B, Cailleteau was Commander-in-Chief (1988-90); Commander of the Trans-Mississippi Department (1985-86); Chief of Staff (1984-86); Parliamentarian (1986-88); Commander, Louisiana Society (1980-83); and Adjutant, Louisiana Society (1979-80 and 1989-present).

In SCV, Cailleteau has served as Commander, Army of the Trans-Mississippi Department (1986-88); Commander, Louisiana Division (1984-86); and Adjutant, Louisiana Division (1986-88). He has served as Parliamentarian of the SCV under five Commanders-inChief and, as acting Parliamentarian under two Commanders-in-Chief. Cailleteau was put in the Chair and presided over the General Convention in Columbus, GA in 1991 when the motion was made, discussed and voted on to purchase Elm Springs at Columbia, TN to serve as the Permanent Headquarters.

Cailleteau established the Louisiana True Delta Division newsletter and edited same from 1984 to 1986 and again from 1995 to 2001.

Cailleteau is a member of Society of the Cincinnati, Sons of the American Revolution, Society of Colonial Wars, Society of the War of 1812, Society of the Sons and Daughters of the Founders of the City of New Orleans, Society of the Sons and Daughters of the Pilgrims, First Families of Tennessee and Founders of Old Mobile Society.

JOHN LYNN ECHOLS, SR.

COMMANDER-IN-CHIEF, MOS&B
1986-1988

Born May 15, 1941 in Memphis, Tennessee, Echols has been a resident of Southaven, Mississippi since 1971. He has been married to Paula Cantrell Echols since May 1963. They have two sons, John Lynn, Jr. and Paul Maitland. John Jr. has been a member of the SCV since 1976. John, Sr. has three grandchildren, Stacey Echols Brown, Justin Woodrow Echols, and Jacob Andrew Echols. He also has one great grandson, Dalton Brown.

Having served in the U. S. Air Force from 1959 to 1961, Echols was Honorably Discharged, and began a 24-year career in the bill collection business. In 1985, he resigned his management position with a corporation in Memphis, and became a college freshman. Having earned an Associate in Education Degree from Northwest Mississippi Community College in 1987, and a Bachelor of Arts Degree in Secondary Education, Summa Cum Laude, from the University of Mississippi in 1989, he began teaching at Southaven High School. He currently teaches U. S History at Southaven High, and proudly displays pictures of President Jefferson Davis and General Robert E. Lee in his classroom.

Echols joined the Sons of Confederate Veterans in August 1965 on the record of Private W. B. Mills, Co. E, 41st Mississippi Infantry, and the Order of the Stars and Bars in September 1971 on the record of Captain James Shelby Lauderdale, 10th Texas Infantry. He is proud to have thirteen other ancestors who wore the Gray.

Since 1971, Echols has held numerous offices in both organizations. In the SCV, he has served as Commander of the N. B. Forrest Camp 215, and James R. Chalmers Camp 1312, both in Memphis, and in the Capt. Edward W. Ward Camp 1452, Southaven. He has served as Commander, Army of Tennessee Department, SCV, as well as Lt. Commander, Tennessee Division, and Commander, Mississippi Division. In addition, he has served on the national staffs of SCV CICs. In the MOSB, he served as National Commander-in-Chief from 1986-1988, as well as Society Commander of both the Mississippi Society and Tennessee Society. He currently serves as editor of various newsletters: *The Southern Comfort,* newsletter of the Capt. Edward W. Ward Camp since 1975, *the Officer's Call,* national newsletter of the MOSB, *the Jeff Davis Legion*, newsletter of the Mississippi Division, SCV, and the *Stars and Bars*, newsletter of the Mississippi Society, MOSB.

Echols has been a member of the Board of Trustees, Beauvoir, Jefferson Davis Home and President Library in Biloxi for 15 years. He currently serves as the Secretary of the Combined Boards of Beauvoir.

He has been the fortunate recipient of recognitions by both these organizations, as well as the United Daughters of the Confederacy, Children of the Confederacy, and Boy Scouts of America.

MARK LEA (BEAU) CANTRELL

COMMANDER-IN-CHIEF, MOS&B
1984-1986

Mark Lea (Beau) Cantrell, the twentieth Commander-in-Chief of the Order, was born March 29, 1951, in Perryton, the county seat of Ochiltree County, Texas, of Virginia M. Cantrell by Donald D. Cantrell. Cdr. Cantrell's mother is a great-granddaughter of James Alfred Estill, 14th Kentucky Cavalry, Morgan's Brigade. His father was the great nephew of Pvt. C.A. Gunn and Capt. Nicholos Gunn Matlock, Co. B., Perkin's Battalion, Missouri Cavalry.

Raised in Texas County of the Oklahoma Panhandle, Beau graduated from high school at New Mexico Military Institute, Roswell, New Mexico, in 1969. After completing a term at the University of Exeter, England, he returned to the New Mexico Military Institute where he took an AA in 1971; a BA from the University of Oklahoma in 1973 in history and political science; a Juris Doctor from the OU College of Law in 1976. Following a brief stint in the office of Oklahoma Attorney General Larry Derryberry in 1977, he has engaged in the private practice of law in El Reno, Oklahoma, from 1977 to the present time.

A member of the U.S. Marine Corps Reserve from 1970-1973, Cdr. Cantrell served as Assistant Staff Judge Advocate of the 45th Infantry Brigade (Separate) OKARNG. While assigned to detached duty in the field in Honduras with A Battery, 160th Field Artillery, Capt. Cantrell was awarded the "Order of St. Barbara" by the Republic of Honduras in the fall of 1986.

Professionally Beau has served as a member of the Ethics Committee, Okla. Bar Association; member of the Board of Directors, Okla. Criminal Defense Lawyers Association; and was a Special Counsel to the Office of the Oklahoma State Treasurer.

Recruited into the SCV in 1973 by his cousin, the late Rev. Hale Bicknell, Jr., former MOSB Chaplain General, Beau joined Brig. Gen. Stand Watie Camp No. 1303, Oklahoma City, and then became a charter member of the Pickens Co. - Chickasaw Nat. Camp No. 1406, Ardmore; R.A. Sneed Camp No.1417, Oklahoma City; Brig. Gen. Albert Pike Camp No.1367, El Reno. He served as commander, Oklahoma Division, from 1977 to 1981. Cdr. Cantrell served as Executive Councilman from the Department of the Army of the Trans-Mississippi on the S.C.V. Executive Council 2002-2004.

Recruited into the MOSB by Commander General Ralph W. Widener, Jr., Beau served as Executive Councilman from 1978 to 1982; Commander, Indian Territory Society from 1981 to 1982; was elected Lt. Commander-in-Chief of the Order in 1982 in Oklahoma City. During the General Convention in Biloxi, Miss., 1984, he was elected the twentieth Commander-in-Chief of MOSB. He was named recipient of the "Robert E. Lee Chalice," the Order's highest award in 1985. He is also a Founding Life Charter Member of the Forrest Cavalry Corps, and Beau has served as the General Commander of the Forrest Cavalry Corps since 1998.

Active in living history, Beau is a founding member of Brig. Gen. Albert Pike Camp No. 1367's re-enactment battery, "Howell's Texas Battery - 11th Texas Light Artillery Battalion, C.S.A.", and has served in the Battery as a private - "No. 1 " - since the founding of the unit in 1979.

Cdr. Cantrell has served as Curator, Confederate Memorial Hall, Oklahoma Historical, since 1980; and Beau has served concurrently as Curator, Union Memorial Hall, O.H.S., since 2002; and as an advisor to the Honey Springs Battlefield Commission since 1987. Mark Lea is the co-author of the book, *Kepis & Turkey Calls; An Anthology of the War Between the States In Indian Territory.*

A communicant of Wesley United Methodist Church of El Reno, Oklahoma, Beau served as Scoutmaster to Troop 388, B. S.A., sponsored by Wesley from 1983 through 1994. Beau also served as Wesley's Administrative Board and Finance Committee, and currently serves on the Church's Bequests & Memorials Committee.

Married to Phyllis Petree Cantrell, they share a family consisting of Zackery Lamarr Hines and wife Melissa of Yukon, Oklahoma; Jeffrey C. Hines and wife Heidi and daughter Haley of Pensacola, Florida; daughter Samantha Houston Gunn Cantrell, and son, Donald Lea Petree Estill Cantrell, twins, who are sophomores enrolled in the University of Oklahoma.

Commanders-General / Commanders-in-Chief

1938-45	Gen. Homer Atkinson, VA
1945-48	Dr George Bolling Lee, DC
1948-53	W. Scott Hancock, MO
1953-54	Dr William R. Dancy, GA
1954-57	Donald B. Todd, TN
1957-59	J. Kyle Senter, TN
1959-61	Alvis I. Downs, TN
1961-63	Frank E. LaRue Jr., TX
1963-64	Col. John Amasa May, SC
1964-66	Tom White Crigler Jr., MS
1966-68	S. Wayne Van Zandt, AR
1968-70	Dr. James M. Edwards, GA
1970-72	H. Paul Porter, VA
1972-74	Dr. Laurence M. Oden, MS
1974-76	Dennis W. Rainocheck, TX
1976-78	Col. Lindsey P. Henderson Jr., GA
1978-80	Dr. Ralph W. Widener Jr., TX
1980-82	John E. Hunter, TX
1982-84	Ronald T. Clemmons, TN
1984-86	Mark Lea "Beau" Cantrell, OK
1986-88	John L. Echols Sr., MS
1988-90	Edward Overton Cailleteau, LA
1990-92	Robert L. Hawkins III, MO
1992-94	Charles H. Smith, OK
1994-96	Perry J. Outlaw, AL
1996-98	James Troy Massey, AR
1998-00	Joe B. Gay, III, VA
2000-02	Albert D. Jones, Jr., NC
2002-04	Jeffery W. Massey, OK

Early Leaders

Gen. Homer Atkins
CIC-UCV 1932-34 & 1936-37
First CIC-OSB 1938-45

Col. Walter L. Hopkins
CIC-SCV, Colonel, Asst. Adj. Gen.,
Maintained records of UCV, SCV, and OSB

John M. Claypool
CIC-UCV (twice) 1937-38 & 1941-42

O.R. Gellatte
Adj. General-OSB 1943-44

Early Leaders

Hon. W. Scott Hancock
Third CIC-MOSB 1945-50

Dr. George Bolling Lee
(Grandson of R.E. Lee)
CIC 1945-48

Dr. William R. Dancy
Fourth CIC-MOSB 1953-54

William Morrison Wood
Adj. General-OSB 19??-43

Organization and History of the Military Order of the Stars and Bars

The success of the organization known as the United Confederate Veterans, whose membership was composed of men who served in the Armed Forces of the Confederate States of America, and who fought not for a price but a principle, and the success of the organization known as the Sons of Confederate Veterans, whose membership is restricted to the male descendants of Confederate Veterans, prompted General Homer Atkinson and a few of his intimate friends to formulate plans to organize a society whose membership would be restricted to those who had served as commissioned officers in the Armed Forces of the Confederate States of America, and their male descendants.

Accordingly, a temporary committee was selected with General Homer Atkinson the chairman. General Atkinson was empowered to contact the living commissioned officers of the Armed Forces of the Confederate States of America, and to send an invitation to the male descendants of commissioned officers of the Armed Forces of the Confederate States of America to meet in Columbia, South Carolina, August 30, 1938, for the purpose of establishing a permanent organization of those eligible for membership.

At 3:00 p.m., on the above mentioned date, in the Jefferson Hotel, Columbia, South Carolina, a total of 17 former officers of the Armed Forces of the Confederate States of America and 47 male descendants of commissioned officers in the Armed Forces of the Confederate States of America were present.

Those present were unanimous in voting that such a society should be organized immediately and the annual meetings should be held at the same time and the same place as the United Confederate Veterans and the Sons of Confederate Veterans.

General Homer Atkinson was elected temporary chairman. In a lengthy discussion of the plans of the Society, it was decided that there would be two types of memberships: Those who had served as commissioned officers in the Armed Forces of the Confederate States of America would be known as original members, and the male descendants of a commissioned officer who had served in the Armed Forces of the Confederate States of America would be known as hereditary members.

The name, Order of the Stars and Bars, was suggested by Clement Wood of New York, an hereditary member who had been an ardent supporter of the United Confederate Veterans and a dedicated member of the Sons of Confederate Veterans. Colonel Walter R. Hopkins, a hereditary member from Richmond, Virginia, was elected Assistant Adjutant-General of the Society. Colonel Hopkins was an attorney-at-law and drafted the first constitution and bylaws of the Society.

The membership certificate was designed by Lieutenant Colonel Edgar Erskine Hume of Carlisle, Pennsylvania, a hereditary member of the Society.

The original insignia of the Society and the Southern Cross of Military Service was designed by John L. Strohl II, of Mt. Morris, New York, a hereditary member.

At the 39th annual meeting of the Order of Stars and Bars in Memphis, Tennessee, the constitution was amended, and the name of the Society was changed to Military Order of the Stars and Bars, effective August 15, 1976.

The Constitution was also amended to provide that the Stars and Bars, the first National Flag of the Confederate States of America, would be the insignia and that the commander's title would be Commander General.

The Military Order of Stars and Bars entered into the purchase of Elm Springs with the Sons of Confederate Veterans and obtained a 10 percent undivided interest in the house and the original purchase of land in December 1991. The Military Order of Stars and Bars pays an annual fee for the upkeep of Elm Springs and operates its national headquarters at that site. Due to delays it was not until June 9, 1995, that the Military Order of Stars and Bars ownership of Elm Springs was conveyed and recorded at Maury County Courthouse.

From Its start, the Military Order of Stars and Bars has held to its founding principles to honor the Confederate soldier and the Confederate Officer Corps.

Original Members

The following are the original members and the hereditary members elected at the meeting in Columbia, South Carolina on August 3O, 1938 in chronological order:

I -0 General Homer Atkinson was elected commander-in-chief of the Order of the Stars and Bars and served until his death March 31,1945. He served as Commander-in Chief of the United Confederate Veterans from 1932-1934 and 1936-1937. For several years he served as the Commander, Army of Northern Virginia, United Confederate Veterans, and was the senior officer of the United Confederate Veterans. The service record of General Homer Atkinson is as follows: Joined Harris 19th Mississippi Brigade, 39th Battalion, Company B, and soon thereafter won a battlefield commission as a second lieutenant. He took part in the Battle of Rivers Farm, in which battle he was captured. However, in the confusion of the battle, he eluded his captors and rejoined his company. Later he was in the Battle of Fort Gregg, where he was made acting captain of his company, and on April 2,1865, he was captured, being then 17 years of age. The few remaining days of the war were spent in a Yankee prison. On April 9, 1865, General Lee surrendered to General Grant at the McLean House at Appomattox, and on April 19, General Atkinson was given parole at City Point. He is buried in Blandford Cemetery, Petersburg, Virginia.

2-0 Captain Samuel A. Ashe, Raleigh, North Carolina, was the last officer commissioned by President Jefferson Davis in the Army of the Confederate States of America. He was elected Vice-Commander-in-Chief of the Order of the Stars and Bars on August 30, 1938. His death occurred the following day, August 31, 1938, in Columbia, South Carolina.

3-0 Captain J. Andrew Jackson Dowdy of the Texas Rangers, Seagoville, Texas.

4-0 Lieutenant Benjamin M. Robinson, Orlando, Florida.

5-0 Lieutenant Wyatt T. Hill died October 4, 1938, just two months after the meeting in Columbia, South Carolina.

6-0 Lieutenant J. Peter Keyser, Rileyville, Virginia, died January 4, 1939, four months after the meeting in Columbia, South Carolina.

7-0 Lieutenant James A. Lowry, Mt. Verde, Florida.

8-0 Colonel James M. Stewart, Little Rock, Arkansas.

9-0 Cadet William Morrison Wood was elected Adjutant-General of the Order of the Stars and Bars and served until his death in Old Hickory, Tennessee, March 2, 1943. He was the last surviving Cadet of the Virginia Military Institute that fought in the Battle of New Market. A member of Company A2.

10-0 Major O. Richard Gellette, Shreveport, Louisiana, was an active and dedicated member of the United Confederate Veterans. He contributed much to the success of the Order of the Stars and Bars and was elected Adjutant-General to succeed General Wood. He served in this office until his death on June 6, 1944.

11-0 Major Stephen Peters Halsey, Lynchburg, Virginia, died five months after the meeting in Columbia, South Carolina on March 1, 1939.

12-0 Lieutenant William McKendree Evans, Richmond, Virginia, had a long and useful career in the United Confederate Veterans. His career was brief in the Order of the Stars and Bars as his death occurred on October 23, 1939. Born in Richmond, Virginia on February 1, 1847, he was a member of a boy's company, the Junior Volunteers, attached to the First Virginia Infantry, from January 1861 to April 18, 1862. He entered Parker's Battery, General Stephen D. Lee's Artillery Department, General Longstreet's Corps, in which he served throughout the war. He was discharged from Point Lookout Prison on June 22, 1865.

13-0 Cadet Carter R. Bishop, Petersburg, Florida.

14-0 Lieutenant Noah Brock was born in Darlington, Indiana, served with Company B, 13th Battalion, North Carolina Cavalry. He was the oldest member present at the meeting in Columbia, South Carolina, being 101 years of age.

15-0 Captain Holland M. Bell, Fayette, Alabama.

Hereditary Members

1. Colonel Walter L. Hopkins was elected Assistant Adjutant-General and upon the death of General John M. Claypool on June 11,1945, he succeeded to the office of Adjutant-General, Richmond, Virginia.
2. W. Scott Hancock, St. Louis, Missouri.
3. Dr. William B. Hopkins, Tampa, Florida.
4. Judge Earl E. Hurt, Dallas, Texas.
5. William O. Smith, Dallas, Texas.
6. Colonel Joseph Wheeler Jr., Wheeler, Alabama.
7. Dr. George Tabor, Oklahoma City, Oklahoma.
8. Dr. James V. Johnson, Miami, Florida.
9. Colonel Carleton B. Cunningham, Chicago, Illinois.
10. Samuel D.D. Deford, Richmond, Virginia.
11. Colonel William Preston Wooten, Washington, DC.
12. Dr. Baylis H. Earle, Greenville, South Carolina.
13, Clement Wood, Delanson, New York.
14. Albert C. McDavid Sr., San Antonio, Texas.
15. James Gardner, Augusta, Georgia.
16. Colonel C. Bascom Slep, Brigstone Gay, Virginia.
17. Charles Pickett, Fairfax, Virginia.
18. Clifton Ratlif, Oklahoma City, Oklahoma.
19. Colonel William W. Old Jr., Norfolk, Virginia.
20. Colonel Robert T. Barton, Richmond, Virginia.
21. William Latta Law Jr., Richmond, Virginia.
22. Henry Taylor Wickham, Ashland, Virginia.
23. Reverend W.H.T. Squires, Norfolk, Virginia.
24. Dr. George Bolling Lee, a grandson of General Robert E. Lee, was elected a Vice Commander and was elevated to the office of Commander-in-Chief to succeed General Homer Atkinson on March 31, 1945. New York City, New York.
25. General Hierome L. Opie, Staunton, Virginia.
26. General B. Frank Cheatham, Stratford, Virginia.
27. Dr. William R. Dancy, Savannah, Georgia.
28. Ernest M. Green, Raleigh, North Carolina.
29. Wayne James Holman Jr., Paris, Tennessee.
30. Hubert Thomison Hohnan, Fayetteville, Tennessee.
31. Roger D. Wharton, Manassas, Virginia.
32. Douglas Wherry, Richmond, Virginia.
33. Major Jere C. Dennis, Dadeville, Alabama.
34. James d'Alvigny McCullough, Honea Path, South Carolina.
35. James Sulliavan Bond, Savannah, Georgia.
36. Oliver B. Burroughs Jr., Augusta, Georgia.

37. Judge Thomas Simmons, Fort Worth, Texas.

38. J. Milton Bailey, Penland, North Carolina.

39. Theodore L. Lesley, Tampa, Florida.

40. Howard P. Wright, Atlanta, Georgia.

41. Colonel James Douglas McLean, Quantico, Virginia.

42. Thomas E. Powe, St. Louis, Missouri.

43. Walker Kirtland Hancock, Gloucester, Mississippi.

44. Harrison Tilghman, Easton, Maryland.

45. Lieutenant Colonel Edgar Erskine Hume, Carlisle, Pennsylvania.

46. John Ashely Jones, Atlanta, Georgia.

47. Judge Alexander W. Stephens, Atlanta, Georgia.

General John M. Claypool was present at the meeting of the Order of the Stars and Bars but did not submit his application for membership for the reason that he was serving as the Commander-in-Chief, United Confederate Veterans, 1937-1938. After his term of office expired, General Claypool submitted his application for membership in the Order of the Stars and Bars and soon became one of its most faithful members. He was again elected Commander-in-Chief of the United Confederate Veterans in 1941 - 1942, and served with honor and distinction.

The service record of General John M. Claypool in the Army of the Confederate States of America is one of valor and devotion to duty. He was born in Nichols County, Kentucky on July 23, 1846. He enlisted in Company E of the 47th Tennessee at Georgetown, Kentucky in September 1862. He served one year and received an honorable discharge due to extreme youth. In 1863 he re-enlisted in the same company, same regiment, which regiment was consolidated with the 12th Tennessee, Company E becoming Company H.

He participated in the Battle of Perryville, Kentucky, and subsequently was wounded in the Battle of Murfreesboro, Tennessee. He participated in the battles from Chickamauga to Atlanta in 1864. He was slightly wounded in Chickamauga. In the Battle of Franklin he was severely wounded and left on the battlefield for two days until taken prisoner. After he was hospitalized he was sent to Camp Chase, Columbus, Ohio. At the close of the war he was paroled at Augusta, Georgia. Having attained the rank of Lieutenant General, John M. Claypool was active in the affairs of Confederate Veterans.

He was one of the Founders of the Order of the Stars and Bars and at the time of his death, which occurred on June 11,1945, he was the Adjutant General of the Order of the Stars and Bars.

He was the last surviving officer of the Armed Forces of the Confederate States of America.

Principles and Purposes

Military Order of the Stars and Bars

Section 1. The General Society shall be literary, historical, benevolent, patriotic, educational and non-political. It shall strive:

a. To cultivate the ties of friendships among descendants of those who shared the responsibilities of Southern leadership in the War Between The States.

b. To provide leadership in the collecting and assembling of data, documents and materials relating to the Confederacy; however, the organization should also preserve the history of the Colonial and Federal periods of our history since the antecedents of The War Between the States are to be found in these periods.

c. To provide for future generations of the descendants of Confederate officers and civilian officials in the Executive and Legislative branches of government an organization to commemorate and honor the leadership of their forefathers.

d. To consecrate in our hearts the flag of the Southern Confederacy, not as a political symbol, but as an emblem of a heroic epoch for which our forefathers fought and died.

e. To maintain a united front against doctrines subversive to the fundamental principles set forth in the Bill of Rights which, as a part of the Federal Constitution, guarantees freedom of speech and the press, together with all other rights and privileges therein provided for the protection of political minorities and of individual citizens.

f. To encourage and support true loyalty to the Constitution of the United States of America.

General Officers
Order of the Stars and Bars
August 30, 1938

Commander-in-Chief	General Homer Atkinson
Vice-Commander-in-Chief	Dr. George Bolling Lee
Vice-Commander-in-Chief	Captain Samuel A. Ashe
Vice-Commander-in-Chief	Lt. Benjamin M. Robinson
Adjutant-General	General William M. Wood
Assistant Adjutant-General	Walter L. Hopkins
Quartermaster-General	Colonel William Beatty
Judge Advocate-General	Lt. James A. Lowery
Surgeon-General	Lt. Wyatt T. Hill
Historian-General	Capt. J. Andrew Jackson Dowdy
Registrar-General	Lt. J. Peter Keyser
Chaplain-General	Cadet Carter R. Bishop

SCV & MOSB Joint Reunions

1938	Columbia, South Carolina	1945	Chattanooga, Tennessee
1939	Trinidad, Colorado	1946	Biloxi, Mississippi
1940	Washington, DC	1947	Chattanooga, Tennessee
1941	Atlanta, Georgia	1948	Montgomery, Alabama
1942	Chattanooga, Tennessee	1949	Little Rock, Arkansas
1943	Atlanta, Georgia	1950	Biloxi, Mississippi
1944	Montgomery, Alabama	1951	Norfolk, Virginia

1952	Jackson, Mississippi	1979	Asheville, North Carolina
1953	Mobile, Alabama	1980	New Orleans, Louisiana
1954	Edgewater Park, Mississippi	1981	Richmond, Virginia
1955	New Orleans, Louisiana	1982	Oklahoma City, Oklahoma
1956	Atlanta, Georgia	1983	Orlando, Florida
1957	Richmond, Virginia	1984	Biloxi, Mississippi
1958	Jackson, Mississippi	1985	Raleigh, North Carolina
1959	Memphis, Tennessee	1986	Nashville, Tennessee
1960	Montgomery, Alabama	1987	Mobile, Alabama
1961	New Orleans, Louisiana	1988	Columbia, South Carolina
1962	Jackson, Mississippi	1989	Oklahoma City, Oklahoma
1963	Lynchburg, Virginia	1990	Fayetteville, Arkansas
1964	Atlanta, Georgia	1991	Augusta, Georgia
1965	Little Rock, Arkansas	1992	Wilmington, North Carolina
1966	Charleston, South Carolina	1993	Lexington, Kentucky
1967	Biloxi, Mississippi	1994	Mobile, Alabama
1968	Nashville, Tennessee	1995	Chattanooga, Tennessee
1969	New Orleans, Louisiana	1996	Richmond, Virginia
1970	Houston, Texas	1997	Nashville, Tennessee
1971	Richmond, Virginia	1998	St. Louis, Missouri
1972	Savannah, Georgia	1999	Mobile, Alabama
1973	St. Augustine, Florida	2000	Charleston, South Carolina
1974	Biloxi, Mississippi	2001	Lafayette, Louisiana
1975	Alexandria, Virginia	2002	Memphis, Tennessee
1976	Memphis, Tennessee	2003	Asheville, North Carolina
1977	Dallas, Texas	2004	Dalton, Georgia
1978	Savannah, Georgia		

Past Commander-Generals / Commander-in-Chiefs

General Homer Atkinson was elected the first Commander-in-Chief, Order of the Stars and Bars and served from 1938-1945. His administration is a record of loyalty and devotion to the Order of the Stars and Bars. His time and his talents were devoted to promoting the Order of the Stars and Bars by personal contact and by letter to all former commissioned officers of the Armed Forces of the Confederate States of America.

Dr. George Bolling Lee, Washington, DC, a grandson of General Robert E. Lee, succeeded General Homer Atkinson as the Commander-in-Chief, Order of Stars and Bars on March 31, 1945 and served until October 5,1948. He attended annual meetings in Chattanooga, Tennessee (twice); Biloxi, Mississippi; and Montgomery, Alabama. He was the son of the illustrious Major General William Henry Fitzhugh "Rooney" Lee, the second son of General Robert E. Lee. The membership continued to increase and sponsored activities were much in evidence.

W. Scott Hancock, St. Louis, Missouri, was elected Commander-in Chief at the annual meeting in Montgomery, Alabama in 1945. He had a distinguished career as a member of the Order of Stars and Bars and Sons of Confederate Veterans. For a period of five years he served as Commander-in Chief, Order of Stars and Bars. His administrative ability was demonstrated at the annual meetings of Little Rock, Arkansas, 1949; Biloxi, Mississippi, 1950; Norfolk, Virginia, 1951; Jackson, Mississippi, 1952; and Mobile, Alabama, 1953.

Dr. William R. Dancy, Savannah, Georgia was elected Commander-in Chief of the Order of Stars and Bars in Mobile, Alabama June 9, 1953. His term in office was brief (too brief). Doctor Dancy only served for a period of one year, June 9, 1953 to September 24, 1954.

Donald B. Todd, Etowah, Tennessee was elected Commander-in Chief of the Order of Stars and Bars on September 24, 1954 and served until November 11,1957. Colonel Todd was vitally interested in the affairs of the Confederate Veteran and sponsored much needed legislation in behalf of the Confederate Veterans such as Confederate Veterans Homes, Hospitals, State Pensions and other benefits that would contribute to their welfare and comfort.

J. Kyle Senter, Elizabethton, Tennessee, was elected Commander-in-Chief of the Order of Stars and Bars on November 11, 1957 and served until October 18, 1959. Alvis I. Downs, Memphis, Tennessee was elected Commander-in-Chief on October 18, 1959 and served until October 1, 1961.

Frank E. LaRue Jr., Farmers Branch, Texas was elected Commander-in-Chief at the meeting in New Orleans, Louisiana, 1961 and served until August 1963.

Colonel John Amasa May, Aiken, South Carolina was elected Commander-in Chief in Lynchburg, Virginia on August 16, 1963. He served until 1964.

Tom White Crigler Jr., Macon, Mississippi was elected Commander-in Chief of the Order of Stars and Bars in 1964 and served with honor and distinction until 1966.

S. Wayne Van Zandt, Little Rock, Arkansas was elected Commander-in Chief of Order of Stars and Bars at the annual meeting in 1966 in Charleston, South Carolina. He served until 1968.

James M. Edwards, Decatur, Georgia was elected Commander-in Chief of the Order of Stars and Bars in 1968. He served until the annual meeting in Houston, Texas, 1970.

H. Paul Porter, Alexander, Virginia was elected Commander-in Chief in Houston, Texas in 1970. Commander Porter served with honor and distinction until the annual meeting in Savannah, Georgia August 3,1972. In recognition of his outstanding service to the Order of Stars and Bars, Commander H. Paul Porter was elected Commander-in Chief, Sons of Confederate Veterans at that convention.

Dr. Laurence M. Oden, Biloxi, Mississippi was elected Commander-in Chief of the Order of Stars and Bars in Savannah, Georgia on August 3, 1972. He still has a record of unselfish service to the Order of Stars and Bars.

Dennis W. Rainoshek, Houston, Texas was elected Commander-in Chief of the Order of Stars and Bars on August 9, 1974 in Biloxi, Mississippi, and is still very active.

Colonel Lindsey P. Henderson Jr., a retired Army officer from Savannah, Georgia was elected Commander General, Military Order of Stars and Bars at the Memphis Convention in 1976.

Dr. Ralph W. Widener Jr. Dallas, Texas, was elected Military Order of Stars and Bars Commander General at the General Convention in Savannah, Georgia in August 1978.

John E. Hunter, Arlington, Texas was elected Military Order of Stars and Bars Commander-in Chief during the August 1980 General Convention in New Orleans, Louisiana.

Ronald T. Clemmons, Murfreesboro, Tennessee, was elected to lead the Military Order of Stars and Bars during the General Convention in Oklahoma City, Oklahoma, in August 1982.

During August 1984, Mark Lea "Beau" Cantrell, El Reno, Oklahoma, was elected Military Order of Stars and Bars Commander-in Chief at Biloxi, Mississippi.

John L. Echols Sr., Southaven, Mississippi, was elected Military Order of Stars and Bars Commander-in Chief at the General Convention held in Nashville, Tennessee during August 1986.

Edward Overton Cailleteau, Baton Rouge, Louisiana, was elected Military Order of Stars and Bars Commander-in Chief at the August 1988 General Convention in Columbia, South Carolina.

Robert L. Hawkins III, of Jefferson City, Missouri was elected Military Order of Stars and Bars Commander-in Chief at the August 1990 General Convention in Fayetteville, Arkansas.

Charles H. Smith, Oklahoma City, Oklahoma was elected Military Order of Stars and Bars Commander-in Chief at the August 1992 General Convention in Wilmington, North Carolina.

Perry J. Outlaw, Fairhope, Alabama was elected Military Order of Stars and Bars Commander-in Chief at the August 1994 General Convention in Mobile, Alabama.

James Troy Massey of Harrison, Arkansas was elected Military Order of Stars and Bars Commander-General at the August 1996 General Convention in Richmond, Virginia.

Joe B. Gay of Franklin, Virginia, was elected Military Order of Stars and Bars Commander-General at the August 1998 General Convention in St. Louis, Missouri.

Albert D. Jones, Jr. of Raleigh, North Carolina, was elected Military Order of Stars and Bars Commander-General at the August 2000 General Convention in Charleston, South Carolina.

Jeffrey W. Massey of Edmond, Oklahoma, was elected Military Order of the Stars and Bars Commander-General at the August 2002 General Convention in Memphis, Tennessee.

Daniel W. Jones of Cary, North Carolina was elected Military Order of the Stars and Bars Commander-General at the 2004 General Convention in Dalton, Georgia.

General William D. McCain

Adjutant General Emeritus

No history of the Military Order of Stars and Bars would be complete without the inclusion and contributions made by General William D. McCain, Adjutant General Emeritus.

General McCain was born at Bellefontaine, Mississippi on March 29, 1907. He graduated from Sunflower Agricultural High School, Delta State College, and the University of Mississippi. In 1935, he received his PhD in history from Duke University in North Carolina, and the honorary degree of Doctor of Letters from Mississippi College in 1967.

Dr. McCain taught at East Central Junior College, Copiah-Lincoln Junior College, Millsaps College, University of Mississippi, Duke University, and Mississippi State University.

He was a historian at Morristown National Historical Park, Morristown, New Jersey; Assistant Archivist at the National Archives, Washington, DC; and served as Director of the Mississippi State Department of Archives and History from 1938 until 1955. In 1955, he was appointed President of the University of Southern Mississippi and retired in 1975.

William D. McCain
ADJUTANT GENERAL
EMERITUS, MOSB

In 1924, he enlisted as a private in the Mississippi National Guard. He served in the Army during World War II and the Korean War and retired as a Major General. He was married to the former Minnie Lenz of Greenville, Mississippi. They had two children, Brigadier General William D. McCain Jr.; and Patricia McCain Boone, and six grandchildren.

General McCain became the Adjutant General of Military Order of Stars and Bars in 1954 and served in this capacity until his death in 1993. He was one of the main reasons for the survival of both the Sons of Confederate Veterans and the Military Order of Stars and Bars, having also served as Adjutant in Chief of the Sons of Confederate Veterans from 1953 until 1993. He operated the national headquarters of the Sons of Confederate Veterans and the Military Order of Stars and Bars at his home until it was transferred to Elm Springs.

Awards

Military Order of the Stars and Bars

1. Robert E. Lee Chalice
2. Gold Awards:
Gen. Samuel Cooper (Department of Northern Virginia)
Gen. Joseph E. Johnston (Department of Tennessee)
Gen. Albert S. Johnston (Department of Trans-Mississippi)
3. Dr. James M. Edwards Award (Distinguished Chapter)
4. Col. Joseph B. Mitchell Award
5. Col. Walter H. Taylor Award (newsletter - society level)
6. Capt. John W. Morton Award (newsletter - chapter level)
7. Distinguished Commander Medal
8. Distinguished Service Medal
9. Col. John Pelham Legion of Merit Award
10. Lt. Charles S. Read Merit Award
11. Meritorious Service Medal
12. Ladies Appreciation Medal
13. Varina Howell Davis Award
14. Joseph Evan Davis Award
15. Law & Order Award
16. Judah P. Benjamin Award
17. Commander General's Award
18. Certificate of Appreciation
19. Honorary Membership Certificate
20. Membership Certificate
21. Rebel Club
22. Lt. Simeon W. Cummings Award
23. Lt. Gen. Simon Bolivar Buckner Chapter Retention Award
24. Gen. William D. McCain Society Recruiting Award
25. Lt. Homer Atkinson Award
26. MOSB Military Service Award
27. John Randolph of Roanoke Cup (Speech Competition)
28. War Service Medal (military service during wartime)
29. John Newman Edwards Media Award
30. Douglas Southall Freeman History Award
31. General Basil Duke Award (for re-issuance of out-of-print books)
32. John Esten Cooke Fiction Award
33. J.E.B. Stuart Award (best Society Scrapbook)
34. T.J. Fakes Award (best Chapter Scrapbook)
35. Dabney Scales Essay Contest (Schools - Gr. 1-12)
36. Lee-Cleburne-Forrest College Scholarships

Medals & Awards by Charles H. Smith, Past Commander General, Jeff Massey, Judge Advocate General, Copyright 1997

1938 UCV Columbia Badge top

1940 OSB Reunion Medal

1938 UCV Columbia Badge drop

First issue MOSB Reunion Medal from 1939. It was Issued to Mr. Paul Ayres Rockwell, Asheville, NC

General Atkinson's 1942 Reunion Medal (never before published)
Courtesy of Museum of Confederacy

1942 Reunion Medal (reverse)
Courtesy of Museum of Confederacy

Literary Awards

The Military Order of the Stars and Bars recognizes and rewards those who communicate the true history of the war through printed media with various literary awards.

In fulfilling its mission as a historical, patriotic, and educational organization, the MOS&B has a wide range of programs at the national level that compliment the work of the state Societies and local Chapters. Among these programs are the following:

DOUGLAS SOUTHALL FREEMAN HISTORY AWARD

The award shall be given annually to encourage research and scholarship in Southern History. The award shall be in the amount of $1,000 paid directly to the author. The winner also shall receive an engraved plaque denoting that he was the recipient of the award. All books to be considered for this year's award shall be submitted to the Freeman History Committee by April 30th.

Invitation to participate in the contest is extended to any person who has written a work published between May 1st of the previous year to April 30th of the current year. All entries must be accompanied by a letter from the publisher giving the official date of publication. All entries must be accompanied by a biographical sketch of the author. The award shall be made for the best published book of high merit in the field of Southern history beginning with the Colonial period to the present time. The award shall be given only to works of high merit. If no work is submitted that meets the high standards of the Freeman History Award regulations, no award shall be given that year. The committee shall consist of nine judges appointed by the Commander General on a biennial basis.

If the winning book goes to a second printing, it shall contain the acknowledgment that it was selected as the winner of the Freeman History Award plus stating the year it was awarded. The book shall also list the previous winners with additions as necessary.

In response to the educational and historical charge set forth in the national Military Order of the Stars & Bars constitution, the Douglas Southall Freeman History Award was established. The Award, named in honor of the premier historian of General Robert E. Lee and the Army of Northern Virginia. This is the seventeenth year of competition for this award.

LIEUTENANT DABNEY M. SCALES ESSAY CONTEST

An annual essay contest for high school juniors and seniors who write on a specified Southern theme.

GENERAL BASIL W. DUKE AWARD

This annual award shall be given to encourage the re-issuance of out-of-print books that accurately present history of the War for Southern Independence. The Award shall be in the amount of $1,000 presented directly to the publisher of the reprinted volume. The publisher shall also receive an engraved plaque denoting that he was the recipient of the award. All books to be considered for this award shall be submitted to the Judging Committee by April 30th. Invitation to participate in the competition is extended to any publisher who issues a book between May 1st of the previous year and April 30th of the current year, that has not been republished since the expiration of the original copyright. All entries must include a letter from the publisher stating the year the book was published originally, and the date the reprint was issued.

The judges shall consider the quality, accuracy, style and value to Confederate historiography when selecting the winning book. Regimental histories, autobiographies, memoirs and biographies of noted Confederate leaders are among he types of books to be considered for this award. If the winning book goes to a second printing, it shall contain an acknowledgment that it was selected as the winner of the General Basil W. Duke Award, plus stating the year it was awarded.

JOHN ESTEN COOKE FICTION AWARD

The award shall be given annually to encourage writers of fiction to portray characters and events dealing with the War Between the States, Confederate heritage, or Southern history in a historically accurate fashion. The award shall be in the amount of $1,000 paid directly to the author. The winner shall receive an engraved plaque denoting that he/she was the recipient of the award. All books to be considered for this year's award shall be submitted to the John Esten Cooke Fiction Award Committee by June 1st.

Invitation to participate in the contest is extended to any person who has written a book-length work of fiction published between May 1st, two years prior and June 1st of this year. All entries must be accompanied by a letter from the publisher stating the official date of publication. Also, each entry must be accompanied by a biographical sketch of the author. The judges will consider the effectiveness of research, accuracy of statement, and excellence of style in selecting the winner. All entries must be book length. The judges shall be appointed by the Commander General on a biennial basis. If the winning book goes to a second printing, it shall contain the acknowledgment that it was selected as the winner of the Cooke Fiction Award along with stating the year the award was made.

HENRY TIMROD SOUTHERN CULTURE AWARDS

Inaugurated in 2000, this is the MOS&B's prestigious award(s) for outstanding excellence and achievement in making contributions toward the understanding, appreciation, and explication of our Southern arts and letters. This is an award for cultural achievement presented by the Commander-General to all those nominated and approved by the awards committee. This can be in the form of - but not limited to - books, treatises, poems, learned articles, Ph.D. theses, sculpture, art forms such as watercolor or oil paintings, the silver screen (cinema), theatre, cuisine, religion, family structure and values, philosophy, musical compositions, finance, television, radio, photographic arts, graphic arts, and architecture. The cultural form should reflect favorably on the sacrifices of our progenitors. In sum, this award can be presented for any positive reflection on our Southern arts and letters.

The awards are named in honor of the famed poet "the Laureate of the Confederacy" Henry Timrod (1829-1867). This Southern poet was born in Charleston, South Carolina. His life was cast in the grandeur of the South and the seething torment of the War. It was Timrod's voice in the dark conflict, in all its gloom of its disaster, and in all the sacred tenderness that clings about its memories, that poured forth all the rich glad life and patriotic pride of the Southern patriot. He has been termed the "poet of the Lost Cause, the finest interpreter of the feelings and traditions of the splendid heroism of a brave people."

The award(s) are established in two distinct categories. Class I is generally presented to only one awardee per annum. The award shall be consistent with the prestigious Douglas Southall Freeman Literary Award. Recipients do not need to be a member of the MOS&B - and, in fact, are anticipated to not be members. The potential award recipient should have made his or her contribution to our Southern arts and letters between 30th April of the previous year and 30th April of the current year of the nomination. Current members of the Executive Council or Society Commanders may make the nominations on the proper forms to the members of the awards committee appointed by the Commander-General on a biennial basis. The recipient(s) receives public recognition at the annual convention and an impressive trophy. They may be requested to address the convention at the annual banquet.

Class II awards are essentially identical to those of Class I except that they are exclusively for MOS&B members. The recipient receives both an attractive certificate and a medal for his achievement. These recipients receive recognition at the annual MOS&B awards convention luncheon.

MILITARY ORDER OF STARS AND BARS SCHOLARSHIP PROGRAM
(GENERAL INFORMATION AND DATA REQUIRED FROM APPLICANTS)

ELIGIBILITY:

Applicants, for a MOS&B Scholarship, must be a genealogically proven descendant of a Confederate Officer or descendant of a member of the Confederate Executive or Legislative branches of government or descendant of a member of the Confederate States' legislatures, judiciary or executive branches of state government.

THE SCHOLARSHIPS:

The MOS&B scholarships shall be named as follows: *The General Robert E. Lee Scholarship* shall be awarded to applicants residing in the Army of Northern Virginia. *The Lt. General Nathan B. Forrest Scholarship* shall be awarded to applicants residing in the Army of Tennessee. *The Major General Patrick R. Cleburne Scholarship* shall be awarded to applicants residing in the Army of Trans-Mississippi.

On recommendation from the committee, scholarship amounts shall be determined annually by the General Executive Council. Funding will be from available resources as determined by the Executive Council.

GENERAL INFORMATION:

TIME SCHEDULES: Scholarship applications must be submitted to the MOS&B Scholarship Committee by March 1st each year. Award winners will be notified as soon as they are selected and funds awarded for scholarships will be forwarded to selected institutions by July 1st.

REVIEW: The committee will review all criteria and provisions and may request additional information or clarification from the applicant. The committee may waive a provision, if extenuating circumstances warrant such a waiver. The provision waived should not significantly affect the merits of the application. The committee's decision as to eligibility and merit is final.

DISBURSEMENT OF FUNDS: Applicants awarded scholarships must be enrolled in an accredited two year or four year college/university, which is a degree-granting institution, before funds are disbursed. Scholarship funds will be placed on deposit at the institution where the person is enrolled, for the benefit of the applicant, and any unused portion shall be returned to the MOS&B by the institution.

SCHOLARSHIP LIMITS: Applicants may not receive a scholarship more than once. However, the committee may consider an award for a previously selected applicant who is entering graduate studies.

JUDGING CRITERIA: Scholarships awarded shall be merit based and applicants will be judged on academic performance, character, school and community activities, ability to express himself/herself in written form, personal motivation, leadership potential, and the strength of the recommendation. JUDGING CRITERIA: Extra Curricular - 10%; Personal Statement - 10%; Academic Performance - 70%; Recommendations - 10%

DATA SUBMISSION REQUIREMENTS:

COMPLETED APPLICATION: Applicants must complete the printed application in its entirety. Signing of the application attests to the accuracy of ALL data submitted for scholarship consideration.

ANCESTOR PROOF: Applicants must be a genealogically proven descendant of a Confederate Officer or a descendent of a member of the national or state Confederate government branches (see Eligibility).

PERSONAL STATEMENT: An applicant will submit a personal letter of application describing his/her academic and career aspirations and include other areas that have influenced the applicants development as a person committed to pursuing his/her educational goals. The applicant may use any approach to completing this assignment. The personal letter is limited to one page back and front.

ACADEMIC RECORDS: The applicant must submit an academic record of courses completed where currently enrolled, and include grade point average and class rank. Scholastic aptitude test scores and/or other pertinent test scores, if not in the applicant's transcript, should also be included. Transcripts not released to the applicant should be sent to MOS&B Scholarship Committee, by the institution transcript officer.

RECOMMENDATIONS: Applicants must submit three letters of recommendation attesting to the applicant's character, ability, dependability and integrity. One of the letters shall be from a teacher, counselor, or principal from the last institution where the applicant was enrolled.

SPONSORSHIP: All applicants must obtain a letter of sponsorship from a MOS&B State Society or Chapter that will be submitted with application material.

Military Order of the Stars and Bars Histories

The membership in the General Society of the Military Order of Stars and Bars is composed of all legitimate male descendants, lineal or collateral, of those who served as officers in the Confederate Army or Navy to the end of the war, or who died in prison or while in actual service were killed in battle, or who were honorably retired or discharged, and descendants of elected or appointed officials of the Confederate or Executive branch of the civil government.

The General Society is divided into Departments, State Societies, and Chapters. There are three Departments: Army of Northern Virginia, Army of Tennessee, and Army of the Trans-Mississippi.

State Societies are formed in states within the three Armies, and these Societies are then divided into local units called Chapters. The following Histories have been submitted for publication:

Army of Northern Virginia Department

The ANV Department consists of four societies: Maryland, North Carolina, South Carolina, and Virginia. Although a state society does not exist in West Virginia, New York, or New England, chapters exist or are being formed in these areas.

The ANV Department continues to show significant growth, with each society gaining membership. New chapters are being formed, and Virginia has led the ANV Department and the MOSB in two recent years with the most new members.

Communications between ANV societies have been improved recently through the expanded use of e-mail between societies and between individual chapters, and through the MOSB's national web site.

Annual conventions are held in each of the state societies, and participation by members from other state societies is encouraged. Recent Past ANV Commanders include Catesby Penniman Jones, Josiah Bynum Gay III, Collin G. Pulley, Jr., Daniel W. Jones, and the Honorable Richard Bender Abell. The current ANV Commander is A. Clarke Magruder, Sr. of Virginia, and the current ANV Committeeman is Larry E. Beeson of North Carolina.

MARYLAND SOCIETY

In 1983, only one Chapter of the Military Order of the Stars and Bars (MOS&B) existed in Maryland. This was the Maryland Line Chapter # 191 chartered in the Annapolis/Baltimore area. In 1986 the Society expanded to three chapters and the Maryland Society MOS&B was chartered.

Of the three, the General Elzey/Admiral Buchanan Chapter on Maryland's Eastern Shore lost its charter in 1991. The Society remained at two chapters until the formation of the Captain Charles Linthicum Chapter # 216 in the Montgomery and Prince George's County areas in 1995. The Maryland Society in 2004 reports 29 members, 5 of whom are life members.

Maryland Society Commanders have been as follows:
1986 to 1988 Robert E. Claggett
1988 to 1992 G. Elliott Cummings
1992 to 1998 Michael K. Williams
1999 to present Donald E. Beck

Major events in the Maryland Society have included:

In March 1997 Society Adjutant G. Elliott Cummings testified before a committee of the Maryland General Assembly on behalf of the MOS&B in support of the Sons of Confederate Veterans license plate logo.

In 2000 Commander Beck successfully nominated Linthicum Chapter member Robert Lyons for the first Jackson Medal awarded with a Star. Compatriot Lyons devoted many hours in the care of the burial sites in Baltimore of General Lewis Armistead and of Colonel Frederick G. Skinner.

In 2001 Commander Beck testified in the successful defense of the Maryland State Song, "Maryland My Maryland," before a committee of the Maryland General Assembly and before a Senate committee the following year.

Commander Beck has delivered welcoming remarks and/or presented the Society wreath and, with assistance of Chapter members, represented the Maryland Society at several annual functions: the Lee/Jackson Birthday Ceremony at the equestrian statues in Wyman Park in Baltimore; the Confederate Memorial Day ceremony at Mt. Olivet Cemetery in Frederick; the Memorial Day ceremony at Veterans Park in Bethesda; the Confederate Memorial Day ceremony in Loudon Park in Baltimore; the Jefferson Davis Birthday and Confederate Memorial Day ceremony at the Confederate Monument in Jackson Circle in Arlington National Cemetery; the Point Lookout Prisoner of War Memorial ceremony at Point Lookout; the Veterans Day ceremony at Veterans Park in Bethesda; the ceremony of the Midshipman's French Club, United States Naval Academy, at the Monument to French Soldiers and Sailors of the American War of Independence in Annapolis; and the ceremony to honor the graves of Captain Heinrich Wirz and Mary Surratt in the Mt. Olivet Cemetery in Washington, DC.

Photo taken in June 2003 at the ceremony honoring the Confederate prisoners of war buried at Point Lookout Cemetery in Maryland. The cemetery is administered by the Veterans Affairs Administration.

Pictured from left to right: Society Adjutant Christopher Russell, Zarvona Chapter; Society Commander Donald Beck, Linthicum Chapter; Patrick J. Griffin III, Linthicum Chapter; past Commander John Stober, Jr., Zarvona Chapter; Adjutant Frank A. Willis, Zarvona Chapter; and George Linthicum, Linthicum Chapter.

Commander Beck has participated in annual Sons of Confederate Veterans functions such as marching in the Presidents Day Parade in Alexandria, Virginia; marching in the Labor Day Parade in Gaithersburg and the placing of luminaries at the Antietam Battlefield Illumination in December.

Commander Beck has attended the National and Maryland SCV/MOS&B Reunions and Conventions each year except Maryland in April 2003 when he was in South Carolina placing the Maryland Society wreath at the grave of his cousin, James A. York, honored in a ceremony there as the last Confederate soldier killed in action in South Carolina.

Commander Beck has worked with the commanders of the Linthicum Chapter 216 and the Norris Camp 1398 to organize and promote the annual MOS&B/SCV jointly sponsored fording of the Potomac River at White's Ford in August to commemorate General Lee's invasion of Maryland in 1862.

Society Adjutant Christopher Russell was instrumental in purchasing a Society flag and pole from Society funds. As a member of the popular Maryland SCV Division Color Guard, he carries the Society flag when the occasion permits.

The Maryland Line Chapter

Baltimore, Maryland

The Maryland Line Chapter was chartered in 1983 as the first Chapter chartered in Maryland. Its commander was Robert E. Claggett. By 1992 it had 15 members in good standing.

The Chapter is now down to 6 members, having provided members to help start up the Zarvona and Linthicum Chapters.

Currently, Michael K. Williams is serving as the commander, G. Elliott Cummings as adjutant.

From the 4th Quarter 1986 until the 3rd Quarter 1990, then Commander Claggett prepared a quarterly Society newsletter named in honor of Captain William Murray of the 2nd Maryland Infantry Battalion, CSA, who was killed at Culp's Hill at Gettysburg.

Commander Claggett was posthumously awarded the General Samuel Cooper Award by Commander-General John Echols. General Echols also awarded Commander Claggett's wife, Romaine, the Varina Howell Davis Award. The Maryland Division of the SCV established its highest award named in honor of Robert E. Claggett.

In 1994 Commander Michael K. Williams conducted the first of several very successful tours of Green Mount Cemetery in Baltimore on behalf of the MOS&B. A number of Confederate general officers, including General Joseph E. Johnston, are buried at Green Mount Cemetery. Commander Williams also planned and conducted several historic tours of the Loudon Park Cemetery in Baltimore under the auspices of the MOS&B.

Currently Commander Williams is conducting an Adopt-a-Confederate Program. This program invites people to adopt the gravesite and marker of a Confederate veteran on Confederate Hill at Loudon Park Cemetery in Baltimore where 610 Confederate soldiers, sailors and one marine are buried.

Captain Charles F. Linthicum Chapter

Darnestown, Maryland

The Charter for the Linthicum Chapter was granted on June 3, 1995. Charter members were Reverend Alister Anderson, Donald E. Beck, Chris Brewer, Larry R. Brown, Gregg S. Clemmer, Daniel L. Denney, Charles Goolsby, Patrick J. Griffin III, Peter M. Griffin, Daniel D. Kessler, Douglas King, Carey O. Leveret, Robert E. Lyons, James F. Powell and Edward F. Romig II. A loss of 5 charter members and a gain of 7 new members give a total of 17 members.

The current officers are Peter M. Griffin, commander; Gregg S. Clemmer, adjutant. Patrick J. Griffin III is the only past commander.

A major project for the Chapter has been the upkeep and refurbishing of Confederate graves and markers at the Monocacy Chapel and Cemetery in Beallsville.

In October 1997 the Captain Charles Linthicum Chapter held its annual picnic at the historic Kennedy Farm near Harpers Ferry, West Virginia, the site from where John Brown staged his infamous 1859 raid on Harpers Ferry. The site is now owned by a member of the Sons of Confederate Veterans.

Since 1998, the Linthicum Chapter has sponsored jointly with the Col. William Norris Camp 1398, SCV, a fording of the Potomac River at White's Ford where General Lee's army entered into Maryland in September 1862. The crossing of the river is followed by a drying off period and a family picnic for children and adults alike. This has been a popular walk-where-your-ancestors-walked event like in the Pan Am Airlines commercial a few years back.

Colonel Richard Thomas "Zarvona" Chapter

Waldorf, Maryland

The Zarvona Chapter was named after Colonel Richard Thomas whose nickname was Zarvona. It was chartered in 1986 with 6 members. The commander was James H. Ball, and the adjutant, James S. Clark. They quickly grew to 7 members. They met in the Public Library in La Plata, Maryland following the meeting of the Pvt. Wallace Bowling SCV Camp 1400.

The current commander is newly recruited and member of the Maryland SCV Division Color Guard, Benjamin Maury Tyler III; the adjutant is the long serving Frank A. Willis.

In 1986 Compatriot Samuel Clark of the Chapter received the UDC War Service Medal for his service with the United States Navy in Vietnam. Compatriot Clark was a 1968 graduate of the United States Military Academy. His untimely death was tremendous loss for the Chapter.

In 1988-1989 the Chapter conducted a successful fund raiser, and on April 28, 1990 used these funds to dedicate a plaque in memory of Colonel Richard Thomas at his grave at Chaptico, Charles County, Maryland.

Because of deaths and loss of members, by 1995 the Chapter required a special effort to rebuild its membership to the required 5 members. Then Society Commander Mike Williams and Zarvona Chapter Commander John B. Stober, Jr. worked together to achieve the restart of the Chapter.

Over the years, the immediate past commander, John Stober Jr., has published an excellent newsletter for the Chapter.

New England Society

C.S.S. Tallahassee Chapter

West Hartford, Connecticut

The C.S.S. Tallahassee Chapter of the MOSB was established in 1994. It covers all of the New England States. It was named for the famous Confederate cruiser which operated off the New England coast where it sank a number of enemy vessels. The commanding officer for much of its history was Captain John Taylor Wood.

The Chapter has held ceremonies marking graves of Confederate officers in the New England area, such as Major General Gustavus Woodson Smith who is buried in New London, Connecticut.

The Chapter publishes a newsletter, *The Capstan*, dealing matters relating to the Chapter, the MOSB, and Confederate Naval History. The Rev. Canon Robert Girard Carron, Past Chaplain General, MOSB, is the Commander and Thomas DiGiuseppe is Adjutant.

New York Society

On December 7, 1949, the Military Order of the Stars and Bars was formed in New York City and the first commander was Lieutenant Colonel David Nye Barrows, M.D. Under his command, on September 26, 1961, the Military Order of the Stars and Bars General Headquarters recognized the New York group as New York Chapter #1.

In 1965, upon the death of Commander Barrows, Colonel H. Harding Isaacson was named commander, a position he held for 21 years. In 1986, Colonel Isaacson retired and was awarded the Legion of Merit Medal and Certificate for his years of service.

On August 5, 1986, under the command of Thomas H. Lipscomb III, the New York Chapter #1 was elevated to full society statue to be known as the New York Society, Military Order of the Stars and Bars, the first in the nation.

In 1992, after being inactive for a few years the New York Society was reorganized through by Colonel H. Harding Isaacson, Lieutenant Commander George Lee Weddington Jr. and David A.S. Brashear. In 1992 David A. S. Brashear was elected commander and Douglas Meier Harding in 1994.

In 1999, Michael Harrison Charles was elected commander after coming to New York from St. Augustine, FL were he was past commander of General William Wing Loring Camp, Sons of Confederate Veterans. Commander Charles is also serving as Treasurer of the General Archibald Gracie Camp, Sons of Confederate Veterans and a member of the Order of the Southern Cross.

Each year the Society participates in numerous events with other New York hereditary societies including Flag Massing Ceremonies, parades, an annual Confederate Ball and wreath laying events. The order is represented at the annual ceremonies at the tomb of General Ulysses S. Grant in conjunction with the Military Order of the Loyal Legion and the Sons of Union Veterans.

North Carolina Society

The North Carolina Society Military Order of the Stars and Bars was organized on February 28, 1978 by Commander Roger Alvis of the NC Division Sons of Confederate Veterans. The first known commander was Thomas F. Davis of Brevard who served in that position until 1985 when Jeff Stepp of Greenville was elected Commander. The Garnett-Pettigrew Chapter located in Greensboro and Danville, Virginia had chartered earlier in September 1984.

In 1987, the Society proposed that the North Carolina Sons of Confederate Veterans and Military Order of the Stars and Bars join together for a Confederate Memorial Weekend and hold a joint, statewide Confederate Memorial Service annually in Raleigh at the State Capitol with a parade. This later became an annual tradition. In 1988, the Captain James I. Waddell Chapter chartered in Raleigh on November 1st and the Lieutenant William C. Ferrell Chapter in Wilson chartered that same year.

In 1989, John Brown of Siler City was elected Commander of the Society. The General William Dorsey Pender Chapter chartered on August 8, 1989.

On January 19, 1990, the first annual Robert E. Lee Birthday Celebration was held at the State Capitol in Raleigh and was sponsored by the Captain James I. Waddell Chapter, Raleigh. The General William R. Boggs Chapter in Winston Salem began sponsoring an annual War Between the States and Antique Only Gun Show each year in April. In May, Commander Brown resigned and Society Lieutenant Commander Danny Moody of Fuquay-Varina took command. The Webb-Bailey Chapter in Raleigh chartered August 1, 1990 and the Colonel Charles Courtney Tew Chapter, Durham, chartered October 1, 1990.

Bob Grimes of Plymouth was elected Commander of the Society in 1991 when the Society Constitution was revised. Commander Grimes resigned in 1992 and Brian Green of Kernersville became the new commander. The Immortal 600 Chapter, Louisburg, chartered on November 12, 1992.

In 1993, Eddie Mauldin of Oxford was elected Commander at the Society Convention in May. On February 14, 1994, the 1st Lieutenant Wiloughby Lynn Hockaday/Black River Tigers Chapter in Sea Level chartered.

At the Society Convention in May 1995, Albert Jones of Raleigh was elected the new Commander. In the spring of 1996 the Society established a newsletter entitled *Farthest to the Front*, which won the Colonel Walter H. Taylor Society Newsletter Award for both 1996 and 1997.

The 1997-99 Officers for the North Carolina Society were Albert Jones of Raleigh, Commander; Ed Martin of Greensboro, Lieutenant Commander; and Byron Brady of Raleigh, Adjutant.

Elected to office for the following term were Steven Blankenship, Commander; Charles Calloway, Lieutenant Commander and Felix Collins, Adjutant.

On August 9, 2001, the Captain Asbury T. Rogers Chapter was chartered in Asheville.

In May 2003 Robert Owens of Bakersville was elected Commander; Larry Beeson of King was elected Lieutenant Commander and George Valsame of Garner was appointed Adjutant. At the time of this publication, these officers continue to serve in their elected positions.

Restoration and rededication of
Brigadier General Lawrence O'Bryan Branch's grave monument by the Captain
James I. Waddell Chapter, Raleigh, NC, August 2002

Shown in the photos from top: row 1: Dan W. Jones; row 2, photo 1: Tom Smith, Sandy Sanderson, Frank Powell, Art Willis, Charles Hawks; photo 2: Darwin Roseman, Byron Brady; photo 3: Byron Brady, Armistead Maupin (great-grandson of General Branch); row 3, photo 1: Frank Powell; photo 2: John Roderick, Tim Carroll, Dan Jones, Randall Lemons; photo 3: Debbie Roseman

Captain Asbury T. Rogers Chapter

Asheville, North Carolina

The Captain Asbury T. Rogers Chapter #266 was organized in Asheville, North Carolina, on August 29, 2001 and chartered on January 15, 2002. Commander General Albert D. Jones presented the chapter with their charter and swore in the following officers: Robert L. Owens, Commander; William Best, Lieutenant Commander; Richard Stowe, Adjutant; Alan Leonard, Judge Advocate; and E. B. Darden, Genealogist. Commander Robert Owens was elected Commander of the North Carolina Society, Military Order of the Stars and Bars, in May 2003 and in November 2003 the following new officers were elected: Tom Vernon, Commander; James Holbrook, Lieutenant Commander; and Derrick Shipman, Adjutant. The chapter's namesake, Asbury T. Rogers, was a Captain in Company A, 62nd North Carolina Regiment.

Brigadier General Rufus Barringer Chapter

Charlotte, North Carolina

The Brigadier General Rufus Barringer Chapter 18, Military Order of Stars and Bars of Charlotte, North Carolina applied for a charter in 1986 under the auspices of Commander Arthur R. Claiborne. Subsequently, commanders have been: Dr. George H. Sutcliffe, Lionel D. Bass Jr., James D. Summers and currently George E. Blow.

This chapter has participated in raising funds for charity, gone on field trips, and restored gravesites with the Major Egbert A. Ross Camp, SVC of Charlotte. It has also participated in memorial ceremonies on Confederate Memorial Day with the Ross Camp at Elmwood Cemetery of that city.

It has helped restore the Brigadier General Rufus Barringer and Brigadier General Thomas Drayton gravesites. Also, 118 stones were placed at gravesites surrounding the Confederate Monument at Elmwood Cemetery with the Ross Camp; thereby, reviving community interest in that cemetery.

Chapter 18 has also helped erect a monument at the site of the North Carolina Military Institute, Charlotte, recognizing the contributions of Pre-War for Southern Independence Superintendent D.H. Hill and graduate Egbert A. Ross to the war effort.

The Brigadier General Rufus Barringer Chapter is proud to host the North Carolina State Military Order of Star and Bars Conference, May 1-3, 1998.

Garnett-Pettigrew Chapter

Greensboro, North Carolina

Garnett-Pettigrew Chapter #67 was chartered on November 6, 1984 by members of the Col. John Sloan Camp, Sons of Confederate Veterans, Greensboro, North Carolina and the Cabell-Graves Camp, Sons of Confederate Veterans, Danville, Virginia. Members decided to name the Chapter for two generals of equal rank, one from Virginia and one from North Carolina.

The Virginian is Richard Brooke Garnett. He was promoted to the rank of Brigadier General in November 1861, and was killed at Gettysburg on July 3, 1863 during the Pettigrew-Pickett charge.

The North Carolinian is James Johnston Pettigrew, who was promoted to Brigadier General on February 26, 1862. General Pettigrew survived the fighting at Gettysburg but was wounded at Falling Waters in rear guard action during the withdrawal to Virginia. He died from his wounds three days later.

Charter members were James E. Anderson, Edwin B. Braswell, Jr., C. Michael Briggs, John J. Brown, Jr., J. T. Ellis, Thomas B. Fowler, E. Clark Graves, Jr., Bertran Hayes-Davis, Gary Lee Hall, F. Lawrence McFall, Jr., H. J. McClendon, Darrell E. Malcom, Arthur W. Miller, Jr., James A. Miller, Jr., Marvin L. Osborne, Kenneth Rockwell, T. J. Sanders, III, Henry C. Siegner, Locke W. Smith, Jr., R. Lester Snyder, Jeffrey H. Stepp, and Joe L. Wade. The charter officers were Arthur W. Miller, Jr., Commander; R. Lester Snyder, Lt. Commander; and F. Lawrence McFall, Jr., Adjutant.

In the years since it was founded, Garnett-Pettigrew members have been involved in numerous projects commemorating our Confederate ancestors. In 1998 the Chapter established a scholarship endowment fund in the name of Lt. General Thomas "Stonewall" Jackson and his wife, Mary Anna, at Oak Ridge Military Academy in Oak Ridge, North Carolina.

The Chapter has also dedicated a state highway marker at the Woodside Inn in Milton, North Carolina, commemorating Major General Stephen Dodson Ramseur. It was at the Inn that Ramseur recovered from wounds received at Malvern Hill and Chancellorsville. It was also the site of his wartime marriage.

Memorial services conducted during the past ten years to remember Confederate officers include General William Hardee and his son, Willie, in 1996; Capt. Isaac Newton Kearns of the 38th North Carolina in 1997; and a memorial service for Lt. Gen. Thomas Jackson in 1998 commemorating the 135th anniversary of the General's unfortunate death.

From 1998 through 2001 the Garnett-Pettigrew sponsored the Guilford Courthouse Battleground Chapter of the Tar Heel Junior Historians. The Junior Historians is a program of the North Carolina Museum of History and is open to all students between the 4th and 12th grades. In 1998, the Guilford Courthouse Battleground Chapter was recognized as the Rookie Chapter of the Year. Also in 1998, their project documenting the preservation efforts of an old family cemetery containing the remains of a Guilford County Confederate soldier was recognized as the Project of the Year in their age group. The Chapter won second and third place project awards each of the next two years.

The Chapter has an ongoing flag preservation project to collect donations at meetings and special events. Contributions are then forwarded to the Museum of the Confederacy in Richmond for their flag preservation efforts.

The Garnett-Pettigrew Chapter has also adopted four markers and monuments at the Gettysburg National Military Park as part of the Park's "Adopt-A-Monument" program. Twice each year members travel to Gettysburg to maintain the markers for the brigades of General Pettigrew, General Scales and General Iverson and the monument of the 11th Mississippi Regiment.

The Chapter's newsletter, *The Garnett-Pettigrew Gray Line!*, was the 1996 recipient of the Capt. John W. Morton Award for outstanding chapter newsletter. In 1998 the Chapter was honored with the Dr. James M. Edwards Distinguished Chapter Award for the most outstanding chapter in the nation.

Each December the membership presents the John Brown, Jr., 161 Award to the Chapter member they deem to have done the most to exemplify the dedication to the South embodied by the actions of 161 Confederate States Military officers, our forefathers, imprisoned by Union forces at Fort Delaware, on May 8, 1865. The award is named to honor the late John Brown, Jr., who was a charter member and past officer of the Chapter, and the 161 Confederate officers who refused to take the Oath of Allegiance without definitive evidence of the surrender of their government and armies.

Garnett-Pettigrew has a dinner meeting and guest speaker at 6:30 on the first Saturday of every "even" numbered month. Visitors and wives are welcomed at our meetings and both can always be found in attendance. The Chapter shares "headquarters" with the Pvt. Lorenzo Dow Williams Camp #1456, Sons of Confederate Veterans and the Rockingham County Chapter #586, United Daughters of the Confederacy. The site is the former Moricle's Country Store at the intersection of highway 65 and Witty Road near the Rockingham and Guilford County line.

General Robert D. Johnston Chapter

Lincolnton, North Carolina

The initial organizational meeting to establish the General Robert D. Johnston Chapter of the MOS&B was held in June 1997 in Lincolnton, North Carolina. General Johnston was born and raised in Lincoln County and was a childhood classmate and close friend to General Robert F. Hoke and General Stephen D. Ramseur. General Johnston was a gallant leader who received five wounds in service to the CSA.

General Robert D. Johnston Chapter was fully chartered in spring of 1998. With the officers being Kirby Sechrist being Commander with Bruce Cloninger, Lt. Commander and Ned Devine as Adjutant.

Mr. Sechrist was Commander until Fall 2001 when Norman Gene Atkins was elected commander, Mr. Atkins was elected for his third term as commander in the fall of 2003.

Current officers of the Chapter are as follows Norman Gene Atkins commander, William Holt Lt. Commander, Bruce Cloninger adjutant, Joe Ginn Chaplain and Dale McKinzie color sergeant.

At this time the General Robert D. Johnston Chapter is working on marking the final resting-places of Confederate officers and Confederate Veterans in the following counties Cleveland, Gaston, Lincoln and Yancey. The members of our Chapter belong to several different SCV Camps.

As commander I have received help to install markers on my Confederate officers and Confederate veterans final resting-places in Yancey County with the help of the local SCV Camp there.

Also the members of our chapter have been asked by a member of the United Daughters of the Confederacy to order several VA markers and install them on veterans resting-places due to the fact that their markers where destroyed or unreadable due to weather. To date we have installed more than forty markers to honor those brave men of the Confederacy.

Respectfully submitted by Norman Gene Atkins

CS Ram Albemarle Chapter

Plymouth, North Carolina

Plymouth, NC was the site and December 2002 saw the beginning of the new MOSB chapter, CS Ram Albemarle. Harry Thompson, Bob Grimes, Walter White, and Albert Jones attended this organizational meeting with Jones elected interim commander and White elected interim adjutant.

From this small but not humble beginning, the Chapter has grown with the potential of thirty plus members.

Heritage goals and community good works are the foundation of this chapter.

Lt. Wilson Bailey Chapter

Raleigh, North Carolina

The oldest Chapter in continuous existence in NC started printing its bimonthly *PRESS ON* in April 1997. Perhaps attributable to its getting the word out is it has announced the dates of all National SCV-MOSB Conventions, pushing the importance of each, —the Chapter has not missed a one! For added interest, it has printed photos, in color, of the Armstrong Gun, the CSS Hunley and a wedding picture of Brandon Hux and his lovely wife, Susan, at Flat Rock Baptist Church in Youngsville on December 5, 1998.

The Chapter attended all the meetings of the NC MOSB Society in its active years. In Feb. 2000, Cmdr. Ed Martin e-mailed congratulations on the success of *PRESS ON* and the donation to Food Lion on Thanksgiving Day 2000. At the last meeting in Matthews in Apr. 2001, Cmdr. Martin presented the Chapter a scroll for the Chapter's perfect attendance plus its enthusiasm. The Chapter was also given $100 for help in cleaning up Lt. Wilson Bailey's gravesite in Bailey. On April 28, 2001, the Chapter attended a Grave Marking Ceremony in Wilson sponsored by the Society for Confederate soldier Pvt. T.E. Page.

The Chapter also joined many Central Brigade SCV's activities, e.g. March in Support of the ill-fated Battle Flag in Columbia SC in 2000, several Confederate Heritage Parades in Richmond, VA, a dedication ceremony in Zebulon on August 21, 1999 honoring two Confederate soldiers.

The Chapter also helped with the Oakwood Burial Project, emplacing new tombstones thru March 1999, thereafter helping with routine maintenance. The Chapter also assists each October in manning the booth at the State Fair.

Each Christmas the Chapter donates money and food to the Food Bank, the Salvation Army, the Raleigh Rescue Mission, and The Ark, all in Raleigh, and others on occasion. The womenfolk prepare luscious pies, cakes and cookies, all delivered by the Cmdr. All members contribute, but Mike Strickland holds the record, donating over 30 lbs of canned goods one year.

The Chapter also helps support the SLRC and the CWPT. And, when feasible, the Masonic Orphanage in Oxford. The Chapter enables a scholarship to the best two-year student of the Electronics Engineering Technology curriculum at Wake Tech CC, whose president, recently retired, is chapter member Dr Bruce I. Howell.

Ron Stacy donated a beautiful Mort Kunslter painting of *Jeb Stuart's Famous Ride Around McClellan* for a Chapter fundraiser. The Cmdr. visited 13 camps, finally collecting $500 from raffles for this painting. The entire amount, thanks to Ron, was placed in the Chapter vaults. Hoping to enjoy profitable sales of his two books soon to be published, *Firing and Flying for the Field Artillery in Korea* and *The Resurgence of the SCV-MOSB in North Carolina,* the Cmdr. hopes to add more to the treasury. With several "wannabes" panting to join, the future for the Lt. Wilson Bailey Chapter looks bright.

Captain James Iredell Waddell Chapter

Raleigh, North Carolina

In 1988, there was no active chapter of the Military Order of the Stars and Bars in Eastern North Carolina. At the suggestion of NC Sons of Confederate Veterans Commander Byron Brady, SCV members from all across eastern North Carolina met in Raleigh at the Cameron Village Regional Public Library August 20, 1988 to form a new chapter. The name of the chapter chosen was Captain James Iredell Waddell, a distinguished Confederate naval hero and Captain of the C.S.S. *Shenandoah*. Captain Waddell was chosen for this honor because he was born July 13, 1824 in nearby Pittsboro, just west of Raleigh. Captain Waddell died March 18, 1886 and is buried in Annapolis, Maryland. Chapter members placed a wreath during a memorial service they held at his grave in September 2002.

The Chapter chartered with 36 members and held their charter banquet April 8, 1989 at Ballentines in Cameron Village. ANV Department Commander Dr. Roy Clemmons delivered the keynote address. The chapter began meeting on a quarterly basis but later switched to bimonthly meetings.

Immediately, the chapter began publishing *The Shenandoah* as their official newsletter, which is published every other month. *The Shenandoah* has won the Captain John Morton Newsletter Award for the best Military Order of the Stars and Bars Chapter newsletter in the Confederation in 1994-95, and 1997-2002. Most of the meetings of the chapter have been held in Raleigh, but in the early years, the chapter tried to have at least one meeting each year down east. Some of the past meetings have been held in Franklinton, Creedmoor, Fayetteville, Williamston, and Windsor, with tours of nearby Fort Branch and Hope Plantation. Chapter field trips were taken to Richmond, Virginia in 1993 and to Durham in 1994. A chapter sponsored Confederate Ball was held at the Moose Lodge in Louisburg on September 30, 1989.

In 1989, the Chapter began sponsoring an annual birthday celebration for General Robert E. Lee at the State Capitol. The ceremony is always held on January 19. Later the General Robert E. Lee Sons of Confederate Veterans Camp 803, Sanford, and the Captain Samuel A. Ashe UDC Chapter 2572, Raleigh, were invited as cosponsors. Every ceremony has had standing room only crowds and the Confederate First National Flag has flown over the Capitol during the ceremony. Some past keynote speakers have been NC Supreme Court Justices I. Beverly Lake and Burley Mitchell Jr., local columnist John Shelton Reed, NC Cultural Resources Secretary Betty McCain and Douglass Knapp, Director of Development of the Museum of the Confederacy in Richmond.

In the summer of 1995, the Chapter began an annual tradition called the Commander's Ice Cream Social which was held at Fred Fletcher Park in Raleigh. The following year in 1996, the Chapter secured a corporate sponsor for the event. The Chapter has always had excellent representation at the Society and national conventions. In Richmond, Virginia in 1996, there were 11 Waddell Chapter delegates in attendance, the largest of any other Military Order of the Stars and Bars Chapter. In 1997, the chapter sent seven delegates to Nashville, Tennessee. At that convention, the Captain Waddell Chapter won the Dr. James M. Edwards Distinguished Chapter Award for the most outstanding chapter in the nation.

Under the leadership of Chapter Commander Dan Jones, the Chapter began a fund raising effort in 2000 to restore the grave of Confederate General Lawrence O'Bryan Branch buried in Raleigh's city cemetery. Funds were collected from members and friends of the chapter from all over the country. The general's grave obelisk was first leveled and cleaned as well as the other tombstones in the Branch gravesite. A Confederate Cross of Honor was place on one side of the monument and a bronze marker denoting the many accomplishments of the general was placed on the other side. The monument was rededicated in a ceremony held on August 18, 2002 with direct descendants of Gen. Branch on hand to accept the restoration on behalf of the family. The Capt. Samuel Ashe UDC Chapter sponsored a reception following the ceremony at the UDC state headquarters in Raleigh.

Editor's note: Waddell Chapter members, Commander Byron Brady and past Commander-General Albert D. Jones, Jr. have received the MOSB's highest award, the *Robert E. Lee Chalice*.

Submitted by Chapter Commander Byron Brady.

Colonel Robert F. Webb Chapter

Raleigh, North Carolina

On July 1, 1969, eleven members of the Private Henry Lawson Wyatt Camp, Sons of Confederate Veterans, Raleigh, North Carolina, organized the Colonel Robert F. Webb Chapter, Military Order of the Stars and Bars. William I. Berryhill, Jr., great-great grandson of Colonel Webb, was elected as the chapter's first commander.

The Chapter received its name from Robert Fulton Webb, the last colonel of North Carolina's famed "Bloody Sixth" regiment. Webb was born in Baltimore, Maryland in 1825. After immigrating to Orange County, North Carolina, he fought in the Mexican War as a second lieutenant. On May 20, 1861, Robert Webb began his Confederate service as captain of Company B, Sixth Regiment, North Carolina State Troops. He rose rapidly through the ranks. On September 19, 1862, while commanding the Sixth North Carolina at the Battle of Sharpsburg, Lt. Colonel Webb suffered a severe arm wound during some of the bloodiest fighting of the war. On July 2, 1863, Robert Webb was promoted to the rank of colonel. He was captured on November 7, 1863, while in command of the Sixth North Carolina at the ill-fated Battle of Rappahannock Bridge, Virginia. Colonel Webb was confined at the Confederate officers' prison at Johnson's Island, Ohio. While a prisoner at Johnson's Island, Webb authored a diary, which is the only history, written during the war, of the Sixth North Carolina Regiment. This diary may be found in the *Mangum Papers*, Southern Historical Collection, University of North Carolina at Chapel Hill and in Judge Walter Clark's *North Carolina Regiments 1861-1865, Vol. IV.* Colonel Webb was released at Johnson's Island on July 25, 1865, after taking the Oath of Allegiance. In March, 1896, a few old soldiers met in Durham and organized the Colonel Robert F. Webb Camp, United Confederate Veterans. Colonel Webb died on January 11, 1891. He is the highest ranking Confederate officer buried in Durham's historic Maplewood Cemetery.

The Colonel Robert F. Webb Chapter has been involved in numerous Confederate preservation projects over the years. The chapter's longest continuous project has been its annual "Ladies Night Confederate Celebration" at the Carolina Country Club in Raleigh. Held for the past eight years, the Webb Chapter's "Ladies Night" has been the premier Military Order of the Stars and Bars event held in North Carolina. This annual celebration has attracted overflow attendance and such notable WBTS speakers as Rod Gragg; Gordon Rhea; Charles Roland; Gary Gallagher, and Robert K. Krick.

For many years, the Webb Chapter cared for the Warren County grave of Anne Carter Lee, youngest daughter of General Robert E. Lee, until Anne's remains were moved to the Lee family crypt in Lexington, Virginia on September 27, 1994.

In 1996, the Webb Chapter financed the North Carolina Division of Archives and History's publication of *North Carolina Petitions For Presidential Pardons, 1865-1868 - An Index*.

In 1997, the Colonel Robert F. Webb Chapter provided funds for the State Capitol Foundation to restore the 1840 House desk of Representative Francis Burton Craige who introduced North Carolina's 1861 Ordinance of Secession. The chapter also donated a full set of the *Southern Historical Society Papers* to Wake County's Olivia Raney Historical Library. On June 12, 1997, the Webb Chapter contributed the funds needed by the State Capitol Foundation to clean and restore to statue of Private Henry Lawson Wyatt on Capitol Square. Wyatt was the first North Carolina soldier to fall during the War For Southern Independence.

In 1999, the Colonel Robert F. Webb Chapter was presented the MOSB's "Lt. General Simon B. Buckner Award" for maintaining 100% membership.

Other more recent Webb Chapter heritage preservation and civic activities have included regular donations to Oakwood Cemetery's Confederate Flag and Light Fund; membership in the Museum of the Confederacy and the Stonewall Jackson Foundation; a donation to the UNC Children's Hospital in Chapel Hill; and sponsorship of an applicant for the MOSB's Robert E. Lee college scholarship.

The Colonel Robert F. Webb Chapter meets quarterly at the Carolina Country Club in Raleigh, North Carolina. The chapter's current commander is John R. Bass of Spring Hope, North Carolina.

Respectfully submitted by William I. Berryhill, Jr., Adjutant

Lt. General Daniel H. Hill Chapter

Wadesboro, NC

The first "official" organizational meeting of the Lt. General Daniel H. Hill Chapter was scheduled for February 28, 2004. The meeting was at the Sullivan Place in Wadesboro, which is owned by the great-niece of the late Hon. General W. A. Smith of the United Confederate Veterans. Smith was a private in Company C, Anson Guards, 14th NC Infantry. After the war he co-authored a book entitled *Anson Guards*. He was also one of the founders of Jefferson Pilot Insurance Company.

On January 30, twenty-five invitations were mailed to MOSB members in the greater area of Wadesboro. This area includes Charlotte, Waxhaw, Monroe, Pinehurst, and Biscoe. Following our organizational-meeting, there will be a brief memorial service for Confederate Congressman Thomas S. Ashe at the nearby Eastview Cemetery. Also, a tour of historic Wadesboro will be lead by Anson County Genealogy Society President Steve Bailey.

The chapter will meet on a quarterly basis. Dates have not been established.

Brigadier General William R. Boggs Chapter

Winston-Salem, North Carolina

The General William R. Boggs Chapter was organized in the summer of 1986 in Winston-Salem and held their first meeting in August of that year. In April 1980 they began publishing **Forsyth Greys** edited by Brian Green.

In 1990 the General Boggs Chapter began sponsoring an annual War Between the States and Antique Only Gun Show each year in March. In 1988 they held their 9th Annual on March 7-9 at the Elks Lodge in Winston-Salem.

The Chapter works very closely with the Captain M.W. Norfleet Camp 1249 Sons of Confederate Veterans in Winston-Salem and participates in Confederate Memorial Services in Salem Cemetery each May. The Chapter also contributes funds to many Confederate related organizations as a result of the profit they make each year at their gun show.

PENNSYLVANIA SOCIETY

John C. Pemberton Chapter

Philadelphia, Pennsylvania

The John C. Pemberton Chapter 229, Philadelphia, Pennsylvania, was chartered in 1996. The signing of the charter was held at General Lee's Headquarters in Gettysburg, Pennsylvania on December 7th of that year, with all charter members present and signing.

The charter officers are still in command, viz Commander Jeffrey S. Prushankin, Lieutenant Commander Herbert E. Dickson, and Adjutant Larry L. Beane II.

Although the chapter is small in numbers, three of its members have been published. Compatriot R. Thomas Campbell is author of four books on the Confederate Navy - including *Gray Thunder* - and has been published in *Confederate Veteran*. Compatriot Thomas Boaz is author of *Guns For Cotton: England Arms The Confederacy*. Adjutant Larry Beane has had articles published in magazines and newspapers, including the *Philadelphia Inquirer*. Commander Jeff Prushankin is a doctoral candidate in American History at the University of Arkansas.

The Chapter has also co-sponsored two memorial services with its brother Sons of Confederate Veterans camp, J.E.B. Stuart 1506 and has donated books to local libraries.

SOUTH CAROLINA SOCIETY

The Military Order of the Stars and Bars (MOSB) was born in South Carolina on August 30, 1938. The 48th Annual Reunion of the United Confederate Veterans and the 43rd Annual Convention of the Sons of Confederate Veterans met at the Jefferson Hotel in Columbia, South Carolina August 30 through September 2, 1938. On August 30, 1938 an organizational meeting was held at 3:00 PM and the Order of the Stars and Bars, as it was known then, was created. The initial membership was composed of 17 former commissioned officers of the Confederate States military and 47 male descendants of Confederate officers. Two South Carolinians, both descendants of Confederate officers, were among the original members of the MOSB. These were Dr. Baylis H. Earle of Greenville and James d'Alvigny McCollough of Honea Path.

The name of the organization was changed to the Military Order of the Stars and Bars at the annual convention in Memphis, Tennessee effective August 15, 1976. As there are no former Confederate officers still living, membership in the MOSB is restricted to male descendants of Confederate officers and elected officials. The survival of the MOSB is due in large part to the late General William D. McCain of Mississippi. He served as Adjutant General of the MOSB from 1954 to 1993. He also served as Adjutant in Chief of the Sons of Confederate Veterans from 1953 to 1993.

The modern history South Carolina Society of the Military Order of the Stars and Bars began on October 1, 1984 when the General Maxcy Gregg Chapter #98 was chartered. The charter members were W. C. Smith, III, David Cooper, Ed Crosby, Dr. Jean LaBorde, Jr. Wesly Drawdy, George Martin, and Henry Durant. This was the only MOSB chapter in South Carolina at that time. It was closely related to the General Wade Hampton Camp, No. 273, Sons of Confederate Veterans of Columbia, South Carolina and shared the same adjutant for several years. For a short time, there was also a Richard Kirkland Chapter #174 Chartered in Camden, South Carolina.

As of July 1, 1999, the South Carolina Society of the MOSB had four active chapters with a total of 57 members. The Society officers for 1998-2000 were Wayne D. Roberts, Commander; William E. DuBose, Jr., Lieutenant Commander; P. Ronald Hamilton, Adjutant; and Michael G. Kelly, Genealogist. The General Maxcy Gregg Chapter #98, chartered in Columbia in 1984, had 25 members in 1999. Officers for the General Maxcy Gregg Chapter were R. Brett Bradshaw, Commander; Harrison Gasque, Lieutenant Commander; Roger O. Harley, Adjutant. The Battle of Dingles Mill Chapter #12, chartered in Sumter, December 23, 1987, had five members in 1999. Officers of the Battle of Dingles Mill Chapter were William E. DuBose, Commander; Benjamin P. McNeese, Jr., Lieutenant Commander; and John A. DuBose, Adjutant. The Major M. C. Butler Chapter #232, chartered in Belvedere June 30, had nine members in 1999. Officers of the Major General M. C. Butler Chapter were R. Jason Goings, Commander and Perry Craig Morris, Adjutant. The Colonel James McCollough Chapter #242, chartered in Greenville June 30, 1997, had 18 members in 1999. Colonel James McCollough Chapter officers were Joseph L. Montgomery, Commander; Samuel T. "Tom" Tucker, III, Lieutenant Commander; and Kenneth Derrell Morgan, Adjutant.

As of January 30, 2004, the South Carolina Society of the MOSB now has a fifth chapter, the General and Colonel Rains Chapter of Aiken, ready to be chartered. The Society currently has a total of 72 members. The Society officers for 2003-2004 are Robert Brett Bradshaw, Commander; Thomas M. Weidner, Lieutenant Commander; P. Ronald Hamilton, Adjutant; and Wayne D. Roberts, Genealogist. The General Maxcy Gregg Chapter, now has 35 members. Officers for the General Maxcy Gregg Chapter are James H. Gressette, Jr., Commander, Tom M. Thomas, Jr., Lieutenant Commander; Steven L. Wolfe, Adjutant. The Battle of Dingles Mill Chapter now has six members. Officers of the Battle of Dingles Mill Chapter are William E. DuBose, Commander; Benjamin P. McNeese, Jr., Lieutenant Commander; John A. DuBose, Adjutant; and Rembert J. Kennedy, Real Son. The Major M. C. Butler Chapter now has ten members. Officers of the Major General M. C. Butler Chapter are R. Jason Goings, Commander and C. Richard Barbare, Lieutenant Commander and Adjutant. The Colonel James McCollough Chapter now has 21 members. Colonel James McCollough Chapter officers are Joseph L. Payne III, Commander; Carroll Wayne Caldwell, Lieutenant Commander; and P. Ronald Hamilton, Adjutant. Danny A. Francis is slated to be Commander of the new Rains Chapter.

The South Carolina Society of the Military Order of the Stars and Bars has been very active with projects over the past several years. In 1993 the Society undertook a series of weekend cleanup expeditions to restore the historic Capers-Guerry cemetery in Sumter. This cemetery was severely damaged by Hurricane Hugo. There has been continuing involvement of the Society in the defense of the Confederate flag atop the South Carolina State House. In 1994, The Society donated $2,000 received from National Headquarters for the defense of the Confederate Battleflag on the dome of the South Carolina State House. In 1995 a new monument in Sumter was dedicated to Confederate Medal of Honor recipient Lieutenant Alexander McQueen. The Society contributed $500 to this project. Also in 1995, the Society donated copies of The Roll of the Dead to several public libraries across South Carolina.

In 1996 The South Carolina Society of the MOSB began holding its Annual Lee-Jackson Banquet in January. This has become a special time for members, wives, and guests to gather and share mementos and stories of their ancestors and Confederate soldiers. The January 2001 Lee-Jackson Banquet was held at Oakley Park in Edgefield. This was the home of Confederate Brigadier General Martin Witherspoon Gary. The Society has donated over $800 toward repairs to the roof at Oakley Park and toward the restoration of the original Company Colors of the Edgefield Hussars, that is on display at Oakley Park. For the 2003 Lee-Jackson Banquet, Society members and guests were treated to a behind-the-scenes tour of the new museum facility of the South Carolina Relic Room, repository of a huge collection of Confederate artifacts. Afterwards, during the Banquet, author Gordon C. Rhea gave a talk about his latest book, *Carrying The Flag.*

In 1997 the South Carolina Society of the MOSB began annual battlefield tours. Many of these tours have been led by Wayne D. Roberts, Society Commander 1993-1994 and 1998-2000. The first tour was at the Battle of Congaree Creek in Lexington County. In 1998, the tour focused on the Atlanta campaign with stops at the Battle of Kennesaw Mountain, the Battle of Kolbs Farm, Marietta, and Kennesaw (Big Shanty during the Great Locomotive Chase). The 1999 tour focused on the campaign for the Charleston and Savannah Railroad with visits to battlefields, earthworks, and sites including the Battle of Pocotaligo, the Battle of Tullifinny Crossroads, the Battle of Coosawhatchie, the Battle of Honey Hill, Stoney Creek Battery, Tomotley Battery, Bees Creek Battery, Pocotaligo Battery, Gardens Corner, Stoney Creek cemetery, Old Sheldon Church, and the Church of the Holy Trinity in old Grahamville. The 2000 tour focused on Sherman's march through South Carolina. Battlefields visited included Rivers Bridge, Broxton's Bridge, and Congaree Creek. The 2001 tour moved down to the Savannah, Georgia area and focused on Old Fort Jackson, Fort Pulaski, and Fort McAlister. The 2002 tour centered on Charleston, South Carolina and was led by National Park Historian Rick Hatcher. There was a tour of Fort Sumter, Fort Magruder, the Battlefield of Secessionville, and of various sites related to the Confederate Submarine Hunley. The tour ended with a viewing of the Hunley, at the Lasch Research Facility. The 2003 tour focused on Potter's Raid into the heartland of South Carolina. Author Allan D. Thigpen led the tour, visiting battlefields and sites along the path of destruction perpetrated by Federal forces from Manning, through Sumter and to Camden, South Carolina. Among the sites visited were the Battle of Dingle's Mill, the Battle of Boykin's Mill, the Battle of Dinkins Mill, the fight on the streets of Manning, and The Borough House, home of Confederate Lieutenant General Richard H. Anderson. Plans are set for the 2004 tour to be in Augusta, Georgia.

As an outgrowth of these battlefield tours, the Society has implemented a plan to place historical markers on South Carolina battlefields. The first historical marker was

2002 South Carolina Society field trip to a home used as a Confederate hospital during the Battle of Seccessionville. Photo taken March 9, 2002

placed at the site of the Battlefield at Pocotaligo in 2002. Current plans are to place a marker at the site of the Columbia Hotel, where the Military Order of Stars and Bars was first founded. Other historical markers have been discussed for the battlefields at Tullifinny Crossroads and Coosawhatchie.

By Wayne D. Roberts (March 29, 2000); Revised by Robert Brett Bradshaw (January 30, 2004)

Colonel James McCullough Chapter

Greenville, South Carolina

Chartered: 2 May 1997
Charter Members:
Thomas M. Weidner
Mark A. Roberts
James J. Baldwin, III
James C. Brice, Jr.
Thomas Brissey
J. Randolph Jackson
James P. Orr
David Jackson Rutledge
Phillip R. Hamilton
Chapter Officers:
1997 – 1999:
Thomas M. Weidner, Commander
Mark A. Roberts, Lt. Commander
Phillip R. Hamilton, Adjutant
2000 -2001
Joseph Lanham Montgomery III, Commander
Samuel Thomas Tucker, Lt. Commander
Kenneth D. Morgan, Adjutant
2002- 2003
Thomas M. Weidner, Commander (Society Lt. Commander 2002 - 2003)
Mark A. Roberts, Lt. Commander
Phillip R. Hamilton, Adjutant (Society Adjutant 2000 - 2004)
2004 -2005 Joseph L. Payne III, Commander
Carroll W. Caldwell, Lt. Commander
Phillip R. Hamilton, Adjutant
The Greenville, SC Museum of Confederate History, which is home to the Col. James McCullough Chapter, is owned and operated by the 16th SC Regiment SCV Camp No. 36.

A proposed new Museum and Library of Confederate History will replace the older structure. This is a joint venture of the Museum Board with support from Camp 36 SCV. Fund raising efforts are on-going at the present time and it is hoped that the expanded space will allow for additional display space dedicated to showing more of the contributions by Women of the Confederacy, and the participation of both the Cherokee Indians and Black Confederates.

The present Museum houses the largest amount of martial weapons of the WBTS period in the State of South Carolina. The library provides researchers seeking information on their Confederate ancestors and WBTS History research materials and books that are not available at any other site in the upstate of South Carolina.

One person who assisted and contributed greatly in the formation of both the James McCullough Chapter, as well as, the Museum was Compatriot Vance Brabham Drawdy (1928-1997).

Past projects of the Chapter have included field trips to Kennesaw Mountain, GA in 1999, Rivers Bridge and Congaree Swamp in 2000 with Compatriot Wayne Roberts serving as the tour guide and finally the cleaning the Iron Crosses of CSA Veterans residing in Springwood Cemetery in Greenville, SC.

Respectively submitted by Joseph L. Payne III, Commander, Col. James McCullough Chapter

VIRGINIA SOCIETY

The Virginia Society, Military Order of the Stars and Bars, was founded in 1977. Past commanders include: 1977-79 Flavius Burfoot Walker, Jr.; 1979-81 Earl Foster Harvey; 1981 Jack K. Wyatt; 1981 Hon Thomas M. Moncure Jr.; 1981-84 Charles R. Higginbotham, Jr.; 198486 James Harrison Monroe; 1986-88 Anthony P. Smith; 1988-90 Catesby P. Jones; 1990-92 Josiah Bynum Gay III; 1992-94 Hon. G. William Hammer; 1994-96 Collin Graham Pulley, Jr.; 1996 -1998 Charles D. McGuire; 1998- 2000 Hon. Richard B. Abell; and 2000-2002 John C. Stinson. The Society's current officers are: Commander, A. Clarke Magruder, Sr.; Lieutenant Commander, Jerrell G. Keathley, DCS; Adjutant, Raymond Warren Gill, Jr.; Genealogist, James E. Cooke, Jr.; 2nd LT. Commander, Norris E. Edgerton; Inspector, Walter E. Rivers, Esq.; Chaplain, Rev. Christopher Agnew; and Aide de Camp, Teddy Mullins.

Since its founding, the Virginia Society has expanded rapidly to become one of the Order's largest societies. It currently has over 250 members in eleven chapters and a Headquarters Chapter, and two additional chapters now are being formed. The Society publishes a membership Directory and two newsletters annually and has established an annual awards system modeled on the MOS&B national awards system in order to honor members and non-members who have made significant contributions to the Virginia So-

Replacement memorial stone erected in 2000 by Virginia Society members at the mass grave site of thirty-four Confederate prisoners who died in Federal hospitals and were re-interred at Christ Episcopal Church, Alexandria, Virginia, in December 1879

ciety or to the Order. The Society's web site is linked to the Order's national web site and lists its chapters by name, location, and points of contact. The Society makes donations annually to institutions or activities which honor and commemorate the history and sacrifices of the Confederacy's officer corps and its elected and appointed governmental officials, most recently to the Museum of the Confederacy, Richmond, and to Confederate Memorial Park, Pt. Point, Maryland. The Society also collaborates routinely with organizations such as the United Daughters of the Confederacy and the Stuart-Mosby and Pickett societies and with other military and historical organizations throughout the state. Society officers participate frequently in local or state heritage activities and ceremonies and are determined to ensure the Virginia Society adjusts rapidly to the challenges of the 21st Century.

General Samuel Cooper Chapter

Alexandria, Virginia

The Cooper Chapter of the Military Order of Stars and Bars is named after General Samuel Cooper, the ranking general officer in Confederate service and Adjutant General of the CSA. General Cooper was a resident of Alexandria both before and after the WBTS and is buried in Christ Church Cemetery. Among his many accomplishments, at war's end General Cooper played a crucial part in safeguarding and turning over to Federal authorities the great majority of Confederate military and personnel records which exist today. The Chapter's address is P. O. Box 2005, Alexandria, Virginia 22301, an address it shares with Robert E. Lee Camp 726, Sons of Confederate Veterans. The Chapter was founded on 31 July 1973 with fifteen charter members. Its charter officers were: Colonel Joseph Brady Mitchell, Commander; George S. Knight, Lieutenant Commander; and DuRoc J. Batte, Adjutant.

The Chapter has had 17 commanders since its founding, and they were as follows: Colonel Joseph Brady Mitchell, 1973; Earl Foster Harvey, 1974; George Stephens Knight Sr., 1975; James Harrison Monroe, 1976 - 79; Charles Rufus Higginbotham Jr., 1979 - 82; Bedford Frederick Penn, 1982; John F. Graham, 1983 - 84; Catesby Penniman Jones, 1984 - 86; Colonel William M. Glasgow Jr., 1986 - 88; Captain Samuel Cooper Dawson, Jr., 1988 - 90; Honorable G. William Hammer, 1990 - 94; Charles Danny McGuire, 1994 - 96; Honorable Richard Bender Abell, 1996 - 98; A. Clarke Magruder, Sr., 1998 -2000 2000; Jerrell Glenn Keathley, 2000 - 02; and Robert Kirk Lindsey, 2002 - 03. Its current officers are: Edward R. Fitzgerald, Commander, and Andrew Knox Ramsay III, Adjutant.

The Chapter has been involved in heritage and community activities since its founding. With R. E. Lee Camp 726, it sponsors Confederate Memorial Day services annually at Alexandria's historic Christ Church where Generals Washington and Lee worshiped. Christ Church contains the remains of Confederate soldiers from all across the South who died in Federal hospitals and were re-interred in a mass grave after the WBTS. Through the generosity of its members and with the support of the Order of the Southern Cross, Cooper Chapter replicated and replaced the mass grave stone marker in 2002. Chapter members are particularly proud their chapter was selected as the MOS&B's Distinguished Chapter in 2000. The Chapter co-sponsors annually a banquet marking the birthday of General Lee at which nationally known historians such as National Park Service Historian Emeritus Ed Bearss and Joseph L. Harsh are featured speakers. The Chapter hosts an annual Christmas party where its members donate toys though the United Christian Ministry to needy children in the Alexandria area. Chapter officers and members also participate in annual Lee Birthday celebrations at Statuary Hall in the U.S. Capitol and at the Lee Mansion at Arlington National Cemetery, and they march in

Alexandria's annual Washington's Birthday Parade, the oldest such parade in the U.S. The chapter also participates in annual Confederate Memorial ceremonies in Arlington and joins with the United Daughters of the Confederacy and other MOS&B chapters in the Northern Virginia area in other heritage activities. It has established a web site with links to the Virginia Society and through it to the national MOS&B. General Samuel Cooper Chapter now numbers nearly 60 members, the highest in its history and is still growing.

Col. Thomas H. Williamson Chapter

Chase City, Virginia

In the early 1990's members of the Military Order of the Stars and Bars at newly organized Southside Virginia SCV camps chose to form their own chapter, rather than continue extended travel to established MOS&B chapters elsewhere in Virginia or North Carolina.

Members selected the ancestor of one Charter Member as a namesake, Gen. Thomas H. Williamson, a professor associate of Stonewall Jackson's at VMI and a veteran of the famed "Foot Cavalry."

Col Williamson Chapter was chartered December 11, 1998 in Chase City, Virginia and holds meetings in various towns in the surrounding Southside area. Members and officers participate in the activities and goals of the MOS&B throughout the South Central area of our State and welcome any qualified men into our fellowship.

Major General John Bankhead Magruder Chapter

Fredericksburg, Virginia

The Major General John Bankhead Magruder Chapter of the Military Order of Stars and Bars is headquartered in Fredericksburg, Virginia. The chapter is named for "Prince John" Magruder.

John B. Magruder was born May 1, 1807 in Velleboro, Port Royal, Caroline County, Virginia. He attended the University of Virginia at Charlottesville and was appointed to West Point in 1826. Magruder graduated in 1830, spent sixteen years in minor assignments and then participated in the Mexican conflict from 1846 - 1848. Captain Magruder was promoted to Brevet Major and then Brevet Lieutenant Colonel in 1847. In 1861 Magruder resigned his commission in Washington and crossed the bridge into Virginia where he wasted no time in applying for a commission in the Confederate Army. Colonel Magruder was assigned to the Peninsula and attained the rank of General in Command of the Peninsula Forces. He successfully defended it, turning back McClellan's troops in the opening engagements of the Civil War. Magruder was promoted to Brigadier General June 1861 and Major General October 7, 1861. He was later assigned to Texas, New Mexico and Arizona District. Gen. Magruder took Galveston from the Union on New Years Day 1863 and successfully defended the Coast.

After the war, General Magruder went to Mexico and served with Maximilian. He later returned to Texas and lived in Houston where he died February 18, 1871. Major General John Bankhead Magruder was buried in Houston but later re-interred in Galveston, Texas.

Chartered as Chapter 258 on August 9, 2000, there were 10 charter members with charter officers being Raymond W. Gill, Jr., Commander, Charles A. Embrey, Sr., Lt. Commander and Jan V. Harvey, Adjutant. Since it's founding, the chapter has dedicated itself to marking the graves of Confederate veterans and is deeply involved in the maintenance of the Confederate Cemetery located in Fredericksburg. The chapter participates in many local parades and ceremonies, including the anniversary of the Battle of Fredericksburg and Memorial Day. The Magruder chapter has won several awards for its newsletter, *The Prince's Dispatch*, as well as recruitment awards. The chapter is committed to creating synergy between the MOS&B, the SCV and the UDC.

Lt. General Jubal Anderson Early Chapter

Hillsville, Virginia

On June 10, 2003 the Lt. General Jubal Anderson Early chapter 277 of the MOSB was chartered in Hillsville, VA. It was formed to cover the area of the New River Valley. The Chapter chartered with 15 members. The Chapter officers elected were Commander Andrew S. Jackson, 1st Lt. Commander Jerry Cooper, 2nd Lt. Commander Steve Williams, Adj. Ivan Robinson, and Judge Advocate Joseph McGrady.

Chapter projects started so far are maintained the grave and family cemetery of 1st Lt. Shardock Collier. The chapter has ordered stones and set for: Lt Franklin Branscome and 1st Lt. Asa Scott. A listening of Confederate Officers buried in Carroll County and surrounding counties is being complied to be kept in chapter archives.

Colonel Elijah Viers White Chapter

Leesburg, Virginia

Colonel Elijah Viers White Chapter was named in honor of the Commanding Officer of the 35th Battalion, Virginia Cavalry, which was composed mainly of Leesburg and Loudoun County citizens. Colonel White played a leading role in the battle of Ball's Bluff, an engagement near Leesburg that resulted in a significant Federal defeat, and led the 35th throughout the War. Afterward, Colonel White returned to Leesburg where he became a prominent banker and businessman, and owner of White's Ferry, a ferry service across the Potomac River to Maryland that is still in operation.

White Chapter was organized in Leesburg in 1983, with eleven members. Its first Commander was Elijah B. White, grandson of Colonel White, and its first Adjutant was W. Emory Plaster, Jr. Today, the Chapter Commander is Robert Giles Brown, and the Adjutant is Wesley Brown. Among the 13 current members is The Reverend Elijah B. White III, great-grandson of Colonel White.

White Chapter participates in community activities such as Memorial Day, when wreaths are placed at the Confederate Statue at Loudoun Court House and the Obelisk to Unknown Confederate Dead at Leesburg's Union Cemetery. In addition, Chapter members march in Alexandria's annual George Washington Birthday Parade, along with dozens of representatives of other Southern heritage organizations. The Chapter is presently engaged in efforts to place a permanent marker at Leesburg's historic Harrison House to commemorate a meeting held there on September 5, 1862 by Generals Lee, Longstreet, Stuart and Armistead to plan the Maryland campaign.

George E. Pickett Chapter

Richmond, Virginia

The George E. Pickett Chapter, Military Order of the Stars and Bars, was formed in Richmond, Virginia and has distinguished itself with several projects through the years. It was members of the Pickett Chapter who suggested in 1994 that the Virginia Society began its ongoing project to donate the entire 100-volume, *Virginia Regimental Series*, to the library at Elm Springs.

The Pickett Chapter meets annually in January at the gravesite of General Pickett at Hollywood Cemetery in Richmond to honor the General. It has also held ceremonies in recent years honoring General William Mahone and General John Imboden. "Real Son" Edward Manry, a great-nephew of General Mahone, was inducted into the Chapter in 1994 and was presented his "Real Son" Medal at that time. The Chapter was also instrumental in presenting a "Real Daughter" Medal to Miss Osa Lee Yates of Richmond. Sadly, both of these links to our Confederate heritage have passed away.

The Pickett Chapter was also responsible for the re-internment of Mrs. LaSalle Corbell Pickett beside the remains of her husband in Hollywood Cemetery in Richmond.

Commanders of the Pickett Chapter have included: Flavius Walker (Charter Commander), Tony Smith, Charles Ridenour Samuel Epes, Allen Thurman, Joe B. Gay III, Richard Owen, Collin G. Pulley Jr., Greg Collins, and W. Samuel Craghead.

Submitted by Collin C. Pulley, Jr., Chapter Adjutant

Hupp-Deyerle-McCausland Chapter

Roanoke, Virginia

The Hupp-Deyerle-McCausland Chapter of the Military Order of the Stars and Bars was chartered on March 11, 1996, and was named for Abraham Hupp, Colonel Andrew Deyerle, and General John McCausland.

Charter members were Don Dye, Jody Goad, Gery Hackney, John Harris, Pat Jefferson, Robert Jorlin, John Kurlander, John Lowman, Keith Maxey, Alexander McCauslander, David Thompson, Callor Thompson, Craston William, Ivan Robinson and Roger Waring. Applications are being completed on Barry Hall and Wayne Powell.

Charter officers were Robert Howlett, Commander; Andrew Jackson, Lieutenant Commander; and Don Lorton, Adjutant.

James T. Jackson Chapter

Suffolk, Virginia

An organizational meeting was held in mid-November 1993. This meeting was for the purpose of organizing a Military Order of Stars and Bars Chapter in southeastern Virginia. The meeting was held at the home of Compatriot and Mrs. B. Franklin Earnest Sr., located at 945 Banyan Drive, Virginia Beach, Virginia.

The name James T. Jackson was suggested by Compatriot B. Earnest. Potential members present voted on this suggestion and it was approved. Although most of us had seen Mr. Jackson's name in print, as James T. Jackson, as well as, James W. Jackson. We chose to honor Mr. Jackson for two reasons. First, our Sons of Confederate Veterans Camp was chartered The Norfolk County Grays to honor, Company "A," 61st Virginia Infantry. Company "A" was also known as The "Jackson Grays," they were honoring Mr. Jackson. In selecting Mr. Jackson's name, our Military Order of the Stars and Bars Chapter wished to honor him, as did the "Jackson Grays," for defending our First National Flag. As most Compatriots know Mr. Jackson owned and operated The Marshall House in Alexandria, Virginia. In 1861, after Virginia had seceded, a Union force under the command of Colonel Elmer E. Ellsworth occupied (invaded) Alexandria. Seeing the "Stars and Bars" atop the hotel, Colonel Ellsworth and some soldiers entered The Marshall House, went to the roof and on coming down with The First National Flag, Mr. Jackson confronted them. Mr. Jackson killed Colonel Ellsworth and was shot and bayoneted by Colonel Ellsworth's men. Thus, Mr. Jackson a civilian became one of the first casualties of the War for Southern Independence.

At the organizational meeting the following provisional officers were elected: Kenneth H. Austin Jr., Commander; B. Franklin Earnest Sr., Adjutant; Billy K. Buck, Chaplain.

The James T. Jackson Chapter #123 was chartered on December 1, 1993, through our efforts and the strong support of Past Deputy Commander-in-Chief W. Baxter Perkinson Sr. The Charter Chapter Officers elected were: Commander, Kenneth H. Austin Jr.; Adjutant, B. Franklin Earnest Sr.; Chaplain, Billy K. Buck. Compatriot, W. Baxter Perkinson was made an honorary member. The other Charter members were David W. Austin, James M. Earehart, Christopher M. Lloyd and Cecil B. Strange. In December 1995, the elected officers were: Kenneth H. Austin Jr., Commander; Edward H. Bittenbender, Adjutant; B. Franklin Earnest Sr., 1st Lieutenant Commander; Christopher M. Lloyd, 2nd Lieutenant Commander; Timothy D. Manning Sr., Chaplain; J. Garry Austin, Treasurer; and Timothy D. Manning Jr., Historian.

On May 30, 31 and June 1, 1997, James T. Jackson Chapter co-hosted The Virginia Division/Society Convention in Norfolk, Virginia with our compatriots in The Norfolk County Grays. Our guest speaker was P. Charles Lunsford. Commander General J. Troy Massey of the Military Order of Stars and Bars and Commander-in-Chief Pete Orlebeke of the Sons of Confederate Veterans were our guests.

In March 1996 The James T. Jackson Chapter had made a beautiful version of The Second National Flag. We were the first Military Order of Stars and Bars Chapter in the Virginia Society to get our Chapter Flag.

Respectfully submitted by Kenneth H. Austin Jr., Commander.

Major Edgar Burroughs & Princess Anne Cavalry Chapter

Virginia Beach, Virginia

During our first year of existence, the Major Edgar Burroughs & Princess Anne Cavalry Chapter did the following:

1. Held meetings once a month, and at 98% of those meetings, a speaker was featured.

2. Actively partook in the following events

a) April Confederate Heritage Parade in Richmond.

b) City of Virginia Beach Veterans Day parade.

c) 2nd Annual Lee-Jackson Day Banquet in Virginia Beach (Joint SCV and MOS&B).

d) Emergency Convention debate.

e) Knotts Island, NC Peach Festival.

f) Back Bay Pumpkin Fling.

g) Joint NC MOS&B, Raleigh NC CWRT, Princess Anne Camp behind the scene tour on the USS Monitor.

h) Supported SB No. 631 (Monument /Memorial Protection Bill).

i) Supported SJR No. 96 (Confederate History and Heritage Month).

3. Chapter Projects:

a) Restored the Burroughs Family Cemetery (3 confederates buried there)

b) Restored the McPherson Cemetery in Camden, NC (2 Confederates buried there)

c) On Veterans Day, placed Confederate flags on all known Confederate graves in Virginia Beach.

d) Ordered three Confederate tombstones from the VA. 1 installed, and 2 waiting for drier weather to install.

e) Installed CSA tombstone at Castleton Cemetery. (5 CSA soldiers buried there).

4. Worked with the Princess Anne Camp # 1993 to submit the following amendments to the VA DIV SCV Constitution:

a) To establish a Guardian Program in Virginia, similar to the Guardian Program in South Carolina and the MOS&B Jackson Medal Program. However, our version would include battlefield preservation

b) To establish Honorary and Associate membership, similar to that in South Carolina.

5. Published an eight page monthly newsletter, including photos. (This is a joint SCV & MOS&B newsletter).

6. Held chapter elections.

7. Established contacts within city government and within other Virginia Beach historical groups.

8. Published a roster of all known units that were formed in Princess Anne County during the War Between the States. This includes Co. A, Burroughs Battalion Partisan Rangers, which until now, was pretty much a mystery unit. Research continues.

9. Responded to the destruction and grave robbery of the Shipp Family Cemetery, where a relic hunter dug into CSA Pvt. Andrew Shipp's grave, looking for Confederate material. This included emergency restoration and contacting the family of this issue. Further restoration work to follow.

10. Chapter #281 charter presentation meeting held March 29, 2004. Charter presented by Virginia Society Commander A. Clarke Magruder, Sr.

11. Chapter membership: 10

12. Chapter officers:

Commander - Oscar F. Baxter V, Lt. Commander - Kenneth R. Harris, Adjutant Treasurer - Col. William D. Andrews, Genealogist - John S. Moscoe

Army of Tennessee Department

The Army of Tennessee Department has been actively engaged in many activities. The current Army Commander is William Earl Faggert from Heidelberg, Mississippi. The current Executive Committeeman is John Thomas Mason from Covington, Tennessee.

Many members have been busy in preparation for the upcoming May 30th opening of the Jefferson Davis Presidential Library at Beauvoir in Biloxi, Mississippi. Numerous memorial services were conducted in the month of April including a newly initiated service in the Vicksburg Cemetery. This project was ably chaired by Commander Lamar Roberts of Vicksburg.

The Department continues to remember the sacrifices of all Confederate soldiers in every way possible.

MAJOR GRAHAM DAVES SOCIETY OF ALABAMA

The Military Order of the Stars and Bars was chartered in Alabama on July 21,1984. At the suggestion of Alfred C. Daves of Mobile, the Society was named in honor of his grandfather, Major Graham Daves.

Major Daves was born in New Bern, North Carolina. He served as adjutant of the 12th Regiment and the regiment later became known as the 22nd when the regiment was re-arranged. He was promoted to major November 5, 1862. He served at Raleigh, Richmond, Wilmington, Petersburg, and in Mississippi where he was assistant adjutant-general on the staff of General Joseph E. Johnston. After the fall of Vicksburg, he returned to North Carolina and served in Raleigh. He was surrendered near Greensboro at war's end and his parole was dated April 26, 1865.

The Society publishes a quarterly newsletter, *The Yellowhammer* with a circulation of approximately 100. Since its inception beginning in October 1987, *The Yellowhammer* has won the Walter S. Taylor newsletter award seven times.

In 1990 the Society began holding semi-annual meetings known as musters. The first muster was held on November 2, 1991 at the home of Lieutenant General Joe Wheeler in Hillsboro, Alabama. Musters have been held statewide in places such as Jacksonville, Cahaba, Tennehill State Park and Mooresville.

On May 11, 1991, the Society adopted its Society Flag based upon the design of the 15th Alabama Infantry upon whose design the current Alabama State Flag is modeled.

The membership has varied since 1984 to between 90 and 130 members. Officers from 1994-1996 were Commander S. Gayden Latture, 1st Lieutenant Commander Thomas L. Alison, 2nd Lieutenant Commander Avery Hudson and Adjutant Cliff Crisler. Officers from 1996- 1998 include Commander Thomas L. Alison, 1st Lieutenant Commander Avery Hudson, 2nd Lieutenant Commander Adam Dasinger and Adjutant Cliff Crisler.

General E.P. Alexander Chapter

Alexander City, Alabama

The General E.P. Alexander Chapter of the Military Order of the Stars and Bars from Alexander City was chartered November 15, 1991 with the following Charter Members: Herman H. Kitchens Jr., Brent Richard Scott, Clifton W. Crisler, William C. Daniel Jr., Jimmy Lee McWhorter, Glenn W. Vinson, Dwight S. Walls, Joseph A. Goggans, Wendell N. White, John M. Taylor, Seth Taylor and Hunter Scott.

Since its chartering the Chapter has had three Commanders: Brent R. Scott, Herman H. Kitchens Jr. and the current commander, Clifton W. Crisler.

The Chapter's namesake, General E.P. Alexander, was chosen by the Chapter because of his prominence in the Army of northern Virginia as well as by the fact that Alexander City, Alabama was named for the General. When the railroad was being planned from Birmingham, Alabama to Columbus, Georgia, a delegation of the representatives of Youngville, Alabama met with General Alexander in Opelika, Alabama with a petition to have the railroad run through their town. This became a reality and in the 1870s the town changed its name to Alexander City in honor of the General.

Though small in numbers, the Chapter is active in support of the local Sons of Confederate Veterans Camp and in doing living history programs and educational programs in the local schools.

Brigadier General St. John R. Liddell Chapter

Bay Minette, Alabama

The Brigadier General St. John R. Liddell Chapter 271 was chartered in April 2002 and had the chartering ceremony on January 14, 2003. Past MOS&B Commander General Perry Outlaw was Master of Ceremonies and swore in Chapter members and new officers. Division-Commander Wyatt Willis was in attendance as well as representatives from three MOS&B Chapters.

Charter members are: Danleigh Corbett, Bert Blackmon, Mike Shipler, Lawrence Morrow, Jeff Boone, Jeffrey Boone, Claude Tuberville, Tommy Rhodes, Robert McMillan, Jr., Henry Barnes, Kiley Barnes and Howard W. Smith. Meetings are on the third Tuesday of each month with a program.

In 2003 we co-sponsored the Lee-Jackson Salute, Jefferson Davis Birthday Party, yard sales, and during the 2003 Division Reunion, we sponsored the MOS&B Business Meeting and the Sunday Prayer breakfast.

In 2004 we are sponsoring the Lee-Jackson Salute, Jefferson Davis Birthday Party, and the First Gulf Coast Civil War and Black Powder Expo, which will become an annual event.

Brigadier General John Herbert Kelly Chapter

Birmingham, Alabama

In May of 1982, Alfred C. Daves, appointed temporarily to the post of Adjutant for the provisional Alabama Society of the MOSB, sent a letter to Alabama MOSB members informing them of plans to formally organize an Alabama Society. Charles Patton Hash, Jr., of the Fighting Joe Wheeler Camp No. 1372, SCV, volunteered to help form a MOSB chapter for the Birmingham area. By July of 1982 the new chapter had formed under the provisional name of the "Thomas Jonathan Jackson-Patrick Ronayne Cleburne Chapter." The chapter was formally organized on October 28, 1982, and the name was changed to honor Alabamian Brigadier General John Herbert Kelly. Jimmy H. Burton was elected Commander, and C. Patton Hash Jr. was elected Adjutant.

In 2003 the Kelly Chapter successfully completed a long-term fundraising project for the professional treatment and conservation of the battle flag of the 2nd Battalion, Hilliard's Alabama Legion, which resides in the collection of Confederate Memorial Hall in New Orleans. Officers since 1998 are John H. Killian, Commander, and Alan Dismukes, Adjutant.

Catesby a.p. Roger Jones Chapter

Selma, Alabama

The Catesby a.p. Jones was chartered October 15, 1995 at Cahaba, Alabama during the annual Military Order of the Stars and Bars fall muster. The Chapter chartered with seven members with Thomas L. Alison appointed Commander and Norman W. Prather appointed Lieutenant Commander. The Chapter counts as its members the State Society Genelogist Nat Rudulph and the current State Society Commander Thomas L. Alison of this date (January 1998). Besides its role in state offices, it renders assistance to the Sons of Confederate Veterans camps located in the Black Belt region of Alabama.

The chapter was named in honor of Catesby a.p. Roger Jones who was the Commander of the Selma Naval Ordinance Works, which was captured by Wilson's raiders in April 1865. Descendants of Commander Jones still reside in Selma and also occupy his home.

Deshler-O'Neal Chapter

Tuscumbia, Alabama

The Deshler-O'Neal Chapter of the Military Order of the Stars and Bars was founded in December 1983 (not certain of exact date), and was named for General James Deshler and General Edward A. O'Neal.

Charter members were William C. Scott Jr., William C. Scott III, Michael B. McCloskey, Colonel Harold Whitlock, Robert S. Dabney and William T. Johnson.

Current Chapter officers are William T. Johnson, Commander and William C. Scott Jr.,Adjutant.

Them Chapter places public notices in local news papers for General Robert E. Lee's Birthday and Confederate Memorial Day.

FLORIDA SOCIETY

The Florida Society is composed of 13 chapters and 232 members. Annually, at the State Convention, the society sponsors the Military Order of the Stars and Bars Prayer Breakfast and the John Randolph of Roanoke Tournament of Oratory.

LT. James Duke	St. Petersburg, FL
MG. James P. Anderson	Pensacola, FL
MAJ. William I. Turner	Sarasota-Bradenton, FL
Marion Dragoons	Ocala, FL
CAPT. William J. Rogers	Kissimmee, FL
LTC. William Baya	St. Augustine, FL
CAPT. Richard Bradford	Madison, FL
GEN. William Miller	Gainesville, FL
CAPT. J.J. Dickison	Jacksonville, FL
BG. Theodore W. Brevard	Indialantic, FL
CAPT. Asa A. Stewart	Lake City, FL
Francis S. Bartow	Bartow, FL
COL. L.M. Park	Orlando, FL

A. Robert Kuykendall Jr., Commander
John W. Adams, Adjutant

Francis S. Bartow Chapter

Bartow, Florida

The Francis S. Bartow Chapter, Military Order of the Stars and Bars was chartered on June 17, 1985 in Bartow, Florida. The Chapter was named for the Francis S. Bartow Camp of the United Confederate Veterans which was organized on June 17, 1893 at the Polk County Court House in Bartow. The Chapter, Camp and City were all named to honor Brigadier General Francis S. Bartow of Savannah, Georgia who gave his life for the Confederacy in the First Battle of Manassas in 1861.

One of the first projects of the Chapter was to identify Confederate Officers and enlisted soldiers buried in local cemeteries. A total of 35 officers were located in Bartow alone and were honored by publication of an Honor Roll. On January 19, 1990 the Chapter erected and rededicated a granite monument marking the site of the home of Confederate Major General Evander M. Law who resided in the city from 1893 to 1920. In addition the Chapter was instrumental in the City of Bartow's Proclamation and establishment of Major General E.M. Law Day. Confederate Memorial Day, April 26th, is annually observed by the placement of flags on the graves of confederate veterans and Confederate Monuments located in the city.

The Chapter has been led by Commanders Wm. Lloyd Harris 1985-1992, Bob Bass 1993-1994, and Robert H. Snead 1995-Present. The Chapter has had one Adjutant Mark A. Hall 1985-Present.

The Francis S. Bartow Chapter holds meetings in conjunction with the Gen. E.M. Law Camp 1323, Sons of Confederate Veterans also in Bartow, Florida.

Brigadier General Theodore W. (Washington) Brevard Chapter

Indialantic, Florida

The Brigadier General Theodore W. (Washington) Brevard Chapter of the Florida Society received its Charter at Indialantic Florida on October 19, 1989 and was assigned Chapter Number 10. The Charter Members were; Major Aubrey R. Bates, Walter E. Hall, Carl E. Smith, Charles H. Bronson and John E. Spooner. At the Chartering Ceremony Dr. Richard M. Lancaster was sworn in as a member.

The Commanders of the Chapter have been, in chronological order, John E. Spooner, James L. Patton, Carl E. Smith and, currently, Dr. Richard M. Lancaster. Other current Officers are 1st Lt. Commander James E. Rowe Jr., 2nd Lt. Commander Robert E. May, and Adjutant Robert R. Murray.

The Chapter is proud to have an Honorary Member of the General Society, Junie Young Williford, Jr.

The Chapter has lost Major Aubrey R. Bates and Robert D. Neill to death, Thomas J. Jenkins as the result of a stroke, Charles K. Bronson as a founding member of another Chapter and Walter E. Hall as a result of job relocation.

One of the Chapter's projects was expanded into the General Society's Ancestral Research Committee and we are looking forward to founding the General Society's Ancestral Research Library.

Submitted by Dr. Richard M. Lancaster, Commander.

Lieutenant Colonel William Baya Chapter

St. Augustine, Florida

The Lieutenant Colonel William Baya Chapter 140, Military Order of the Stars and Bars, was chartered on April 26,1991. Chartering ceremonies were held on December 18,1991 at the home of its first and only commander, Colonel John J. Masters Sr., U.S. Army Retired, at 3000 Usina Road, St. Augustine, Florida. The Charter was presented by E. Price Landrum III, Commander, Florida Society, Military Order of the Stars and Bars.

Charter members were Colonel John J. Masters Sr., Commander, and his sons, Major John J. Masters Jr., Florida Army National Guard, Adjutant/Treasurer, and Captain Burton L. Masters, U.S. Army; Kenneth Beeson; N. Putnam Calhoun, Lieutenant Commander; Michael H. Charles; Captain Benjamin Hudgins; James V. Perry Sr.; John G.R. Rountree and his son Robert I. Shreve-Rountree. Four of the charter members, the three Masters, and Kenneth Beeson are cousins of Lieutenant Colonel Baya. Another cousin, Charles E. Stevens Jr., joined later.

Lieutenant Colonel William Baya was born in St. Augustine, Florida on January 23,1834. He served as an orderly sergeant early in the war. He then was a 1st Lieutenant CS Marines, aboard the CSS Jeff Davis. He organized and commanded a company of Grayson's Artillery which was re-designated Company D, 8 Florida Infantry CSA and mustered into Confederate Service in May of 1862. Promoted to Lieutenant Colonel he commanded the 8th Florida Infantry at the Battle of Gettysburg. He was wounded twice and captured three times, the last being at Saylors Creek, Virginia on April 6, 1865. Lieutenant Colonel Baya died July 1, 1903 in Jacksonville, Florida and is buried in Evergreen Cemetery.

Commander Masters has been a committee of one in locating the graves of over 167 Confederate soldiers and sailors in St. Johns County and mounting 32 Veterans Administration headstones on graves of Confederate soldiers. The results of this work will be published soon.

The Chapter donated part of the funds for the purchase of the just published six volume set of the *Biographical Rosters of Florida Confederate and Union Soldiers, 1861-1865* to be donated to the St. Augustine Genealogical Society to be put in the main public library of St. Augustine.

Commander Masters has attended the last seven State and National SCV/MOSB conventions. The Chapter co-hosted the Florida Division Sons of Confederate Veterans and the Florida Chapter Military Order of the Stars and Bars annual convention at St. Augustine, Florida, in June 1994. It provides leadership to the General Loring Camp's Sons of Confederate Veterans as Commander, 3rd Lieutenant Commander, and Adjutant/Treasurer.

The Chapter has participated in all the Sons of Confederate Veterans Camp and the Ancient City Chapter, UDC activities since its founding. Chapter activities also include Lee/Jackson and Lieutenant Colonel Baya's birthday dinners in January, CSA Memorial Day in April, cemetery ceremonies when mounting CSA headstones each fall and commemoration of General Loring's birth and death in December.

The Chapter has lost one member in death, Robert I. Shreve-Rountree on May 11,1992, one transfer out, Michael Charles, who remains an associate member; and gained three members: Fred Chauvin, Charles E. Stevens Jr., and one transfer in, Robert Kuykendall Jr., Commander of the Florida Society Military Order of the Stars and Bars and Commander Army of Tennessee Department Sons of Confederate Veterans.

The Chapter now has 13 members. Officers are elected every two years. At its last election on March 30, 1995, Colonel John J. Masters Sr. was re-elected Commander; Major John J. Masters Jr., Adjutant/Treasurer, and G. Fred Chauvin was elected Lieutenant Commander due to the resignation of N. Putnam Calhoun on March 21, 1995, from that position. Charles E. Stevens Jr. was elected Chaplain. Other members are Kenneth H. Beeson, N. Putnam Calhoun, Carleton P. Drew, Captain Benjamin Hudgins, A. Robert Kuykendall Jr., Major Burton L. Masters, USAR, James H. Perry Sr., John G.R. Rountree and William D. Chisholm Jr.

Chapter Officers:
Paul M. Pomar, Commander
George F. Chauvin, 1st Lt. Commander
James S. Davis, Adjutant
Michael C. Greenleaf, Chaplain
Col. John J. Masters Sr., Genealogist

GEORGIA SOCIETY
Captain William A. Fuller

When the organizational meeting of the Order of Stars and Bars took place in Columbia, South Carolina on August 30, 1938, three Georgians were present. Dr William R. Dancy of Savannah, John Ashley Jones of Atlanta and Judge Alexander W. Stephens of Atlanta. Dr. Dancy would later in life become Commander of the MOS&B and Mr. Jones would go on to be CIC of the Sons of Confederate Veterans.

The Georgia Society was named for Captain William A. Fuller, famous railroad conductor of the *General*. Captain Fuller was the Hero in the *Great Locomotive Chase*.

The Fuller Society was organized during the centennial by Clyde A. Boynton of Atlanta. He would serve as the first commander. Later Leslie A. Owens of Augusta would serve in 1968. Since then Jack Bledose, Col. Mac Pryor, Robert B. Turbyfill, Jimmy Fouche, P. Charles Lunsford, Henry B. "Hank" Googer, and Thomas W. "Woody" Highsmith have all served as Commander.

In 1993, then Commander Lunsford gave the Society and then National, the John Randolph of Roanoke Oratory Contest. Under the leadership of Command Highsmith, (1996-1998), the Society saw amazing growth in not only membership, but in the mission of the MOS&B. Events were held each year for the Last Confederate Cabinet meeting in Washington, Georgia and Alexander H. Stephens Birthday Jubilee in Crawfordville, Georgia. Also the Society reprinted the *Defense of Battery Wagner, July 18th, 1863: Shattering the Myth of the 54th (Coloured) Massachusetts.*

Today, the Georgia Society is the largest. Under the leadership of Charles Kelly Barrow since 1998, the Society has been involved in many events. The events in Washington and Crawfordville continue to grow. New events have come on board. The Jefferson Davis Birthday Celebration in Irwinville, Georgia continues to grow. A National Confederate Memorial Service at Stone Mountain Confederate Memorial Park is held every April. This idea was conceived Woody Highsmith. The Society also co-sponsors events such the Annual Captain Henry Wirz Memorial in November in Andersonville, Georgia, Patrick Cleburne Society Banquet in March, and the Immortal 600 project at Fort Pulaski. The Society was also responsible for making the Confederate Memorial Tartan the Official Tartan of the Georgia Society, Georgia Division, SCV and the National MOS&B and SCV. Also the Society reprinted *Truth of the War Conspiracy of 1861.*

Like the name of our Society, we will continue to grow, move, and lead for all to follow in our Glorious and Noble Cause.

Colonel Emory Best Chapter

Cassville, Georgia

Emory Best grew up in Cassville Georgia and was the son of a local pastor. During the Civil War, Emory was appointed Colonel of the 23rd Infantry Company C.

On November 3, 2001 a Luminary Service was held in the old Cassville Cemetery in honor of the sacrifice and loss of the citizens of Cassville. The city was burned on November 5, 1864 at the hands of federal troops. This service is an annual event.

The Colonel Emory Best Chapter #265 of The Military Order of the Stars & Bars was chartered at this service with Society commander Kelly Barrow officiating.

Commander: Eddie Fain Boswell

Lt. Commander: Barry Lynn Colbaugh

Other members are: David Joe Ferguson, James M. Gaston, Jr., Denson Baltzelle Hamby, Derek Sean Hamby, Jerry Lane Luffman, Cecil Ray Palmer, Tommy V. Smith, and Ralph Franklin Treadaway.

Quarterly meetings are held locally in the old town of Cassville. This chapter has been represented at the 2002 and 2003 National MOS&B Conventions, local July 4th parades, and Confederate Memorial Day services in Bartow County and Gilmer County, GA. We have also served as volunteer honor guard for the crew of the H.L. Hunley in Charleston, SC. Our goal is to uphold the good name of the Confederate soldiers and Officers Corp.

Lieutenant General William J. Hardee Chapter

Jonesboro, Georgia

The Lieutenant General William J. Hardee Chapter was founded in 1993 after the great-grandfather of charter member William Elder. Other charter members include Scott Gilbert, Bill Gilbert, Ben Huiet, Caleb Huiet, Gary Helton, James Pollard, Mark Pollard, Ed Reynolds, Matt Thomaston and David Helm.

Charter officers are Commander Scott Gilbert and Lieutenant Commander Mark Pollard.

Past Commanders are Scott Gilbert (twice), Bill Elder (deceased) and Gary Helton. Current Commander is Gary S. Helton.

The Chapter donated the Georgia State flag to the city of Lake City, Georgia in Clayton County; they donated library books to the library in McDonough, Georgia in Henry County; and held three consecutive Jefferson Davis birthday suppers.

General Alfred Holt Colquitt Chapter

Macon, Georgia

The General Alfred Holt Colquitt Chapter was founded in 1995, and was named after Confederate Brigadier General, Congressman, U.S. Senator and Governor of Georgia, A.H. Colquitt.

Charter members were John T. Clark, Hendley V. Napier III, D. Mark Baxter, Dr. Charles Kellum, Joseph Cogbill, William R. Elliott and William Nisbet.

Charter Officers were John T. Clark, Commander; D. Mark Baxter, Lieutenant Commander; William R. Elliott, Adjutant; and Hendley V. Napier III, Treasurer.

John T. Clark is past Commander and D. Mark Baxter is the current Commander. The Chapter meets quarterly in the Macon Volunteers Room of the Washington Memorial Library, Macon, Georgia.

The Chapter donates a book on southern history each year to a library and maintains the grave of General Colquitt at Rosehill Cemetery.

ILLINOIS SOCIETY

and

Deo Vindice Chapter

The roots of an MOS&B presence within Illinois lie with the founding of the oldest existing Illinois SCV organization, that which became Camp Douglas 1507. Jim Barr, along with Andy Wilson, were the moving force(s) in that organizational endeavor in the mid 1980's, at which time Jim realized that there was no opportunity for the descendents of the Confederate Officer Corps to gather organizationally, as his MOS&B membership was originally begun in the Texas Society under Tulane Gordon in 1980. Some twenty years later he approached the then IL SCV Division Commander Charles Edward Briggs to request his assistance to organize an Illinois Chapter, and address the men of Illinois at a Divisional Convention.

With the unqualified support of the succeeding Illinois Division Commanders, Gale Franklyn Red and Robert F. Herr (both now MOS&B proud members), the one Chapter, named "Deo Vindice" soon flourished to become a full Society under CDR Barr's leadership. The name was chosen as it was the least controversial of any Chapter name suggested. The remarkable growth and success of the Chapter and Society would not have been possible without three national officers, whose support was unwavering. Those were Genealogist General Rodney Patrick Williams, COS GEN Curtis Hopper, and CDR GEN Jeffrey Wayne Massey, all of whom have supported the infant Illinoisans as their numbers have exponentially grown. It is anticipated that there will be thirty members of the Illinois Society by the publication of this edition.

The originally petitioners and officers were: James F. Barr, ABA, ATP as CDR, the Very Rev. William W. Barr, MA. M Div as ADJ and the Hon. Gary L. Corlew, Esq. as Judge Advocate. Joining them to form the original Chapter 270 were Gale Franklyn Red, and Karl Federer. The Illinois Society and Deo Vindice Chapter 270 were installed on

May 10th, 2003 at Springfield, Illinois by COS GEN Curtis Hopper, IN SOC CDR John Forrest, and Physician GEN Neal Pitts, MD. There were 17 members at that time.

Elected at the installation for a full term were: CDR James F. Barr, ABA, ATP; Lt CDR Roger Heinrich; ADJ Charles Edward Briggs. The Society and Chapter function as one unit, with joint officers and compatible Constitutions, with grateful acknowledgement to Dr. Fred McNary of the Florida Society for his assistance with documentation.

At the Memphis Annual Meeting the Chapter presented its first report, reflecting nine members and various outreach programs for membership. At the Asheville Annual Meeting the Society and Chapter then numbered 21, and reported joint participation in several Illinois and national events. They were nationally awarded Best Newsletter and Best Scrapbook at that time, and also awarded the Distinguished Chapter Award for the Year 2003. (This was the first time a new Chapter had ever won the award, as well as the first time a chapter located in a Northern State had won this prestigious award.)

The future of the MOS&B in Illinois is indeed bright with the ever growing membership numbers, and the adaptability of their leadership corps to integrate new projects and new ideas into the ever present changing role of the hereditary society within the counter culture of today's society.

Illinois Society, MOS&B, Deo Vindice Chapter 270

MOS&B Member	Officer Forebearer	Unit Of Leadership
James Falvy Barr	Col. James Barr	10th Miss. Inf.
	Brig. Gen. J.J. Alfred A. Mouton	La. Acadian Reg.
	Capt. Edward Littleton Belcher	35th Tn. Cav.
	Sen. Alexandre Mouton	Pres. La. Succession Conv.
William W. Barr	Col. James Barr	10th Miss. Inf.
	Brig. Gen. J.J. Alfred A. Mouton	La. Acadian Reg.
	Capt. Edward Littleton Belcher	35th Tn. Cav.
	Sen. Alexandre Mouton	Pres. La. Succession Conv.
Eugene T. Beals	Brig. Gen. William N.R. Beall	48th Tn. Inf.
Randall W. Becker	Capt. William James Epps	19th Reg. 2nd Batt. Va.
Charles E. Briggs	Brig. Gen. Turner Ashby	7th Va. Cav.Ashby Brig.
Stan D. Buckles	Brig. Gen. Joseph O. Shelby	Iron Brigade, Mo. Cav.
William H. Burnman	Capt. Edward Littleton Belcher	35th Tn. Cav.
Gary L. Corlew	Capt. Martin Gore Corlew	Poindexter's Reg. Mo. Cav.
Karl M. Federer	Hon. Paris L. Simms	Tn. Civil Servant
Marc K. Finnegan	Flag Off. Samuel Barron III	Nc.
Timothy L. Garrett	Enr. Off. Isaac Garrett	Ga. Militia
Jon Michael Gentry	Pres. Jefferson Davis	Confederate States of America
Dale R. Halemeyer	Lt. John Woodard Methvin	27th Ar. Inf.
Roger L. Heinrich	Maj. Richard Woodrum	26th Va. Co. F, Thrasher's Brig.
Robert F. Herr	Brig. Gen. P.G. Beauregard	La. Acadian Reg.
Wayne J. Holman	Col. Daniel W. Holman	10th Tn. Cav.
	Capt. Walter B. Grizzard	Greer's Tn. Partisan Rangers
Patrick J. McGee	Capt. John Wesley McGee	60th Ga. Inf.
Randy Peacock	Capt. Thomas C. Lott	26th Ga. Inf. Co. F
Gale Franklin Red	Lt. Alson Red	8th Miss. Inf.
Bobbie Samuel	Gen. Robert E. Lee	Army of Northern Virginia
John Stillwell	2nd Lt. James M. Barbee	4th Va. Cav. Co. A
Terry R. Warren	2nd Lt. Thomas B. Smith	42nd Tn. Inf. Co. F
James A. Wilson, Jr.	2nd Lt. Larkin Fletcher	37th Va. Inf. Co. 1
Kyle Wilson	2nd Lt. Larkin Fletcher	37th Va. Inf. Co. 1
Steven Woodfall	Gen/St. Surg. William A. Leelan	41st Al. Inf.

Illinois Society Commander Jim Barr at work

INDIANA SOCIETY

The Indiana Society of the Military Order of the Stars and Bars consists of two chapters:

1. General Francis Asbury Shoup Chapter chartered at Bluffton, Indiana
2. General Adam R. Johnson Chapter chartered at Indianapolis, Indiana.

The Military Order of the Stars and Bars society was originally called by the name of the first chapter, Francis Asbury Shoup. Since the chartering of a second chapter, Adam R. Johnson, it was decided to include both these chapters under the title of Indiana Society of the Military Order of the Stars and Bars.

The following are the officers for the Indiana Society of the Military Order of the Stars and Bars for 1994-96:

Colonel John T. Forrest, Commander
Adam Taylor, First Vice Commander
Kenneth E. Dixon, Second Vice Commander
Robert A. Brown, Adjutant
Neal Chase Pitts, M.D. Genealogist

This Society has assisted the Indiana Sons of Confederate Veterans with every project to date including being an added driving force in the accomplishment of the Dedication of Confederate monument in the Crown Hill Cemetery project, Indianapolis, Indiana and in conducting memorial services for Confederate soldiers in the area.

Northwest Rebel is the official newsletter of Society and Indiana Division Sons of Confederate Veterans.

Francis Asbury Shoup Chapter

Bluffton, Indiana

Five members (camp status) started the Francis Asbury Shoup Camp in the spring of 1988. With the increase in membership from a camp status to that required of a chapter, we were now ready to apply for the charter. An organizational meeting for the General Francis Asbury Shoup Chapter was held in Indianapolis, Indiana in November 1988. The Charter was applied for in December 1988 with the following members:

Don E. Brown
Kenneth E. Dixon
John T. Forrest
Neal Chase Pitts, M.D.
Frank Vandy
Robert A. Brown
James T. Forrest
Gale Jones
Terry Rickerson

The charter was granted in January 1989 with the following officers:

Neal Chase Pitts, M.D., Acting Commander
John T. Forrest, Acting Lieutenant Commander
Robert A. Brown, Acting Adjutant

In April of 1989, a slate of officers was selected to be voted on at the August 1989 meeting, held in Indianapolis. The following officers were elected to hold office until 1992:

Neal Chase Pitts, M.D., Commander
John T. Forrest, Lieutenant Commander
Robert A. Brown, Adjutant
Roger Pruitt, Color Sergeant at Arms

Commander Pitts was to contact Reverend Frank Vandy and inquire if he would accept the office of Chaplain. Reverend Vandy accepted.

In April 1990 Commander Pitts was elected Commander of the Indiana Division Sons of Confederate Veterans. Commander Pitts did not feel that he should be Commander of both organizations and therefore resigned. Lieutenant Commander John T. Forrest filled out his term.

The following are the officers for 1994-96 of the General Francis Asbury Shoup Chapter:

Monte D. Ice, Commander
Neal C. Pitts, M.D., Lieutenant Commander
Robert A. Brown, Adjutant

Along with the Indiana Division Sons of Confederate Veterans, they coordinated the Dedication of Confederate Monument in the Crown Hill Cemetery, Indianapolis, Indiana and conducted Memorial services for the Confederate soldiers buried in the area.

Northwest Rebel is the official newsletter of Society and Indiana Division Sons of Confederate Veterans.

General Adam R. Johnson Chapter

Indianapolis, Indiana

The Charter for the General Adam R. Johnson Chapter was applied for in November 1990 and granted December 1990 with the following Charter members:

Edward Burbank
Reverend Frank Vandy
Kenneth E. Dixon
Reverend John H. Killian
Terry Rickerson

Kenneth Eugene Dixon transferred from the General Francis A. Shoup Chapter and was elected the first Commander and Reverend John H. Killian, Adjutant. The following are the officers for 1994-96 of the General Adam R. Johnson Chapter: Kenneth Eugene Dixon, Commander and Charles E. Dixon, Adjutant.

This Chapter has assisted the Indiana Sons of Confederate Veterans with every project to date including being an added driving force in the accomplishment of the Dedication of Confederate monument in the Crown Hill Cemetery project, Indianapolis, Indiana and in conducting memorial services for Confederate soldiers in the area. *Northwest Rebel* is the official newsletter of Society and Indiana Division Sons of Confederate Veterans.

KENTUCKY SOCIETY

Although the Kentucky Society of the Military Order of the Stars and Bars was not formed until 1979, Kentuckians played an essential role in the formation and early growth of the order. In 1938, when the Military Order of Stars and Bars was organized, Sons of Confederate Veterans national officer Colonel William Batty of Ohio County, KY, was a key player in the formative stages of the organization. Col. Batty was proposed as one of the original members, but poor health prevented him from making formal application. Another early supporter of the Order was Lieutenant Colonel Edgar E. Hume, who joined in 1938 and was member #45. Col.. Hume served the Military Order of Stars and Bars as Vice Commander-in-Chief and proposed the original membership certificate which was adopted in 1941. He also chaired the committee which designed the Order's insignia and badge. Because he was a career military officer, Col. Hume's place of residence changed regularly, but with the admission of his son to the Order as member #86, their permanent residence was established as Frankfort, KY.

In spite of this early support, prior to 1978 only 14 Kentucky Compatriots joined the MOS&B. Compatriot Frank G. Rankin Jr. of Louisville, KY, started a one-man campaign to establish the MOSB in Kentucky as a permanent and powerful historical voice. Less than a year after joining the Order Compatriot Rankin formed the Kentucky Society on April 11th 1979 and became it's first Society Commander

Compatriot Rankin served as Society Commander until 1987. During his tenure, he was responsible for over 200 new members from Kentucky. He developed the Robert E. Lee Award for journalism, and was active in seeing that Confederate Literature received recognition from the national organization. He served in almost every staff position for the national MOSB and received the coveted Robert E. Lee Chalice in appreciation for his service.

In 1987 Compatriot Rankin was succeeded by Compatriot Robert Daniels of Covington, KY who continued Rankin's work. After one year terms as Society-Commander in 1989 and 1990 by Marcus Whitt of Georgetown, KY and William C. Gist of Louisville, KY.

The KY Society Commandership went to John B. Wells III in Paintsville, KY in 1991. Commander Wells continued as Society Commander until 1999, when he was succeeded by the Rev. Dr. Thomas M. Yoder of W. Paducah. Dr. Yoder has served in various positions in the Order in Arkansas including Commander of that Society. Dr. Yoder is the only member of the KY MOS&B to have served in two separate states to date, and is the first to serve from W. Kentucky. He is currently serving his second term as Commander after being appointed by Commander-General Jeff Massey to fill the position vacated by Commander Richard Davis, who was also Commander of the local National Guard Armory which was activated for service to Iraq early in 2003.

Today the KY Society contains three chapters; the George Johnson Chapter, Louisville; the Mountain Partisan Ranger Chapter, Paintsville; the George Basil Duke Chapter, Lexington. Kentucky Compatriots continue to honor the memory of their brave Confederate Officers who sacrificed so much for their beloved land.

Respectively submitted by Dr. Tom Yoder

MISSISSIPPI SOCIETY

The Mississippi Society Military Order of the Stars and Bars has been searching for some type of celebrations that they could use to further the cause of preserving Confederate history. One of the ways that has been tried and seems to be successful is to have a prayer breakfast for events like Confederate Memorial Day, Confederate heritage month, and Lee-Jackson Birthdays.

The Mississippi Society celebrated Confederate Memorial Day with a service at the Confederate Officer's plot in Vicksburg's city cemetery this year with Clayton Faggert of the Captain Rufus K. Clayton chapter as the speaker. The event was well attended for a first time event. The Mississippi Society has planned a workshop in November 1998 that will cover subjects of interest to members researching their ancestors, wanting to preserve their artifacts, and also how to preserve and repair tombstones. The society has been urging each chapter to meet regularly. The Captain Ike Whitaker Chapter of Vicksburg has met each month for the past year. Two other chapters are now beginning to have meetings. Plans are underway to re-charter one chapter and also to charter a chapter. The society now has seven chapters.

Mississippi Society Commander	Lamar Roberts
1st Lieutenant Commander	Billy Ray Hankins
Adjutant	Eddie Cresap
1st Brigadier Commander	Paul Reese
2nd Brigadier Commander	Jeff Mayo
3rd Brigadier Commander	Bill Woods
Captain. Rufus K. Clayton Chapter, Heidelburg,	Billy Ray Hankins, Commander.
President Jefferson Davis Chapter, Southahve,	John Paul Goss, Commander.
General Nathan B. Forrest Chapter, Corinth	
Captain William R. Mitchell Chapter, Holly Springs	Norman Vaden, Commander
Father Abram Ryan Chapter, Biloxi,	John Stewart, Commander
General Jacob Sharp Chapter, Columbus,	Wheeler Watson, Commander.
Captain Ike Whitaker Chapter, Vicksburg,	Eddie Cresap, Commander.

TENNESSEE SOCIETY
John Hunt Morgan Society

Dr. B.H. Webster of Nashville was appointed as commander of the John Hunt Morgan Society by the CIC of the Military Order of the Stars and Bars. Shortly after his appointment, Dr. Webster became ill and was unable to carry out the duties of the society commander. Dr. Webster had proposed the name for the society to honor his relative who had served under General Morgan during the War Between the States.

On September 14, 1980, at the State Capitol in Nashville in the Senate Chamber, the first election of officers of the John Hunt Morgan Society was held. Three of the four active chapters in the state were represented. R.T. Clemmons of the General Joseph B. Palmer Chapter was elected society commander. Lynn J. Shaw of the Shaw-Battle Chapter was elected lieutenant commander. Albert Baxendale of the General Morgan Chapter was elected adjutant. Among items approved were a two-dollar per member society dues, society awards program and the appointment of a constitutional committee. *The Vidette,* the society newsletter, was started shortly afterwards by Commander Clemmons. By the spring of 1981, a constitution had been proposed and later approved. Since that time, the John Hunt Morgan Society has been represented at every national reunion of the Military Order of the Stars and Bars. Two of its members, R.T. Clemmons and John L. Echols, have been elected CIC of the MOSB. A number of members have served as national officers of the MOSB.

Shaw-Battle Chapter

Brownsville, Tennessee

Shaw-Battle Chapter was chartered in Brownsville, Tennessee on June 3, 1977. The chapter was named for Capt. D.A. Shaw and General Cullen Battle. Lynn J. Shaw of Brownsville was elected the chapter's first commander and has held this position to this present time. Though never more than a few dedicated members, the chapter has worked with the local SCV and UDC groups on many projects. Among them, the hosting of the SCV and MOS&B state reunion held in Brownsville in 1988; helping to sponsor the annual Robert E. Lee birthday party; this year's celebration marking the 28th time in a row that it has been held; the monument dedication and erection to the unknown Confederate dead in Oakwood Cemetery in 2001; and helping with the 96th UDC Memorial Service at Stanton; and many other important events that the chapter has been a part of.

The chapter is hard at work with plans to work with the local SCV camp to host the state reunion to held in Brownsville in 2006. The chapter has been represented at every state and national reunion held since 1977. It is the motto of the Shaw-Battle Chapter to lead by example.

Patrick R. Cleburne Chapter

Chattanooga, Tennessee

The Patrick R. Cleburne Chapter was founded August 29, 1993 and named after Patrick R. Cleburne. Charter members include Thomas Cook, C. Anthony Hodges, Steve Goodner, Blanton Govan, Jim Landress and Peter Snyder.

Charter Officer, Jim Landress, was commander from 1993-95 and John S. Sims was Commander, 1995-1997.

The Chapter provided leadership in the Chattanooga Confederate Cemetery renovations in the 1990s and they co-hosted the SCV/MOSB reunion in Chattanooga.

Captain Zillman Voss Chapter

Medon, Tennessee

The Chapter was founded April 15, 1995 with the following officers and members: Commander Ken Anderson Sr., 1st Lieutenant Commander Mike Lambert Sr., 2nd

Lieutenant Commander B.A. Montgomery, Adjutant Malcom Wilcox, Treasurer Mike Lambert II, Chaplain Billy Jack Goodrich, Quartermaster Perry Blakeman, Color Sergeant Mitch Hatchett Sr., Jerry L. Austin, Vince Hatchett, Charles Locher, John Paul Jones, Howard M. Thomson, Clark Tippens III.

Ken Anderson Sr. has been the Commander of the Chapter since conception, 1995-98. The first and largest project of the Chapter is the placing of a large brick marker with marble insert. This being the Confederate Burial Trench at Mercer, Tennessee. Herein lie the remains of 28 Confederate soldiers killed at a nearby crossing on the Hatchie River. We have dedicated and re-dedicated numerous graves and sites and furnished speakers to different Sons of Confederate Veterans and Confederate groups in our area. We formed the 154th Senior Tennessee Infantry Regiment Honor Guard for services conducted by the Chapter and to also assist local Sons of Confederate Veterans Camps in their ceremonies. In 1998 the chapter dedicated with full services, a Union soldier, Ben Lacefield of Tarltons Command, who was killed in action near Medon, Tennessee. The Chapter has located six Union grave sites in their area. These men were never honored in any manner.

Awards consist of the "Rebel Club" Certificate and Ribbon awarded to Commander Anderson Sr. for 1996 and 1997.

Five members of the Chapter are descendants of Confederate generals. Commander Anderson is a descendant of six Confederate officers. 2nd Lieutenant Commander W. Clay Crook III is a prolific writer of southern articles, "Hurst" in the *Confederate Veteran* and "J.W. Dodd", this in the *United Daughters of the Confederacy Magazine*. These are only two of many that have been printed. The officers who have "passed over" are Chaplain Billy Jack Goodrich and 2nd Lieutenant Commander Billy A. Montgomery.

The officers and members of the Chapter now consist of the following: Commander Ken Anderson Sr., 1st Lieutenant Commander Mitch Hatchett Sr., 2nd Lieutenant W. Clay Crook III, Adjutant/Treasurer Charles Merritt, Chaplain Howard M. Thomson, Quartermaster Perry Blakeman, Color Sergeant Vince Hatchett, Kenneth Merritt, Kevin Merritt, John Paul Jones, Jerry Austin, Charles Locher

The Captain Zillman Voss Chapter #223 meets monthly and publishes a monthly newsletter, *The Confederate Officer*. Their motto is "To repudiate revisionism."

Army of Trans-Mississippi Department

At the General Convention in New Orleans in 1980, the Order amended its Constitution and created Departments with the same configurations as Departments in the SCV. At the first meeting of the Trans-Mississippi Department, MOS&B, George Hawes Sutherlin, Jr. of New Orleans was elected Commander.

Serving as Commander from 1982 to 1984 was James E. Meadows, Jr. of Shepherd, Texas.

Elected Commander at the 1984 General Convention in Biloxi was Comp. Joseph A. Winkler, Jr.; Comp. Winkler died in 1985 and Edward Overton Cailleteau was appointed by the Commander-in-Chief, Mark Lea (Beau) Cantrell, to fill the unexpired term.

Serving as Commander from 1986 to 1988 was W.L. (Lou) Acker of Texas.

The Department Commander from 1988 to 1990 was Paul Tulane Gordon, III of Houston, Texas.

At the 1990 General Convention in Fayetteville, Arkansas, Joseph A. Winkler, III of Lafayette, LA was elected Commander of the Department.

In Wilmington, North Carolina in 1992, Dr. Patrick J. Hardy, Jr. was elected and served until 1994.

James Troy Massey of Harrison, Arkansas was elected Commander in Mobile in 1994 and served until 1996.

J. Evetts Haley, Jr. of Midland, Texas was elected Commander in Richmond in 1996 and served until 1998.

K. Patrick Sohrwide of Stillwater, OK was elected Commander in St. Louis in 1998 and served until 2000.

Curtis Hopper of Jefferson City, MO was elected Commander in Charleston, SC in 2000 and served until 2002.

Michael McCullah of Russellville, Arkansas was elected Commander in Memphis in 2002.

Submitted by Edward Overton Cailleteau, Commander (1985-86) Trans-Mississippi Department

ALASKA SOCIETY

Captain James Iredell Waddell Chapter
Anchorage, Alaska

This Chapter was chartered on November 5, 2000 as a sister Chapter to the CSS Shenandoah Sons of Confederate Camp #1820. Both are based in Anchorage, Alaska. These are probably the northernmost organizations honoring Confederate heritage in the world today. The Commander of this Chapter is also the Commander of the Sons of Confederate Veterans Camp. Monthly meetings are held concurrently. Membership is steady and there is interest from prospective members.

We are set up to specifically honor the heroic feats of our Chapter's namesake who commanded the historic journey of the Confederate Raider, CSS Shenandoah around the world. In 1865 the CSS Shenandoah destroyed much of the Union whaling fleet in Alaska waters. We are proud of all Confederate Officers and Soldiers who served their Country.

Current members include:

Robert James Casey, Ph.D., of Kiana, Alaska

John Edward Crowder, Adjutant, of Big Lake, Alaska, Real Great Grandson, Forrest Lee Gartin of Ketchikan, Alaska

Robert Scott Gartin, P.E., Commander, of Anchorage, Alaska

Edward Charles Willis, Lieutenant Commander, of Eagle River, Alaska

Curtis Hopper, Honorary Member, MOSB Chief of Staff, of Jefferson City, Missouri

In 2001 the members contributed to the Florida Battle Flag monument in north Florida. Adjutant John Edward Crowder was present at the dedication of that monument. A plaque on the flag base there commemorates our Chapter.

The Honorable Curtis Hopper provides great encouragement and help to our Chapter. He swore in the Commander by telephone. Curtis keeps us informed on Confederate issues. The Honorable Edward Charles Willis is a former State Senator of Alaska. He brings great wisdom and leadership to our Chapter. Dr. Robert James Casey is a Special Education Teacher in Kiana. He teaches Alaska Native children with special needs.

Forrest Lee Gartin is a High Lead Logger in southeast Alaska who is training as a helicopter pilot in the off-seasons. He is the son of the Commander. Robert Scott Gartin, P.E., is a registered professional Civil Engineer serving as the State Pavement Management Engineer with the Alaska Department of Transportation and Public Facilities.

Web Site: http://home.gci.net/~css-shenandoah-1820/

GENERAL PATRICK R. CLEBURNE, ARKANSAS SOCIETY

The Arkansas Society was formed on April 13, 1985, at the Arkansas Division, Sons of Confederate Veterans Convention in Harrison. Elected officers were Commander James Troy Massey; 1st Lieutenant Commander Bill Ferguson; and Adjutant E. Wayne Cone. The two chapters were: Abner-Cone-Langston-Shaver-Wright Chapter of Harrison with fourteen members and the Wayne Van Zandt Chapter of Little Rock with nine members. At that convention, they voted to place a Military Order of the Stars and Bars plaque at the Arkansas History Commission to honor their Confederate ancestors. Also, a project was to name all known Confederate Arkansas officers. The next year a new chapter, General Dandridge McRae, at Searcy, Arkansas, was formed with seven new members.

In 1993, the Arkansas Society had a name change. It voted to be renamed the General Patrick R. Cleburne, Arkansas Society. Past commanders include: James Troy Massey, Jeff Massey, Sam Massey and Thomas Yoder. At present the Arkansas Society Commander is Steve Muller of Harrison, 1st Lieutenant Commander Jerry Stroud of Cabot, and Adjutant J. Troy Massey of Harrison.

Lieutenant Silas A. Henry Chapter

Dardanelle, Arkansas

The Lieutenant Silas A. Henry Chapter was organized at Dardanelle, Arkansas in May of 1996. The Charter was presented by Commander General J. Troy Massey in November 1996.

Charter members were Jerry Chasmar Stroud, Commander; Paul Marcus Slaton, Lieutenant Commander; Arlis Michael McCullah, Adjutant; Wilbur Lucius Palmer III; Thomas Michael Singleton; and Jerry Chasmar Stroud Jr. Since the founding of the Chapter additional members enrolled are William Bullock Jr. and Ott Holliman. The Chapter holds its monthly meetings on the fourth Thursday at the Dardanelle Public Library in Dardanelle, Arkansas.

Abner-Cone-Langston-Shaver-Wright Chapter

(Renamed Captain James Tyrie Wright Chapter)
Harrison, Arkansas

The Abner-Cone-Langston-Shaver-Wright chapter was formed November 4, 1983 from Confederate officer corps ancestors of charter members of the chapter. Abner was an ancestor of Steve Muller; Lieutenant Cone, an ancestor of E. Wayne Cone; Langston, an ancestor of Charles and Harold Hammett; Colonel Robert G. Shaver, a great-great uncle of Ron Shaver; and Captain James Tyrie Wright, a great-great-great-grandfather of James Troy Massey, Sammy Joe Massey, Jeffery Wayne Massey and John David Massey.

The first elected officers were Commander James Troy Massey, 1st Lieutenant Commander Jeff Massey and Adjutant E. Wayne Cone.

In 1994 the name was changed to the Captain James Tyrie Wright Chapter of Company C, 11th Regiment, 8th Division, Missouri State Guard. Past Commanders of this chapter are James Troy Massey and John David Massey. Officers for 1997 are: Commander Steve Muller, 1st Lieutenant Commander Marty Garrison and Adjutant James Troy Massey.

Major General James F. Fagan Chapter

Jonesboro, Arkansas

Officers:	Ancestor/Relative
W. Danny Honnoll; Commander	2nd Lt. James Wiseman Honnoll
	Co. E, 11th Mississippi Cavalry
William Edwin Dudley; 1st Lt. Commander	Capt. Pleasant A. Peeples
	Co. K, Mississippi Infantry
	* mortally wounded at Gaines Mill
Dale Howard Barnett; 2nd Lt. Commander	2nd Lt. Joseph B. Clark
	Co. l, 23rd Arkansas Infantry
M. Ray Jones, III Adjutant/Treasurer	Major General James Fleming Fagan
	Arkansas Division; ATM
James Allen Langley, Recording Sec.	1st Lt. James Louis Young
	Co. l, 15th Missouri Cavalry

Chartered June 30, 2003
Dedicated MOSB Marker at Craighead County Courthouse on Veterans Day (Nov. 11) 2003. Three MOSB life members; W. Danny Honnoll, W. Ed Dudley, and M. Ray Jones III. The Fagan Chapter helped the SCV Shaver Camp #1655 with three memorials in 2003. Dudley, Jones, and Honnoll attended Cleburne Society Meeting at Pine Bluff in April of 2003. Adj. Jones and Cmdr. Honnoll attended national convention at Asheville, NC.

CALIFORNIA SOCIETY

John B. Hood Chapter

Los Angeles, California

The John B. Hood Chapter 89 Military Order of the Stars and Bars was named after the California Sons of Confederate Veterans Camp 1208 (founded in 1951), and was organized on May 18, 1980 at a meeting held at the Eaton Canyon Nature Center in Pasadena, California. Arden H. Brame Jr. II, then Camp 1208 Commander, invited quali-fying Camp members in California to apply for membership, and some "at large" Sons of Confederate Veterans and Military Order of the Stars and Bars members also transferred into the new organization.

Subsequent meetings, always sparsely attended, were held in the early 1980s in the Southern California communities of Arcadia, Placentia, Reseda, Hollywood, Riverside and La Jolla.

The Chapter was plagued in the early years with loss of members who would be-come discouraged by the gradual increase in membership; in 1984, for example, there were 11 paid and 17 delinquent members. After a strenuous campaign for membership recruitment and retention, the count inched up to 13 by the end of 1985. The dues in-crease of 1987 reduced membership to its low point, a mere nine members.

Current membership in the Chapter (1997) is 17 paid members. We will achieve a slow but steady growth in years ahead, but members are widely scattered over this large state and it is not yet time to visualize a well-attended Military Order of the Stars and Bars undertaking independent of the California Division Sons of Confederate Veterans.

Submitted by Maner L. Thorpe, Ph.D., Commander.

COLORADO SOCIETY

Captain John S. Sprigg Chapter

Denver, Colorado

Captain John S. Sprigg Chapter 263 of the Military Order of the Stars and Bars was chartered on Jun. 16, 2001 in Colorado Springs. Elected as the first Chapter officers were: Commander O.J. Mooneyham; Lt. Commander Patrick Gerity, and Adjutant Troy Tofflemeyer. Charter members include BJ Blackerby, Rev. Armistead Boardman, Dr. James Bush, Patrick Gerity, John Leudecke, OJ Mooneyham, Robert Mooneyham, Myron Smith and Troy Tofflemeyer. Honored guest was Curtis Hopper, MOSB Army of Trans-Mississippi Commander, who presided over the Chapter charter Ceremony.

Due to our small Chapter size, our main goal is to compliment SCV activities. However, we have taken on a couple of additional projects that include assisting in the Glorieta Pass Battlefield preservation in New Mexico, and the creation of Colorado's Confederate History Book. As Colorado has a rich Confederate history, it is one of our main objectives to assemble and bring this information to public light.

Chapter 263 currently has six members. The current command structure is: Commander Marc Hollingsworth, Lt. Commander Patrick Gerity, Adjutant Troy Tofflemeyer, and Chaplain Rev. Armistead Boardman.

LOUISIANA SOCIETY

The Louisiana Society, MOS&B was organized in 1979-80 by the late George Hawes Sutherlin, Jr. and Edward Overton Cailleteau. Both men are sons of Alexandria, Louisiana. In fact, when Colonel George Sutherlin and his wife were married, their only attendant was the lady who later was the mother of Edward Overton Cailleteau. Sutherlin, a relative of the man who owned the home in Danville, VA in which the last meeting of the Confederate Cabinet took place, had done some preliminary work toward organization earlier in 1979. Cailleteau became a member of Headquarters Camp No. 584, SCV and a member at-large of the General Society, MOS&B earlier in 1979. Sutherlin was appointed Organizing Commander of the LA Society by then Commander-in-Chief Dr. Ralph W. Widener of Dallas. Sutherlin appointed Cailleteau as Adjutant. The Society held its first meeting on June 28, 1980 at Toby's Four Corners Restaurant in Lafayette. Over dinner, those in attendance considered and adopted a Constitution which had been drafted by Adjutant Cailleteau.

When the 1980 General Convention at New Orleans amended the Constitution of the Order to create Departments, George H. Sutherlin, Jr. was elected the first Commander of the Trans-Mississippi Department and Edward O. Cailleteau became Commander of the Louisiana Society.

Those who have served as Commander are: George H. Sutherlin, Jr. of New Orleans, 1979-80 (died 1986, age 46); Edward Overton Cailleteau of Baton Rouge, 1980-83; Joseph A. Winkler, Jr. of Hammond, 1983-85 (died 1985); Bruns D'Aunoy Redmond of New Orleans, 1985-89; Joseph A. Winkler, III of Lafayette, 1989-95; Alvin Young Bethard of Lafayette, 1995-97; Miller D.M.F. Dial of Baton Rouge, 1997-99; Charles E. McMichael of Shreveport, 1999-2001; Robert Williams Crook of Baton Rouge, 2001-2003; and Dr. Ernest St. Clair Easterly, of Watson (Livingston Parish), 2003-2005. Those who have served as Adjutant include: Edward Overton Cailleteau, Charles Owen Johnson, and Claudius Augustus Mayo.

Submitted by Edward Overton Cailleteau, Commander (1980-83), Louisiana Society, MOS&B

C.S.S. Arkansas Chapter

Baton Rouge, Louisiana

The C.S.S. Arkansas Chapter of Baton Rouge was organized to commemorate the feisty ironclad, which, if it had been in good running order, might well have provided invaluable aid to John C. Breckinridge in the expulsion of the federal forces occupying Baton Rouge. The Charter, dated January 19, 1987, was presented at a luncheon in Baton Rouge on February 20, 1987. The Organizing Commander was Edward Overton Cailleteau. The Adjutant was Joseph A. Winkler, III.

The second Commander was Miller D.M.F. Dial who served from 1994 to 1998. At a meeting held on January 14, 1998 Dr. Ernest St. Clair Easterly, III was elected Commander and Robert Williams Crook was elected Adjutant. In 2000 William Glen Griffin was elected Commander and John A.R. Hebert was elected Adjutant. Serving as Commander since 2002 is Compatriot John Alvery Richard Hebert of Gonzales.

Governor Alexandre Mouton Chapter

Lafayette, Louisiana

The Governor Alexandre Mouton Chapter of Lafayette applied for Charter under date of May 12, 1987. Commanders have included Joseph A. Winkler, III and Alvin Young Bethard.

Lt. Isaac Ryan Chapter

Lake Charles, Louisiana

The Lt. Isaac Ryan Chapter of Lake Charles was chartered in 1994. The Organizing Commander was Claudius Augustus Mayo. Compatriot G. Scott Thorn has served as Commander of the Chapter. After a period of dormancy, the Chapter has revived and the Commandancy has devolved to Compatriot Michael Dan Jones of Iowa, Louisiana, a byline reporter with the Lake Charles *American Press*.

Major Winfrey Bond Scott Chapter

Minden, Louisiana

The Major Winfrey Bond Scott Chapter of Minden was organized in 1997. In 2002 the Winfrey B. Scott Chapter was renamed the Colonel Leon Dawson Marks-Major Winfrey B. Scott Chapter and the bases of the Chapter became Shreveport and Minden. Several members of the Brigadier General Henry Gray Chapter transferred to the Marks-Scott Chapter. The Commander of the Chapter is George Mark Camp.

Major General Earl Van Dorn Chapter

New Orleans, Louisiana

The Major General Earl Van Dorn Chapter of New Orleans was the first MOS&B chapter in Louisiana and was chartered on January 6, 1983. Organizing Commander was David Wayne Powell. Organizing Adjutant and the only Adjutant the Chapter has ever had is Edward Overton Cailleteau. CDR Powell was succeeded by Edward

Church Bush. When he became Commander of the Col. Charles Didier Dreux Camp No. 110, SCV, Bush was succeeded by the great nephew of the Chapter's namesake, Hon. Earl Van Dorn Wood. Cdr. Wood died in office on May 15, 1997. At a special meeting of the Chapter held at Antoine's Restaurant on October 10, 1997, Dr. Philip D. Mollere was elected to fill the unexpired term of Cdr. Wood as Commander of the Chapter.

MISSOURI SOCIETY

The Brigadier General Francis M. Cockrell Chapter was formed on September 26, 1987, and in a month the Chapter had grown sufficiently to be granted Society status. The Society had tripled in size by the next year and the Maj. Gen. John S. Marmaduke Chapter, Jefferson City, MO was formed. The Maj. Gen. John Stevens Bowen Chapter was formed in St. Louis in July of 1990 and the Colonel Ben Elliott Chapter was formed in Warrensburg, Missouri in 1991. The year 1996 saw growth and the formation of two new chapters, the Colonel Upton Hayes Chapter, Springfield, Missouri and the Lt. Colonel John Boyd Chapter in Independence, Missouri. In 1997 the Brig. Gen. M. Jeff Thompson Chapter was formed in Dexter, Missouri. In 2001 the Governor Claiborne Fox Jackson Chapter of Stockton, Missouri was formed.

The first Missouri Society Commander was Gaylord Patrick (Pat) O'Conner (1916-95) of Louisiana, Missouri. Pat was later re-elected to this position. Lynn N. Bock of New Madrid, Missouri was elected in 1988 and re-elected in 1990 as Society Commander. In 1992 William Gordon Buckner of Marshall, Missouri was elected Society Commander serving one term. Keith I. Daleen of Sedalia, Missouri was elected Society Commander in 1994 and re-elected in 1996. Gene Dressel, Jonesburg, Missouri was elected Society Commander in 1998 serving one term, followed by John Wolfe of Springfield, Missouri, being elected in 2000, serving one term. Gary Ayres of Humansville, Missouri elected in 2002 as Society Commander.

Lt. Colonel John R. Boyd Chapter

Independence, Missouri

This Chapter was formed in 1996. It has always been a small chapter. In 2002 we shrank to only 4 members. With the patient help & encouragement of Society Commander Gary Ayres, and a loan from one member, we kept this Chapter from loosing it's Charter & disbanding. From January to Dec 2003 we went from 5 to 11 members. All taken from a pool of what is now only 24 SCV members.

Little is known or written about Lt Col John Boyd. After the Battle of Corinth, Ms., he was sent to MO, by General Sterling Price, along with Shelby, Hughes & Thompson. They joined up with MO, State Guard & Quantrill's Partisan Rangers in the Battle of Independence, MO, Aug 11, 1862. B/G John T. Hughes was in charge. He & Boyd were both killed. They lay side by side in Woodlawn Cemetery in Independence. On Confederate Memorial Day, we decorate their graves and help put flags on all CSA graves. During memorial services we have a roll call and ring in their names.

We will soon be replacing unreadable and broken stones with Gov. Issue. We are doing research now. We have recently ordered and installed headstones for two of Quantrill's Raiders in Elmwood Cemetery in Kansas City, MO.

Hughes SCV Camp # 614 share their meeting place and their recruiting tent. We try to attend every reenacting event on the western side of MO. We have jointly adopted a one mile section of Noland Road in Independence for clean up.

James M. Bagby was re-elected as Commander & Adjutant for 2004. Larry Yeatman is Lt. Commander. He is also the Editor of our Hughes Camp News letter, *Hughes News*.

2004 will be another recruiting year. More members living in the Independence, MO. area are needed.

Submitted by Adjutant, James M. Bagby

Major General John Sappington Marmaduke Chapter

Jefferson City, Missouri

The Major General John Sappington Marmaduke Chapter of the Military Order of the Stars and Bars was founded on August 5, 1988, and was named for Major General John Sappington Marmaduke.

Charter members include Robert L. Hawkins Jr., Robert L. Hawkins III, Robert L. Hawkins IV, Thomas Holloway, James M. Keown, John C. Scruggs, Gary W. Beahan, Gordon W. Jones, K.C. Jones Jr., Royal Cooper, Camden R. Fine, Adam Neise, and Reginald Jankowski.

Charter officers include Robert L. Hawkins III, Commander; James M. Keown, Lieutenant Commander; and Gary W. Beahan, Adjutant.

Past Commanders include Robert L. Hawkins III, Thomas Holloway, Richard Caplinger and Kenneth Wilks.

The Chapter publishes a joint newsletter, *The Governor's Guard*, along with M.M. Parsons Camp #718, Sons of Confederate Veterans.

Commanders:

2002-2004-Commander - Curtis Hopper

2001-2002-Commander- Curtis Hopper

1998-2000-Commander Curtis Hopper

1996-1998-Commander- Kenneth Wilks

1995-1996- Commander- Richard E. Caplinger

1994- No record who was the Commander

1992-1993-Commander- Thomas L. Holloway

1990-1991-Commander-James C. Edwards (On 09-11-1990-Robert L. Hawkins III went to office of MOSB as CIC for Missouri)

1988-1989-Commander- Robert L. Hawkins, (First Chapter Commander)

Governor Claiborne Fox Jackson Chapter

Stockton, Missouri

Eligible members to the Military Order of Stars & Bars of the Colonel John T. Coffee #1934 met outside of Greenfield, Missouri at Compatriot John Ayres' home in May, 2001. This meeting was to form a new Chapter in the Missouri Society. Camp members forming this Chapter would be Alfred Ayres, Gary Ayres, Jgade Ayres, Kelly Ayres and Johnny Ayres, all brothers.

The Charter was approved August 15, 2001 and initiation ceremonies held at Collins, Missouri in December 2001. Presiding over the ceremony was ATM Commander Curtis Hopper and presenting the Charter was Missouri Society Commander John Wolfe. Gary Ayres was the first Commander elected, Alfred Ayres elected as first Lt. Commander and Jgade Ayres as first Adjutant. After the first year of charter, Gary Ayres was reelected as Commander, Harold Hicks elected as Lt. Commander and Jerry Fast as Adjutant. They will hold office until January 2005.

The Chapter established the Governor Claiborne Fox Jackson Birthday Dinner, held the first of April each year in honor of the Governor.

The Chapter works with the Col. Coffee Camp #1934 in projects as providing books to libraries, erecting gravestones and the placement of the Missouri Brigade Monument in St. Clair Co. It also sponsored a young lady, Carrie Phillips, for the General Patrick Cleborne scholarship, which she was awarded.

The Chapter is seeing steady growth and will continue to be a strong presence in the Order.

Colonel Ben Elliott Chapter

Warrensburg, Missouri

Colonel Ben Elliot Chapter was founded December 30, 1990 with the following charter members: Paul Porter, Lindsey Whiteside, James Roll, Delbert Field, Keith Daleen and Delbert Field.

Charter officers are Commander Lindsey Whiteside and Adjutant Paul Porter. Past commander is Lindsey Whiteside.

INDIAN TERRITORY SOCIETY

The Indian Territory Society, MOSB, had its origin in the formation of the Brig. Gen. Douglas H. Cooper Chapter, Oklahoma City. In February of 1979, Charles H. Smith spoke at a meeting of Brig. Gen. Stand Watie Camp No. 1303, SCV, urging formation of a MOSB chapter in Oklahoma. The following month on March 23, 1979, the Brig. Gen. Douglas H. Cooper Chapter was formed and Smith was elected commander. Dr. Ralph Widener, Dallas, Texas, MOSB Commander-in-Chief, made a formal presentation of the chapter charter at a dinner meeting.

During a chapter meeting at the 45th Infantry Division Museum, Oklahoma City, in March 1981, Cdr. Mark Lea "Beau" Cantrell proposed forming a society now that the chapter had grown. This was warmly received and on June 16, 1981, the Indian Territory Society was formally chartered.

Elected to lead the new society was Mark L. Cantrell, El Reno, Commander; Rev. Alvin Baker, Weatherford, Lt. Commander; and Larry A. Walls, Konawa, Adjutant.

In the following years chapters were formed: George Washington Caddo Frontier Battalion Chapter, El Reno; Col. Roswell W. Lee Chapter, Edmond; Eppa Hutton Chapter, Tulsa; Capt Clem Vann Rogers Chapter, Okla. City; and Maj. Gen. Patrick R. Cleburne Chapter, Mustang.

Indian Territory Society Commanders:
1981-82 - Mark L. "Beau" Cantrell
1983-84 - Alvin Lee Baker
1985-86 - Charles H. Smith*
1986 - Richard E. Rea
1987-88 - Daniel K. Almond
1989-90 - Richard Almond**
1991-92 - Robert E. Henson, Jr.**
1993-94 - Daniel K. Almond
1995-96 - K. Patrick Sohrwide
1997-98 - Dr. James G. Caster
1999-2000 - Paul D. Zapffe

2001-02 - J. David Massey
2003-04 - Dr. Philip E. Isett
*Resigned when elected MOSB Lt. CIC
** Deceased
Commanders-in-Chief:
The Indian Society has provided the following gentlemen to lead the national Order.
Dr. James M. Edwards, 1968-70
Mark L. "Beau" Cantrell, 1984-85
Charles H. Smith, 1992-93
Jeffery W. Massey, 2003-04

General Stephen Dill Lee Chapter

Broken Arrow, Oklahoma

The General Stephen Dill Lee Chapter was founded on March 24, 1997 with the following charter members Commander William D. Brocker, great-great-grandson of General S.D. Lee; M.B. Stewart, W.H. Tydings, Francis Stewart, Douglas M. Stewart and Steven H. Tydings.

Charter officers include William D. Brocker, Commander; Murray B. Stewart, Lieutenant Commander; W. Harold Tydings, Adjutant.

Colonel Roswell W. Lee Chapter

Edmond, Oklahoma

The exact date of the founding of the Colonel Roswell W. Lee Chapter of the Military Order of the Stars and Bars is unknown but the adjutant has records starting in 1988. Colonel Roswell W. Lee is the namesake of the Chapter.

Charter members include Edwin L. Deason, Jamie Howard, Forest Schooling, Charles H. Smith and Roy P. Stewart.

Charter officers include Commander Charles H. Smith and Adjutant Edwin L. Deason. Past Commanders are Charles H. Smith, Richard Hull and Edwin L. Deason.

The membership of this Chapter are dedicated to the preservation of Southern history and to protect and defend the honor and dignity of the Confederate Officer Corps and the officials of the civilian Confederate Government.

General Patrick R. Cleburne Chapter

Mustang, Oklahoma

The General Patrick R. Cleburne Chapter was founded in April 1997 with the following charter members: Jeff Massey, David Massey, Charles W. Britton, Mark Atchley and Joe Atchley. Charter officers include David Massey, Chapter Commander; Jeff Massey, Chapter Adjutant; Charles Britton, Chaplain; Mark Atchley, 1st Lieutenant Commander; and Joe Atchley, Historian. The Chapter hosted the 1998 Lee-Jackson Memorial Day Luncheon in Oklahoma City. Their newsletter is called the *Cleburne's Charge* and is published quarterly. The Cleburne Chapter upholds the finest traditions of the Confederate Officer Corps by regularly participating in national and local events affecting our Confederate history.

Brig. Gen. Douglas H. Cooper Chapter

Oklahoma City, Oklahoma

Chartered: March 23, 1979
Officers:
Commander -Charles H. Smith
Lt. Cdr. - Dr. C.W. Buck
Adjutant - Donald G. Church
Charter Members: Charles H. Smith, Dr. C.W. Buck*, Mark L. "Beau" Cantrell,
Rev. Alvin Lee Baker, Donald G. Church, Richard B. Harris, and Hale Bicknell, Jr.*
* Deceased

Accomplishments: Brig. Gen. Douglas H. Cooper Chapter was responsible for the formation of the Indian Territory Society. The Chapter also established the longest running event at the Oklahoma Historical Society, the "Lee-Jackson Memorial" held during January each year. The Chapter was selected as the Outstanding MOS&B Chapter two consecutive years: 1995 & 1996. The Chapter has provided three Commander Generals: Mark L. Cantrell, Charles H. Smith, and Jeffery W. Massey. Many members have served on the General Staff: Jeffery W. Massey, Leslie R. Tucker, Daniel K. Almond, Robert E. Henson Jr., John David Massey, and K. Patrick Sohrwide.

TEXAS SOCIETY

Currently the Texas Society has 15 chapters located in Houston, Dallas (2), Midland, Austin, San Antonio, Plano, Ft. Worth (3), Tyler, Comanche, Ennis, Alvin, and Orange. In recent months we have instituted new chapters in Ft. Worth and Alvin.

Among the activities of our chapters are two web sites, members@aol.com/mosb264/ and www.bl7.com/mosb/. Most chapters are active in dedication of grave markers, living history/school programs, many joint activities with the SCV, providing speakers to heritage groups, recruiting booths at fairs/expos, and special monument drives.

Our Society has the very best working relationship with the Texas Division SCV and we regularly cooperate and work together.

Submitted by Dale Fowlkes, Commander

Col. Isaac E. Avery Chapter

Alvin, Texas

This new chapter was granted an official charter on January 10, 2004 by Texas Society Commander Dale Fowlkes. At the time of the chartering ceremony, 17 members were on the roster making this the fourth largest chapter in the state of Texas.

Organization, membership recruitment, and chartering took place in perhaps record time, just six short months. Efforts to organize a chapter were begun June 29, 2003 by SCV compatriots Henry B. Seale and Carl R. Adams, who canvassed those members of John Bell Hood Camp # 50 (Galveston) and 13th Texas Infantry Camp # 1565 (Lake Jackson) with officer ancestors, to determine their level of interest in forming an MOSB chapter. Encouraged, they also located former MOSB members who lived within driving distance of Brazoria and Galveston Counties and solicited their membership.

The decision was made to locate the chapter in Alvin, Texas, and to name it in honor of Col. Isaac E. Avery of the 6TH North Carolina Infantry Regiment, who died at Gettysburg. As he lay dying, Col. Avery wrote a note to his kinsman, Major Samuel

McDowell Tate, which said, "Major, Tell my father I died with my face to the enemy." We believe these final words of Col. Avery are indicative of the spirit of our Confederate ancestors.

The chapter had organizational meetings (before chartering) in September, October, November, and December of 2003, with a speaker at the October meeting. At the November meeting, the bylaws were amended and officers were elected for 2004. The bylaws had been drafted by Henry Seale and Carl Adams, before being voted upon by the membership. Chapter officers for 2004 are Henry B. Seale, Commander; Carl R. Adams, Lt. Commander; James E. Bagg, Jr., Adjutant; Carroll D. Dodgen, Treasurer; Ronald R. Strybos, Chaplain; and Andrew J. Strybos, Sergeant at Arms / Color Sergeant.

The chapter already has a Web site (www.geocities.com/ieachapter282), which was designed and set up by Lt. Commander Adams, and it is lining up speakers for 2004 meetings. The chapter will be actively participating in the MOS&B's "Books For Beauvoir" project and welcomes opportunities to cooperate with area SCV camps and UDC chapters for the preservation of Confederate history and to honor our heritage.

Major John Loudermilk Chapter

Comanche, Texas

The Major John Loudermilk Chapter held its Charter Ceremony in Comanche Texas in June of 2001 with five members present. As of June 2004 the Chapter will have more than quadrupled its membership with over 20 members. We also now have a web page and newsletter.

The Chapter is named for a Confederate veteran who was Commander of Company D, 36th Georgia Volunteer Infantry, Army of Tennessee. John enlisted in June of 1861 and during his service he participated in many battles including: Cumberland Gap, Perryville, Dog Walk, Baker's Creek, Missionary Ridge, Chattanooga, Lookout Mountain, Pea Vine Creek, Rome, Resaca, Tunnel Hill, Buzzard Roost, Dalton, Adairsville, Dug Gap, Cassville and New Hope Church. John was captured at Baker's Creek, but shortly escaped and rejoined his men after the fall of Vicksburg. He was shot in the head at the battle of New Hope Church and died in a field hospital in Atlanta in June of 1864. He is buried in the Confederate section of the Oakland Cemetery in Atlanta.

The Chapter is fortunate in that it has members from four different SCV Camps and has had the opportunity to participate with these camps in many monument dedications, grave marker ceremonies, memorial days, parades and other celebrations of our heritage. In May 2003 the Chapter was the lead organization in a cemetery memorial ceremony honoring one of Major John's brothers who fought with him.

Among our major events, we co-sponsor a Christmas Party and Robert E. Lee Memorial Ceremony with one of our SCV Camps. In 2002 and 2003 we participated in the placing and dedication of five new Confederate monuments, and we look forward to continued growth and even greater support of our Southern history and heritage.

MOSB # 264 web site address: <http://members.aol.com/mosb264/>

General Tom Green Chapter

Corsicana, Texas

On November 15, 1995, a chapter charter application was submitted to General Headquarters of the Military Order of the Stars and Bars for the formation of a chapter at Corsicana, Texas, to be know as the General Tom Green Chapter. The application was subsequently granted.

Charter members include Gerry D. York, Commander; David W. Franklin, Lieutenant Commander; Norman Stubbs, Adjutant; and members Harrell D. Simpson, Roger Womack and Bobby Dan Bell.

The chapter's members are also members of the J.L. Halbert Camp #359, Sons of Confederate Veterans. The Halbert Camp also meets in Corsicana, Texas. The chapter's namesake, Tom Green, was a native Virginian but made his mark as a Texan. General Green fought with the Texas Revolutionary Army when the Republic of Texas won its independence at the victory over Santa Anna at the Battle of San Jacinto in 1836. General Green served Texas in many areas and commanded a cavalry division, including the 5th and 4th Texas Cavalry, and was killed serving the south on April 1, 1864, at Blair's Landing, Louisiana. General Green is buried in the State Cemetery in Austin, Texas.

The new chapter has taken a particular interest in preserving cemetery sites of Confederate veterans. In 1996, the chapter aided in the dedication of a new marker at Oakwood Cemetery in Corsicana as well as the marking of Confederate veterans' graves who previously had none. The ultimate goal of the General Tom Green Chapter is to always uphold the honor and good name of the fighting men of the Confederate Officer Corps.

Submitted by David Franklin and Gerry York, General Tom Green Chapter, Military Order of the Stars and Bars.

Gaston Gregg Chapter

Dallas, Texas

Members of the Gaston Gregg Chapter recently located the Lincoln Cemetery containing 204 acres of black gravesites, including WWII veterans, which we cleaned. The chapter also took part in the marker dedication service honoring a Confederate soldier, Ahana Butler, in the Coon Creek Cemetery, within Smith's Bend of the Brazos River in Bosque County.

Several chapter members have visited 161 cemeteries out of 240 in Dallas County during 2002-03. Our goal was to find all of the Confederate veterans in Dallas County. Thus far we have located the graves of 1,200 soldiers, two sailors, and one marine. We also located the graves of two CSA black washer-women and one black CSA Cavalry soldier, all of which are documented on the muster rolls. We clean all veterans' graves (Union & Confederate, Spanish/American War, WWI, WWII, etc.) and record the G.P.S. so that others in the future can find the cemetery.

Lone Star Chapter

Dallas, Texas

The Lone Star Chapter was organized in Dallas, Texas, on January 21, 1975. The chapter name was selected to honor the gallant military history and contributions of the men in gray from Texas. We are proud to state that our members have honorably and faithfully served the organization and our ancestors in levels from the chapter up to and including the highest office. Two of our members, Dr. Ralph Widener and John Hunter, served as Commander-in-Chief of the MOS&B.

Meeting regularly, we coordinate our activities and projects with the SCV camp with which we are associated, the General W.L. Cabell Camp 1313. Our members take part in recruiting and informational activities, community affairs such as the Adopt-a-Highway project, parades, memorial services including Confederate Memorial Day, and honor guards.

Colonel W.H. Parsons Chapter

Ennis, Texas

The Col. W. H. Parsons Chapter #273 was chartered in Ennis, Texas on August 16, 2002, with fourteen charter members. The chapter meets quarterly on the fourth Thursday of the first month of each quarter. The charter officers are Robbie Keever, Commander, Glenn Toal, Lt. Commander, and Jim Templin, Adjutant.

The chapter has been active, providing color guards for several events, donating books to the Ennis Public Library, and obtaining a section of the new metal picket fence at the local cemetery with the name of "Col. W. H. Parsons" on it. Col. Parsons gave the original land for the cemetery. We are now raising funds to obtain markers to place at the gravesites of Confederate Officers that will tell of their activities during the war, such as "Led a charge at the Battle of Gettysburg" or "Commanded the Fifth Texas Field Artillery at the Battle of Calcasieu Pass."

At our first National Reunion, we won first place for our scrapbook, thanks to the work of Glenn Toal and his wife, Susie.

D.W. Snodgrass Chapter

Ft. Worth, Texas

The D.W. Snodgrass Chapter 254 was chartered at the turn of the century (year 2000).

The first commander was Jerry Betsill. We named our chapter after an ancestor of the Betsills who is buried in Trickham, Texas. We were fortunate to have the Loudermilk Chapter honor that gravesite this year. We are greatly indebted to them for such.

From the very beginning, our members were the laborers for our SCV Camp when gravemarkers were to be installed. That has been and continues to be our role. At one day, we set 17 markers in the Upper Greens Creek Cemetery in Dublin, Texas. We have not confined ourselves to our own geographic area. Sometimes we travel many miles to set one to three markers. But, we do primarily work in our home town. As an example, our most recent action saw us place four markers for Confederate Veterans in Hebrew Rest Cemetery, one of the oldest in Fort Worth, Texas.

The following is a list of our membership: Daniel Betsill, Jerry Betsill, John Betsill, Charles Boldt, Jonathan Boldt, Kevin Boldt, Michael Sewell, Gary Whitfield, Jeff Whitfield, Caleb Williams, and Douglas Williams.

Texas Chapter

Houston, Texas

The Texas Chapter, Military Order of the Stars and Bars, the first chapter in Texas, was chartered on June 30, 1970, in Houston, Texas. It was affiliated with Dick Dowling Camp, #1305 Sons of Confederate Veterans, The Chapter was named for the Lone Star State of Texas and the present address is P.O. Box 2221, Conroe, Texas 77305, Conroe being a suburb of Houston, Texas.

Most of the records of the Texas Chapter were lost during Hurricane Alicia, August 15-21, 1983. In the ensuing years many of the charter members have died or have moved away. We have found bits and pieces here and there and a few members have furnished information from memory or personal files. Therefore our early history is not complete. However we trust that what we have is fairly dependable.

Charter Members

Fred G. Aylott	Travis S Helpenstell	Mark E. Price
A B. Banowsky	William Henley	Dennis W. Rainoshek
Lynne O. Beall	Charles M. Hines	George P. Red
Thomas G. Bousquet	James W. Hines Jr.	James A. Saye Jr.
William P. Boyd	James W. Howell	Palmer D.T. Schweppe
V.H. Caraway	Phillips C. Huck	Col. Eugene E. Skinner
Durrell M. Carothers	F. Allen Johnston	Lyonel L. Tatum
Joseph A. Collerain	Sherman Kendall	Dr. Heyl G. Tebo
William P. Deese Jr.	Lilbourn A. Lewis	Frank E. Tritico
Larry N. Doherty	Weaver Moore	Toni Richard Turk
Adrien F. Drouilhet	W.T. Nettles	John B. Waller
Msgr. Anton J. Frank	Larry Mac Owens	Dr. Ralph W. Widener
Dorsey B. Hardeman	Mallory D. Price	

Charter Officers

Commander	Dennis W. Rainoshek
Lieutenant Commander	F. Allen Johnston
Adjutant-Treasurer	Larry N. Doherty
Chaplain Msgr.	Anton J. Frank
Past Commander	Weaver Moore (deceased)

At a later date Msgr. Anton J. Frank was named Honorary Chaplain for life.

MOS&B Texas Society Commanders
1971 -73 Dennis W. Rainoshek
1973-74 F. Allen Johnston
1974-75 Larry W. Hays
1975-76 W.T. Nettles
1977-79 Michael O. Shannon

Past Commanders
Weaver Moore
Dennis W. Rainoshek
Larry N. Hays
Timothy Wheatley
Michael O. Shannon
Frank T. Harrowing

MOS&B Commanders-In-Chief
1974-76 Dennis W. Rainoshek
1978-80 Dr. Ralph Widener Jr.

SABINE PASS MEDAL

The Sabine Pass Medal was presented to Dick Dowling and the Davis Guards by the grateful citizens of Houston after the spectacular victory at Sabine Pass, September 8, 1863. It was the only medal presented to Confederate Soldiers during the war. When the Texas Chapter of the Stars and Bars was organized in 1970, the late Weaver P. Moore, Commander, conceived the idea of presenting a replica of the medal, in gold or silver, in recognition to members of the hereditary Confederate organizations, who have made substantial contribution to the cause for which they stand, or to those who through their research, preservation, or presentation, have contributed to the preservation of our southern heritage.

Recipients of the Sabine Pass Medal

Msgr. Anton J. Frank	Catherine Knowles. UDC
Mrs. Katherine Wilcox, UDC	Charles Bracelon Flood
Dr. William D. McCain	Gregory T. Hector
Dr. Frank Vandiver	Martin J. Johnson
Tom White Crigler	James M. Edwards
Col. Harold B. Simpson	Peter W. Orlebeke

Ralph Green
Dr. Heyl Tebo
Craig Watkins
Mrs. Carlatta Barnes, UDC
Frank T. Harrowing
Michael O. Shannon
Gordon Hayslip
William J. Willmann
Frank E. Tritico
J. Douglass Moore
Charles Smith

Joseph B. Mitchell
Mr. and Mrs. Howell Pursue
Mack Neal
Ed Arnold
Dr. Ralph Widener Jr.
Dr. Keith King
Larry J. Miggins
James E. Meadows
James N. Vogler
Helen Ramsey. UDC

1997 Texas Chapter Roster

John Benjamin Aderhold
Randall Wayne Connell
Leonard W. Craig
Earl E. Dunson (life member)
David Quysenberry Hammond

Frank Thomas
Harrowing
Michael F. Harrowing
Clayton Floyd Lee Jr.
James N. Vogler Jr.

None of the above are "Real Sons"

Note: Out of 38 Charter Members in 1970, none are still active on the rolls of the Texas Chapter.

Requiescat in Pace

Deo Vindice

Activities include recruiting new members for both the Sons of Confederate Veterans and Military Order of the Stars and Bars; placing Confederate flags on Confederate graves in area cemeteries; periodically cleaning such graves as necessary; furnishing speakers for various organizations such as Rotary Club, PTO, UDC, School Assemblies, etc. They also attended and participated in local chapter meetings and functions; attended and participated in Texas Society Conventions and National Sons of Confederate Veterans and Military Order of the Stars and Bars Conventions.

Haley-Holt Chapter

Midland, Texas

Haley-Holt Chapter was chartered October 1, 1986, Midland, Texas. Charter members include:

John Conrad Dunagan
Frank Jefferson Haley
J. Evetts Haley Sr.
J. Evetts Haley Jr.
James Evetts Haley III
J. Holt Jowell
William Holt Jowell
Clifon Vincent

John Vincent
Carr Vincent
Robert Carr Vincent
Jack Tyler
Evetts Haley Jr., First Commander
W. Carr Vincent, Second Commander
J.M. Simpson, Current Commander

John L. Echols was the Commander-in-Chief of the Military Order of the Stars and Bars at the time of the chartering of this chapter. In 1990 the Chapter sponsored a new award program for the benefit and support of the entire Texas Society of the Military Order of the Stars and Bars. A bronze medallion, called the M.E. Bradford Military Order of the Stars and Bars Bronze Service Award, is to be presented to a deserving individual who by his or her endeavor with the written word is effective in the preservation of southern history and traditions. It is the intent with the award to honor those people who have actively defended southern culture in writing, or through other thoughtful action, have helped to accurately portray and preserve southern history for future generations. It is also appropriate for those individuals who have helped provide a forum for the accurate portrayal of southern history. Dr. M.E. Bradford was the first recipient of this award.

Also a silver medallion, called the Dr. Larry Arnold Military Order of the Stars and Bars Silver Service Award, is to be presented to an individual who illustrates a knowledge of southern history and personifies its best traditions. He or she must also have shown the determination and character to continue the fight for the preservation of our southern ideals. It is to honor a real fighter, in the best tradition of General Robert E. Lee and his officers and men. Ralph Green was the first recipient of this award.

Colonel Benjamin H. Norsworthy Chapter

Orange, Texas

We were recently chartered in June of 2003. We are fortunate that the "Walter P. Lane" camp #1745 in Orange, Texas has always been active in many activities. Living Histories at local schools and various events, Memorial Ceremonies and reenacting through the 3rd Texas, a local reenacting group. The majority of our new charter membership have been active in the past through these groups. This has allowed us to participate as members of these groups as well as to represent our newly established Colonel Benjamin H. Norsworthy chapter at the same time.

Since our conception, in the past six months we have had members present at several reenactments, which we feel helps to keep the interest in the war alive. We have been part of two living histories, one at the Heritage House in Orange, Texas and one in Hemphill, Texas. The later was in conjunction with the "Walter P. Lane" camp and a newly formed heritage group in Hemphill to raise money for the preservation and restoration of an old original home, the "Pratt House". These living histories allow our members to set up camp and demonstrate many activities from the time of the war. We have rifle and cannon firings, we put out displays of guns, swords, uniforms, original paper money and a flag display where each flag's true history is told. The most important thing is we are able to talk to the public one on one, young and old, black and white. We have the ability to tell our ancestors' side of the war and answer questions with a true history of their struggle. Through our local camp, some of our members have also participated in living histories set up at local schools.

Some of our members ventured off to Bolivar, Texas (about 80 miles from Orange) to work with three SCV camps. We were there to help with the rededication ceremonies of a Confederate soldier at a small family grave plot located a hundred yards off of the Beach Road going toward Galveston. It was a small gathering of family members UDC, SCV and MOSB members. We posted flags, fired volleys from rifles and a mortar, and preformed the ceremony of giving the soldier the last drink. The family members were grateful and we were honored to have been there.

The first official activity of our chapter was a night ceremony at the gravesite of Colonel B.H. Norsworthy our chapter's name-sake at Evergreen Cemetery in Orange, Texas. We had a short prayer and handed out membership certificates to our charter members. There is a Texas State Historical Marker at Colonel Norsworthy's grave which was previously damaged by the moving crew. Working in conjunction with the local "Orange County Historical Commission" (which one of the board members is part of our MOSB membership) the marker has been removed and repaired awaiting reinstallation. At that time we will have a rededication ceremony at the gravesite. We are also working again with the "Orange County Historical Commission" and our local camp #1745 "Walter P. Lane", Orange, Texas. We will contribute to the funds to help replacing a State Historical Plaque that was destroyed. The plaque acknowledged the Confederate unites formed in Orange County with a brief description of the role Orange had during the war. Hopefully this will materialize this year along with a small sign that we are working with our local SCV camp with to be placed on the access road of I-10. The sign will have the SCV camp, our local "Order of Confederate Rose", and the MOSB chapter recognized at the entrance of our meeting location.

I see our chapter as one to work with and support other heritage organizations. We have and will continue to take the lead when able, but to support the activities our brother heritage groups have initiated is just as important. Hopefully we will help in bridging our local SCV camps together, and support any activity that would honor our ancestors.

Submitted by Commander Granvel J. Block

Major Chatham Roberdeau Wheat Chapter

Plano, Texas

The Major Chatham Roberdeau Wheat Chapter was chartered on January 8, 1996, in Plano, Texas. Major Wheat commanded the famed 1st Louisiana Special Battalion, "Louisiana Tigers." He was seriously wounded at 1st Manassas, July 21, 1861, while leading his troops, but returned to command during the Peninsula Campaign of March-July 1862. When his brigade commander, Colonel Seymour, was killed in battle at Gaines's Mill on June 27, Major Wheat took command and was also killed with a bullet through the brain. He is buried in Hollywood Cemetery, Richmond, Virginia. His descendant, Melvin C. Wheat, was the founder of this Chapter.

Charter members include Melvin C. Wheat, Commander; David Wetzel, 1st Lieutenant Commander; Lamar Davis, 2nd Lieutenant Commander; William Moore Hurst, Adjutant; Elmor Harris, Chaplain; Chris Tankersley, Color Sergeant; Dennis Todd, Gilbert H. Keathley, Robert E. Dodd Sr., Robert E. Dodd Jr., Danny L. Lewis and Michael Deweese.

Officers for 1997 are Dennis Todd, Commander; Danny Lewis, 1st Lieutenant Commander; David Wetzel, 2nd Lieutenant Commander; and Gilbert H. "Sandy" Keathley, Adjutant. Current active membership is 14.

In 1966 the Wheat Chapter "adopted" a heavily traveled street in Plano. Street signs there prominently display the name of the Military Order of the Stars and Bars.

Starting in the spring of 1997, we held the first annual MOSB Ancestor Dinner. Members and their wives had a catered, southern style dinner, then held a ceremony in which candles were lighted for each ancestor as he was named.

In 1997, in conjunction with the William H.L. Wells Camp of Sons of Confederate Veterans, we launched a Web Site on the Internet. Developed by Adjutant Sandy Keathley, the complete site includes pages for our Sons of Confederate Veterans Camp, our Military Order of the Stars and Bars Chapter, information on genealogical research and grave marking, unit histories for the 8th Texas Cavalry and 1st Tennessee Infantry, background on the War for Southern Independence, and external links to about 50 sites of interest to Confederates and genealogists, including the Texas Division Page and the Sons of Confederate Veterans IHQ Page.

To honor our ancestors, our chapter has sent magazine subscriptions to VA hospital, participated in the "adopt a highway' program, donated history books to the local elementary schools, lectured at the local library, donated books to the local library, sponsored tours at the cemetery, provided a Color Guard for UDC events, provided Color Guard for memorial day services, and have spoken to fifth graders at schools in Collin County. We present an outdoor "living history' every spring to students in McKinney ISD.

Our biggest accomplishment was to mark the graves of 150 CSA veterans buried in Pecan Grove Cemetery in McKinney, Texas.

We could not locate the graves of all the veterans buried in Pecan Grove so we decided to raise money for a large monument that had the name of every War Between the States veteran buried in the cemetery on the monument. The names of two US veterans are also on the monument.

To raise the money for the monument we sold tee shirts, books, had bake sales, garage sales, and we put on a large reenactment that made us $10,000.00.

We did this with the help of the SCV Wells camp in Plano, Texas.

Submitted by Dennis Todd

Sul Ross Chapter

San Antonio, Texas

Approximately 20 members from four SCV camps are members of this chapter. Those camps are Hood's Texas Brigade and The Alamo Camps in San Antonio, and the camps in New Braunfels, and Junction, TX.

Past commanders include Albert Lee Jamison, John Wilmeth, Glen "Randy" Hartman, Judge Edward F. Butler, Sr., John Fargarson and John Dunkley.

The camp conducts four meetings each year and also participates in a joint picnic in October and a Christmas party in December with the Hood's Texas Brigade. Judge Ed Butler served as Deputy Judge Advocate General of the national society in 2001-2002, following his second year as chapter commander.

The chapter instituted a gift program in 2000, whereby members could be recognized for gifts to the MOSB chapter. Those donating $75.00 became a "Colonel Of Confederate Calvary."

Those so appointed were:

Col. Joe Ware

Col. John Fargarson

Col. Ed Butler

In June 2000, Judge Ed Butler received the national MOSB Meritorious Service Medal, and in August of that year he was awarded the Lt. Charles W. Read Legion Of Merit Award. In August 2000, the Sul Ross Chapter was awarded the MOSB Merit Award.

Colonel Richard Bennett Hubbard Chapter

Tyler, Texas

The Richard Hubbard chapter was chartered February 6, 2001 with twelve members. Dale Fowlkes and Bob Davidson were the driving forces behind the formation of the camp, with Bob acting as temporary commander. After the chartering of the chapter, Dale was elected as its first regular commander. Current officers are Larry McClellan, commander; Dr. Tom McCall, lieutenant commander; John Haynes, adjutant; and Rev. Don Majors, chaplain.

The Hubbard chapter acts in close concert with the James P. Douglas SCV camp, also centered in Tyler. Four of the camp's original members were former commanders of the Douglas camp.

Members of the Hubbard chapter help promote Southern history in numerous ways. Each year, for example, the camp helps man the clubs and organizations booths at the

East Texas State Fair in Tyler, passing out literature and talking to men interested in their Confederate heritage. MOS&B members discuss the South and the WBTS in area schools, visiting schools in Fruitvale and Hawkins as well as Tyler. This year the chapter held a ceremony at the grave of Colonel Hubbard honoring his service in the war and as governor of Texas. One unusual fact is that two Hubbard members sing in a quartet specializing in songs of the Confederacy. Several MOS&B members belong to a cannon squad, participating often in area ceremonies. Marker dedications are common, with MOS&B compatriots always helping with organization as well as participating as rifle squad members, flag carriers, and speakers. Not only do members of the Hubbard chapter speak at events honoring the Confederacy-massing of the flags, UDC meetings, memorial dedications, SCV camps-they also speak at meetings of other clubs and organizations.

Two facts give special pride. First, Amy Bounds, the granddaughter of Hubbard compatriot Joe Harris, received the Patrick Cleburne Scholarship this year. Second, two Hubbard members hold state offices, Dale Fowlkes being the State Commander and Bob Davidson the Chief of Staff.

MOSB Active Chapters

State	City	Ch #	Chapter Name	Mbrs
AK	ANCHORAGE	259	CAPTAIN JAMES IREDELL WADDELL	5
AL	ALEXANDER CITY	78	GEN. E. P. ALEXANDER CHAPTER	15
AL	ATHENS	57	COL. STEPHEN F. HALE CHAPTER	5
AL	AUBURN	204	NICOLA MARSCHALL	1
AL	BAY MINETTE	271	BRIG GEN. ST. JOHN RICHARDSON LIDDELL	13
AL	BIRMINGHAM	90	GEN. JOHN HERBERT KELLY CHAPTER	12
AL	HUNTSVILLE	17	BRIG. GEN. JOHN HUNT MORGAN CHAPTER	2
AL	JACKSONVILLE	172	PELHAM-FORNEY CHAPTER	2
AL	MOBILE	58	ADMIRAL FRANKLIN BUCHANAN CHAPTER	17
AL	MONTGOMERY	199	WILLIAM WIRT ALLEN CHAPTER	1
AL	SELMA	41	CATESBY AP JONES CHAPTER	8
AL	TALLADEGA	274	MAJ. GEN. EDWARD CARY WALTHALL CHAPTER	7
AL	TUSCUMBIA	60	DESHLER-ONEAL CHAPTER	2
AR	DARDANELLE	231	LT. SILAS A. HENRY	2
AR	HARRISON	33	CAPT. JAMES TYRIE WRIGHT CHAPTER	25
AR	JONESBORO	280	MAJOR GENERAL JAMES F. FAGAN CHAPTER	5
AR	PINE BLUFF	262	GEN. JOHN EDWARD MURRAY	6
AR	SCOTT	178	S. WAYNE VAN ZANDT CHAPTER	2
AZ	BOWIE	248	CAPTAIN JAMES HENRY TEVIS	10
CA	LOS ANGELES	89	GEN. JOHN B. HOOD CHAPTER	18
CO	DENVER	263	CAPTAIN JOHN S. SPRIGG	8
FL	BARTOW	65	FRANCIS S. BARTOW CHAPTER	42
FL	DAYTONA BEACH	252	CAPT. JOHN N. MAFFITT, CSN	8
FL	FORT LAUDERDALE	278	CAPT. LESLIE T. HARDY CHAPTER	11
FL	GAINESVILLE	111	GEN. WILLIAM MILLER CHAPTER	14
FL	INDIALANTIC	10	B/G THEODORE W. BREVARD CHAPTER	17
FL	JACKSONVILLE	29	CAPT J. J. DICKISON CHAPTER	26
FL	KISSIMMEE	212	CAPT. WILLIAM J. ROGERS CHAPTER	12
FL	LAKE CITY	24	CAPT ASA A. STEWART CHAPTER	7
FL	OCALA	164	MARION DRAGOONS CHAPTER	8
FL	ORLANDO	52	COL. L. M. PARK CHAPTER	13

FL	PENSACOLA	156	MAJ. GEN. JAMES P. ANDERSON CHAPTER	2
FL	SARASOTA-BRADENTON	161	MAJ. WILLIAM I. TURNER CHAPTER	17
FL	ST. AUGUSTINE	140	LT. COL. WILLIAM BAYA CHAPTER	16
GA	ATHENS	176	ROBERT TOOMBS CHAPTER	25
GA	ATLANTA	88	GEN. JOHN B. GORDON	26
GA	ATLANTA	188	THE ATLANTA COUNCIL CHAPTER	2
GA	AUGUSTA	50	COL. GEORGE W. RAINS CHAPTER	23
GA	CASSVILLE	265	COL EMORY BEST	10
GA	COLUMBUS	104	GEN. PAUL JONES SEMMES CHAPTER	3
GA	GAINESVILLE	272	PRESIDENT JEFFERSON DAVIS CHAPTER	9
GA	IRWINVILLE	206	JEFFERSON DAVIS MEMORIAL	11
GA	JONESBORO	143	LT. GEN. WILLIAM J. HARDEE CHAPTER	9
GA	MACON	70	GEN. ALFRED HOLT COLQUITT CHAPTER	5
GA	MARIETTA	112	GEN. WILLIAM T. WOFFORD CHAPTER	1
GA	NEWNAN	245	LT. COL. ROBERT P. TAYLOR	7
GA	SAVANNAH	97	GEN. LAFAYETTE MCLAWS CHAPTER	30
GA	THOMASTON	134	KING COTTON CHAPTER	5
IL	CHICAGO	270	DEO VINDICE CHAPTER	24
IN	BLUFFTON	82	GEN. FRANCIS A. SHOUP CHAPTER	11
IN	INDIANAPOLIS	69	GEN. ADAM JOHNSON CHAPTER	10
KS	KANSAS CITY	268	CAPTAIN WILLIAM H. GREGG CHAPTER	7
KY	COVINGTON	85	GEN. GEORGE BAIRD HODGE CHAPTER	9
KY	GEORGETOWN	71	GEN. BASIL W. DUKE CHAPTER	1
KY	LOUISVILLE	118	GEORGE W. JOHNSON CHAPTER	9
KY	PADUCAH	250	COL. ALBERT P. THOMPSON	3
KY	PAINTSVILLE	167	MOUNTAIN PARTISAN RANGER CHAPTER	1
LA	BATON ROUGE	21	C.S.S. ARKANSAS CHAPTER	16
LA	LAFAYETTE	120	GOV. ALEXANDRE MOUTON CHAPTER	5
LA	LAFAYETTE	138	LOUISIANA SOCIETY	1
LA	LAKE CHARLES	205	LT. ISSAC RYAN	7
LA	NEW ORLEANS	154	MAJ. GEN. EARL VAN DORN CHAPTER	11
LA	SHREVEPORT	218	BRIG. GEN. HENRY GRAY	11
LA	SHREVEPORT-MINDEN	214	COL. LEON DAWSON MARKS-MAJ. WINFREY B SCOTT	7
LA	ST. JOSEPH	286	ISAAC HARRISON'S TENSAS CAVALRY	7
MA	CHARLEMONT	209	C.S.S. TALLAHASSEE	6
MD	ANNAPOLIS	191	THE MARYLAND LINE CHAPTER	5
MD	DARNESTOWN	216	CAPTAIN CHARLES F. LINTHICUM	18
MD	WALDORF	54	COL. RICHARD THOMAS "ZARVONA" CHAPTER	6
MO	DEXTER	238	BRIG.GENERAL M. JEFF THOMPSON	5
MO	INDEPENDENCE	236	LTC JOHN R. BOYD	12
MO	JEFFERSON CITY	150	M/G JOHN SAPPINGTON MARMADUKE	34
MO	LOUISIANA	84	GEN. FRANCIS M. COCKRELL CHAPTER	7
MO	SPRINGFIELD	235	COL. UPTON HAYS	7
MO	ST. LOUIS	157	MAJ GEN JOHN S BOWEN CHAPTER	9
MO	STOCKTON	267	GOVERNOR CLAIBORNE FOX JACKSON	11
MO	WARRENSBURG	46	COL BEN ELLIOT	8
MS	BILOXI	63	FATHER ABRAM RYAN CHAPTER	10
MS	BROOKHAVEN	275	CAPT. JAMES ALBERT BASS CHAPTER	10
MS	DE SOTO COUNTY	173	PRESIDENT JEFFERSON DAVIS CHAPTER	11
MS	HEIDELBERG	213	CAPTAIN RUFUS K. CLAYTON CHAPTER	14
MS	HOLLY SPRINGS	197	WILLIAM R. MITCHELL CHAPTER	9
MS	INDIANOLA	253	BRIG GEN CHARLES CLARK	9

State	City	No.	Chapter	Members
MS	JACKSON	110	GEN. WILLIAM BARKSDALE CHAPTER	1
MS	YAZOO CITY	257	LT. COL. WILLIAM H. LUSE	2
NC	ASHEVILLE	7	ASHEVILLE CHAPTER	13
NC	ASHEVILLE	266	CAPTAIN ASBURY T. ROGERS CHAPTER	15
NC	CHARLOTTE	18	BRIG. GEN. RUFUS BARRINGER CHAPTER	40
NC	GREENSBORO	67	GARNETT-PETTIGREW CHAPTER	42
NC	LINCOLNTON	247	GENERAL ROBERT D. JOHNSTON CHAPTER	15
NC	RALEIGH	195	COLONEL ROBERT F. WEBB	32
NC	RALEIGH	32	CAPT. JAMES I. WADDELL CHAPTER	32
NC	RALEIGH	208	LT. WILSON BAILEY	6
NC	WILSON	148	LT. WILLIAM C. FERRELL CHAPTER	10
NC	WINSTON-SALEM	19	BRIG. GEN. WILLIAM R. BOGGS CHAPTER	2
NY	NEW YORK	169	NEW YORK CHAPTER	8
OH	AKRON	256	GENERALS LEE & JACKSON	15
OH	CINCINNATI	159	MAJ. GEORGE DOWNS CHAPTER	3
OK	EL RENO	22	CADDO FRONTIER BATTALION CHAPTER	6
OK	OKLAHOMA CITY	77	GEN. DOUGLAS H. COOPER CHAPTER	25
OK	OKLAHOMA CITY	240	MAJOR GENERAL PATRICK R. CLEBURNE	5
OK	OKLAHOMA CITY	177	ROSWELL W. LEE CHAPTER	1
OK	TULSA	16	BRIG. GEN. EPPA HUNTON CHAPTER	7
PA	PHILADELPHIA	229	JOHN C. PEMBERTON	1
SC	BELVEDERE	232	MAJOR GENERAL MATTHEW CALBRAITH BUTLER	5
SC	COLUMBIA	98	GEN. MAXCY GREGG CHAPTER	36
SC	GREENVILLE	242	THE COL. JAMES McCULLOUGH	20
SC	SUMTER	12	BATTLE OF DINGLES MILL CHAPTER	6
TN	BRENTWOOD	109	GEN. WILLIAM B. BATE CHAPTER	11
TN	CHATTANOOGA	158	MAJ. GEN. PATRICK R. CLEBURNE CHAPTER	7
TN	COLUMBIA	1	PRESIDENT JEFFERSON DAVIS	201
TN	COLUMBIA	8	AT-LARGE	30
TN	COLUMBIA	163	MAJ GEN WILLIAM D McCAIN CHAPTER	14
TN	COVINGTON	73	GEN. CADMUS M. WILCOX CHAPTER	13
TN	JACKSON	223	CAPTAIN ZILLMON VOSS	7
TN	MEMPHIS	141	LT. DABNEY M. SCALES CHAPTER	6
TN	NASHVILLE	91	GEN. JOHN HUNT MORGAN CHAPTER	15
TN	PARKER'S CROSSROAD	142	LT. GEN. NATHAN B. FORREST CHAPTER	3
TN	SMYRNA	94	GEN. JOSEPH B. PALMER CHAPTER	5
TN	TULLAHOMA	210	COL. JAMES W. STARNES	27
TX	ALVIN	282	COLONEL ISAAC E AVERY	12
TX	AUSTIN	127	JOHN H. REAGAN CHAPTER	10
TX	COMANCHE	264	THE MAJOR JOHN LOUDERMILK	20
TX	DALLAS	137	LONE STAR CHAPTER	22
TX	DALLAS	68	GASTON GREGG	11
TX	ENNIS	273	COL. W. H. PARSONS CHAPTER	16
TX	FORT WORTH	279	COL. BENJAMIN MORRIS CHAPTER	14
TX	FORT WORTH	254	CAPT. DAVID WHITFIELD SNODGRASS	11
TX	FORT WORTH	194	WAULS TEXAS LEGION CHAPTER	1
TX	HOUSTON	5	ALBERT SIDNEY JOHNSTON CHAPTER	55
TX	MIDLAND	121	HALEY-HOLT CHAPTER	13
TX	ORANGE	276	COL BENJAMIN H NORSWORTHY CHAPTER	10
TX	PLANO	224	MAJOR CHATHAM ROBERDEAU WHEAT	13
TX	SAN ANTONIO	184	SUL ROSS CHAPTER	21
TX	TYLER	261	COL RICHARD BENNETT HUBBARD	17

This photograph of four Confederate Veterans living in the Confederate Soldiers' Home in Raleigh, NC appeared in the Raleigh News and Observer on May 14, 1938. These gentleman (left to right) are Andrew J. Wise, William Holcombe, Walton Barfield, and Thomas S. Arthur. Photograph courtesy of North Carolina State Archives.

Eulogy to the Confederate Soldier

By Lt. Gen. Jubal Anderson Early, CSA

I believe that the world never produced a body of men superior in courage, patriotism, and endurance to the private soldiers of the Confederate armies. I have repeatedly seen these soldiers submit with cheerfulness to privations and hardships which would appear to be almost incredible; and the wild cheers of our brave men (which was so different from the studied huzzahs of the Yankees) when their lines sent back opposing hosts of Federal troops, staggering, reeling and flying, have often thrilled every fiber of my heart. I have seen with my own eyes ragged, bare-footed and hungry Confederate soldiers perform deed which if performed in days of yore by mailed warriors in glittering armor, would have inspired the harp of the minstrel and the pen of the poet.

United Confederate Veterans Reunions (1889-1951)

Location	Date
Organizational Meeting, New Orleans	June 10, 1889
1. Chattanooga, Tennessee	July 3-5, 1890
2. Jackson, Mississippi	June 2, 1891
3. New Orleans, Louisiana	April 8-9, 1892
No Reunion due to financial depression	1893
4. Birmingham, Alabama	April 25-26, 1894
5. Houston, Texas	May 22-24, 1895
6. Richmond, Virginia	June 30-July 3, 1896
7. Nashville, Tennessee	June 22-24, 1897
8. Atlanta, Georgia	July 20-23, 1898
9. Charleston, South Carolina	May 10-13, 1899
10. Louisville, Kentucky	May 30-June 3, 1900
11. Memphis, Tennessee	May 28-30, 1901
12. Dallas, Texas	April 22-25, 1902
13. New Orleans, Louisiana	May 19-22, 1903
14. Nashville, Tennessee	June 14-16, 1904
15. Louisville, Kentucky	June 14-16, 1905
16. New Orleans, Louisiana	April 25-27, 1906
17. Richmond, Virginia	May 30-June 3, 1907
18. Birmingham, Alabama	June 9-11, 1908
19. Memphis, Tennessee	June 8-10, 1909
20. Mobile, Alabama	April 26-28, 1910
21. Little Rock, Arkansas	May 15-18, 1911
22. Macon, Georgia	May 7-9, 1912
23. Chattanooga, Tennessee	May 26-29, 1913
24. Jacksonville, Florida	May 6-8, 1914
25. Richmond, Virginia	May 31-June 3, 1915
26. Birmingham, Alabama	May 15-18, 1916
27. Washington, D.C.	June 3-7, 1917
	(June 5-7 MOC)
28. Tulsa, Oklahoma	Sept. 25-27, 1918
29. Atlanta, Georgia	Sept. 6-10, 1919
30. Houston, Texas	Oct. 6-8, 1920
31. Chattanooga, Tennessee	Oct. 24-27, 1921
32. Richmond, Virginia	June 19-22, 1922
33. New Orleans, Louisiana	April 10-13, 1923
34. Memphis, Tennessee	June 3-6, 1924
35. Dallas, Texas	May 19-22, 1925
36. Birmingham, Alabama	May 18-21, 1926
37. Tampa, Florida	April 5-8, 1927
38. Little Rock, Arkansas	May 8-11, 1928
39. Charlotte, North Carolina	June 4-7, 1929
40. Biloxi, Mississippi	June 3-6, 1930
41. Montgomery, Alabama	June 2-5, 1931
42. Richmond, Virginia	June 21-24, 1932
43. Atlanta, Georgia	Sept. 5-6, 1933
44. Chattanooga, Tennessee	June 6-8, 1934

45.	Amarillo, Texas	Sept. 3-6, 1935
46.	Shreveport, Louisiana	June 9-12, 1936
47.	Jackson, Mississippi	June 9-12, 1937
48.	Columbia, South Carolina	Aug. 30-Sept. 2, 1938
49.	Trinidad, Colorado	Aug. 22-25, 1939
50.	Washington, D.C.	Oct. 8-11, 1940
51.	Atlanta, Georgia	Oct. 14-15, 1941
52.	Chattanooga, Tennessee	June 23-26, 1942
53.	Atlanta, Georgia	Sept. 13, 1943
54.	Montgomery, Alabama	Sept. 27-28, 1944
55.	Chattanooga, Tennessee	Sept. 25-26, 1945
56.	Gulfport, Biloxi, Mississippi	Oct. 7-8, 1946
57.	Chattanooga, Tennessee	Oct. 7-8, 1947
58.	Montgomery, Alabama	Oct. 5-7, 1948
59.	Little Rock, Arkansas	Sept. 27-29, 1949
60.	Biloxi, Mississippi	Sept. 27-30, 1950
61.	Norfolk, Virginia	May 30-June 3, 1951

United Confederate Veterans Commander-Generals

Dates	Name	City
1889-1904	John B. Gordon	Atlanta, GA
1904-1908	Stephen Dill Lee	West Point, MS
1908-1909	W.L. Cabell	Dallas, TX
1909-1910	Clement A. Evans	Atlanta, GA
1910-1912	George W. Gordon	Memphis, TN
1912-1913	C. Irvine Walker	Charleston, SC
1913-1916	Bennett A. Young	Louisville, KY
1917-1918	George P. Harrison	Opelika, AL
1918-1921	K.M. Van Zandt	Fort Worth, TX
1922-1923	Julias S. Carr	Durham, NC
1923-1924	Gen. B. Haldeman	Louisville, KY
1924-1925	James A. Thomas	Dublin, GA
1925-1926	Walker B. Freeman	Richmond, VA
1926-1927	M.D. Vance	Little Rock, AR
1927-1928	J.C. Foster	Houston, TX
1929-1930	Albert T. Goodwyn	Elmore, AL
1930-1931	Richard A. Sneed	Oklahoma City, OK
1931-1932	L.W. Stephens	Coushetta, LA
1932-1933	C.A. DeSaussure	Memphis, TN
1933-1934	Homer Atkinson	Petersburg, VA
1935-1936	Harry Rene Lee	Nashville, TN
1937-1938	John M. Claypool	St. Louis, MO
1938-1939	John W. Harris	Oklahoma City, OK
1939-1940	Julius Franklin Howell	Bristol, VA
1941-1942	John M. Claypool	St. Louis, MO
1942-1943	John W. Harris	Oklahoma City, OK
1943-1944	Homer T. Atkinson	Petersburg, VA
1945-1946	Henry T. Dowling	Atlanta, GA
1948-1949	William Mercer Buck	Muskogee, OK
1949-1951	James W. Moore	Selma, AL

All Living Real Sons

Bennett Y. Allen	Cibolo, TX	Clay W. McIver	Winters, TX
Grover Anderson	Washington, WV	John N. McPherson	Northport, AL
Alexander Apperson	Clearwater, FL	L. L. Merdith	Dewitt, VA
Evin J. Atkins	Denver, CO	Thomas J. Moore	Bowdon, GA
Yates Dewey Beam	Lawndale, NC	Clyde J. Morris	Fair Bluff, NC
Joseph Oscar Beaugh	Church Point, LA	J. Z. Murphy	Atmore, AL
Rupert Blue	Laurel, MS	James L. Nelms	Corinth, MS
H. V. Booth	Elberton, GA	William B. Oliver, Sr.	McDonough, GA
William D. Bowen	Virginia, VA	Paul B. Phipps	McLeansville, NC
Edgar Boyles	Tillman, VA	Clifton Pierce	Glen Allen, VA
John C. Briggs	Ft. Worth, TX	Charles G. Pinkston	Mtn. Home, AR
Walter Broome	Bolton, MS	Woodrow Plaugher	Orcutt, CA
James F. Brown, Sr.	New Smyrna Beach, FL	Barney M. Pool	Caldwell, TX
James F. Brown	MaltaBend, MO	Rupert C. Preacher	Marion, SC
Thomas N. Bruce	Knoxville, TN	W. A. Rich	Burlington, NC
Dr. W.R. Burris	Doddsville, MS	Woodrow W. Sagers	Oriah, AL
Agnew Campbell	North Augusta, SC	Oakey H. Scarce	Dry Fork, VA
Samuel B. Campbell	Murfreesboro, TN	Ernest J. Scarce	Dry Fork, VA
Aaron B. Carpenter	Moulton, AL	William Scroggins	Anniston, AL
Willie J. Cartwright	Cornith, MS	Thomas O. Seabolt	Gainesville, GA
William M. Cobb	Bells, TN	Marion Sessions	Conway, SC
Albert L. Comer	Lavale, MD	Cullie W. Sessions	Conway, SC
Calvin Crane	Roanoke, VA	Jack Sexton	Memphis, TN
Tyus K. Denney	Tarrant, AL	William L. Sinclair	Paris, TN
Frank E. Dickerson, Sr.	Fincastle, VA	Everette Smith	Butler, KY
George W. Doss	Java, VA	Brant Staford, Sr.	St. James City, FL
John Davis Dunivant	High Point, NC	Jessie C. Stone	Hattiesburg, MS
William A. Dysard	Lewisburg, WV	Thomas E. Tatum	Durham, NC
Lattie C. Edge	Fayetteville, NC	Thomas L. Trimble	Roanoke, VA
Leonard Ellis	Chatsworth, GA	D. Crayton Vaughn	Hendersonville, NC
Quincy A. Ellis	Arlington, TX	Sam Hale Ward	Rural Retreat, VA
Louis Fite	Benton, AR	Robert E. Lee Webb	Claremore, OK
James W. Follin	Annandale, VA	John H. Webb	Claremore, OK
Joe D. Fox	Statesville, NC	Wilburn R. West	Wynnewood, OK
Jacob P. Garvin	Wagner, SC	George M. Wheatley	Glen Cove, NY
Robert Gober	St. Augustine, FL	David W. White	High Point, NC
Henry O. Gober	Millbrook, AL	Marion E. Wilson	Amarillo, TX
Clifford B. Hamm	Gastonia, NC	Boss R. Wood	Renton, WA
John P. Hopping, Jr.	Williston, FL	Mike Y. Yancey	Cordova, TN
Alcus F. Huff	Meadville, MS	Samuel Young	Verona, MS
Benjamin D. Hunter	Colquitt, GA		
William E. Hunter	Oglethorpe, NC		
Eddie L. Jordan	Selma, AL		
Thomas Keith	Franklin, KY		
Rembert J. Kennedy	Sumter, SC		
Grover Kesterson			
James H. King	Lovelady, TX		
Amos B. Little	Richton, MS		

Editor's Note: Five years ago we were honored to list 255 names. Now only 89 Real Sons remain. We must cherish these men who are our last remaining direct link to our past.

Real Sons Biographies

H.V. BOOTH was born 12-28-1918 and has always lived in the Hart and Elbert Co., Ga. area and now lives in Elberton, Ga. He is a retired car salesman. He served in the Navy in the South Pacific during WWII. He  is a active member of the Lt. Dickson L. Baker Camp 926 in Hartwell, Ga. He was first married to Sara Dickerson, and they had two boys Edwin and Virgil Booth. Sara died in April 5, 1999. H.V. has remarried to Margaret M. McClanahan

H.V.'s daddy was Isam Johnson Booth, born Feb. 7, 1847 in the Tallow Hill area of Elbert Co., near the little town of Dewy Rose, Ga. At the age of 16, Isam went with his two older brothers to the Mustering grounds at Antioch Church to join the Confederate Army. Young Isam entered as a Private in the 1st Georgia Reserves Co. D "Fannis Regiment". He was sent to Andersonville Prison as a guard. As H.V. was growing up, Isam told H.V. of the hardships that were suffered, not only to the Yankee prisoners but also on the Confederates stationed there. He told of the guards dying the same rate as the prisoners did with the "fever". Pvt. Booth caught the fever and was put on a mule and sent home to recuperate. This was a long trip back to Northeast Georgia, the trip took him six days and six nights to reach home. When Pvt. Booth got home, he was very ill and the mule was nearly dead.

With good care from his family, Pvt. Booth got over the fever and started back to Andersonville, but to find out the war was over. Isam J. Booth returned to farming and married Larkin Ann Parham and had nine children. Then Larkin Ann died in 1913, and he then married Lou Maranda and had one child, H.V. Booth.

Mr. Isam Booth died in Feb. 3, 1934 and is buried at Antioch Baptist Church, Dewy Rose, Ga. on the same grounds where he joined the Confederate Army.

WILLIAM DAVID BOWEN, Compatriot Bowen was born in Mecklenburg County, Virginia on November 27, 1913 to John William (Jack) Bowen and Myra Rice Bowen. He attended Piney Grove School in Mecklenburg County and is a retired farmer. He is a member of Aarons Creek Baptist Church and is also a member of Armistead-Hill-Goode-Elam Camp 1624, SCV, in Chase City, Virginia.

On January 12, 1935, William David married Mary Ellen Baylous in Mecklenburg County. Four children were born to the Bowens: Elizabeth, Alton, Lacy and Joey. William David has nine grandchildren.

William David's father, "Jack", died in Mecklenburg County in 1930, at age 85. Jack served in the Home Guard and the 59th Regiment, Virginia Infantry. William David was 16 at the time of his father's death and recalls that "Dixie" was his father's favorite song. He also recalls his father telling of stepping behind a tree as he was fired at and missed by a Yankee soldier; when the Yankee attempted to reload, Jack came out from behind the tree and shot him.

(We're very lucky to have this information on Mr. Bowen, who lives alone and, at age 90, was recently beaten and robbed by three "men". Fortunately he is recovering, but it was difficult to contact him. Our thanks to Commander Norris Edgerton of Colonel Thomas Williamson Chapter 249, Chase City, Virginia, who made a special effort to visit and interview him to obtain this biographical data.)

CALVIN ROBERTSON CRANE, born Feb. 27, 1917 in Pittsylvania County, VA. His parents were James Anthoney Crane and Anna Eanes. He attended Danville City School and worked for the post office, from which he retired.

He is a member of the Republican Party, Christian Disciple of Christ Church, American Legion Post #3 and the DAV. He served in the US Army during WWII as a private and received the American Defense Medal and Upper Africa Campaign Medal.

Calvin R. Crane married Mary Christine Harth in December 1923 at Roanoke, VA. Mary Christine was born July 23, 1921 to David C. and Lonna (Browning) Harth in Roanoke, VA. Their children are Cynthia Ann James and Sharon A.J. Bohon

He is a member of Fincastle Rifles Camp #1326, Roanoke, VA. His father had 16 children by his first wife and five by his second wife (Galvin's mother) and he is the youngest. He was 16 months old when his father died and has three sisters still living.

FRANK ELMER DICKERSON, born Sept. 17, 1925 in Christiansburg, VA to Eli Dickerson and Nora Martin. He attended school in Salem, VA and worked as a carpenter.

He belonged to both parties, was a member of the Baptist Church, Lions Club and VFW. He served in the US Navy Seabees during WWII in the South Pacific and attained the rank Petty Officer 3/c.

Frank Elmer married Iasbelle Simpson, born Aug. 12, 1927 in Fincastle, VA to David Lee and Marada M. (Spangler) Simpson. They were married Dec. 14, 1946 in Roanoke, VA and had three children: Frank Dickerson Jr., David Bruce, and Dennis Wayne Dickerson

He is a member of Botetourt Artillery Camp #1701, Buchannan, VA and remembers that his father had a long white beard.

Pvt. Eli Dickerson served with Co. K, 22nd Regt. VA Cav. with Commanding Officer Bowen. He was born Oct. 11, 1841, died July 8, 1930, and is buried in Floyd Cemetery (private). He married (1) Eliza Jones and (2) Noria Martin. Buried Montgomery Cemetery (private). He was a farmer and had 11 children Homer H., Wilburt H., Mary A., Costillo M., Peter, Asa, Addie, William H., Adelphia, Maggie and Frank.

JOHN DAVIS DUNIVANT, is a member of the Col. John Sloan Camp #1290 in Greensboro, NC. John was born Feb. 5, 1912, the son of Lycurgus Hannibal Dunivant and Celestia Davis Dunivant.

John graduated from Greensboro, High School in Greensboro, NC. During the 1930s he was employed by Meyer's Dept. Store in Greensboro; in the 1940s by S&W Hosiery Co.; and in the 1950s and 1960s by the E. Harllee Dept. Store in High Point, NC.

John has been active in the United Methodist Church and has served on his church's administrative council. He is a Mason and has also served as President of the Golden K Kiwanis Club. He was also a member of the National Guard.

John is married to the former Julia Stanford. Julie was born June 5, 1916, in Greensboro, NC. She is the daughter of Gaston William Stanford and Lydia Denton Stanford. She and John were married June 1, 1937, in Greensboro. They have two children: (l) John Davis "Jack" Dunivant

born July 28, 1938 and married to Susan Meredith (2) and Julia Ellen Dunivant Sessoms, born April 17, 1944.

John's father, Lycurgus Hannibal Dunivant, was born Nov. l, 1843, in Caswell County, NC. He was a private in Co. H of the 56th NC Inf. during the War for Southern Independence. Lycurgus Dunivant died Oct.21, 1913.

John's mother was Celestia Davis Dunivant, born Sept. 14, 1874 and died May 15, 1960. She and Lycurgus Dunivant are both buried in Mt. Pleasant Cemetery east of Greensboro. Lycurgus Dunivant's grave is marked with a bronze and stone Confederate marker.

Lycurgus and Celestia married Jan. 19, 1898. He was 55 and she was 23. Lycurgus had a son and a daughter by a first wife (the first wife died) and five daughters and four sons by Celestia: George Lynwood, born Nov. 10, 1898; Cora Griffin, born Oct. 19, 1899; Elizabeth Ledbetter, born March 1, 1902; Robert Lee, born May 28, 1903; Violet Baldwin, born Nov. 2, 1904, died Oct. 16, 1905; Lelia Ann, born June 24, 1906; Dorothy O'Dell, born March 25, 1908; John Davis, born Feb. 5, 1912, married Julia Stanford; Lycurgus Hannibal, born Oct. 26, 1913.

Lycurgus Dunivant was a "rugged individual" skilled in masonry and carpentry. He built the stone entrances to Green Hill Cemetery, as well as other works, that still remain standing in Greensboro today.

JAMES W. FOLLIN, born Oct. 16, 1918 in Fairfax County, VA to John N. and Lillian (Lowe) Follin. He attended nine years of school in McLean, VA and worked as Mgr. Safeway Grocery Co., Washing-

ton, DC and was organizer and vice president of Meat Cutters Union.

He was a member of the First Christian Church and served as deacon and chairman of trustees. He served in the military as Petty Officer l/c.

James married in Washington, DC to Bina R. Hutchison, born Feb. 7, 1923 in Fairfax County, VA to Dallas P. and Ethel N. Hutchison. They had three children: Walton L., born March 23, 1939; Thomas N., born Sept. 30, 1952; and Lynda D., born July 5, 1950. He is a member of Robert Lee Camp #726, Alexandria, VA.

Pvt. John Nelson Follin served in C-35, 35th VA Cav. He was wounded at the Fairgrounds, Petersburg, VA; broke out of prison in 1863; was at the Fort Monroe Hospital and later joined Mosby Rangers. He was wounded twice. John was born Aug. 20, 1847, died Oct. 5, 1937 and buried at Andrew Chapel Cemetery in Fairfax, VA with Southern Cross marker. He was a farmer and married Lillian Lowe. She was born March 14, 1879 and died March 1929 and is buried in Andrew Chapel Cemetery. They had two children, John R. Follin, born 1913, died 1965 and James Walton Follin, born October 1918 and still living.

CLIFFORD BLAIR HAMM was born on August 22,1923 and is a proud member of the Major Charles Quinn Petty Camp SCV Camp #872 in Gastonia, North Carolina. Mr. Hamm's father, John Berry Hamm, served in Company D, second North Carolina Junior reserves from 1864 until the close of the war. Mr. Clifford Blair Hamm served in the military as a member of the United States Marines from 1943 thru 1945. He is a respected Elder in Onley Presbyterian Church in Gastonia, North Carolina. The members of the Charles Q. Petty Camp are honored to have Mr. Hamm as our Real Son.

LUCA LEWIS MEREDITH JR., born March 3, 1924 in DeWitt, VA to Lucas Lewis and Mary Frances (Gregory) Meredith. Attended Norfolk Navy Yard Apprentice School, 1941-43; William and Mary, 1948-51  and earned BS degree. From 1951 to present, he has worked as a florist at The Flower Mart, Inc., Petersburg, VA.

He held office with Board of Supervisors, Dinwiddie County, 1964-68; was a deacon at Second Presbyterian Church, 1946-93; member of Rocky Run U.M. Church, 1993-present; Commander of the American Legion #149 for four years; life member of VFW Post #622; BPO Elks #237; IPA; Dinwiddie Ruritan Club, 1956-present (president for three years). He served in the US Navy 1943-46 as B3/c. Lucas is a member of A.P. Hill #167, Petersburg, VA.

Lucas married Hattie Pittman on Aug. 16, 1952 in Richmond, VA. Hattie was born Jan. 30, 1930 in Sims, NC to Hazel and Collin Pittman. They had three children: Janet Meredith, born Feb. 17, 1956 and married F. L. Wyche; Lucas Lewis III, born June 20,1958 and married Dolore Foster; and Nancy, born Jan. 16,1967 and married Andrew Keldehouse.

Pvt. Lucas Lewis Meredith served in Co. C, 3rd VA Inf. with Lt. Thomas Scott as commanding officer. He was born March 15,1842, son of Charles and Mary Chambers Meredith. He enlisted and was sworn into service at Dinwiddie Courthouse, Dinwiddie, VA on May 23,1861. He participated in numerous Civil War battles including the Battles of Manassas (Bull Run), Gettysburg, where he carried the Confederate Battle Flag for Co. C, 3rd Virginia Inf. in Pickett's Charge on July 3, 1863; Antietam; South Mountain; and his last battle was the Battle of Five Forks, where he was captured April 1, 1865 and held as a prisoner of war in the Union Stockade at Ford, VA until paroled on April 16, 1865.

On Aug. 15, 1866 he married Mary Ann E. "Mittie" Grammer, born Oct. 10, 1851, died July 20, 1907. They had six children: I.aura Verdaline (Chambers), born Jan 26, 1868, died March 1, 1946; Mary Ann E?? (Puss), born Sept. 29, 1871, died unknown; Erma T. (Wilkinson), born June 18, 1877, died July 22, 1964; John Chambers Meredith, born Aug. 1, 1879, died Sept. 17, 1953; Lottie J. (Mertens), born Oct. 16, 1881, died Oct. 6, 1968; Charles William Meredith, born April 14, 1883, died July 25, 1883.

On July 10, 1910, he married Mary Francis "Fannie" Gregory, born Jan. 5, 1886, died April 15, 1976, and is buried at Rocky Run UMC Cemetery.

They had three children: Lois, born Sept. 3, 1911, died March 4, 1912; Ida Lee (Boze), born July 22, 1914, died Sept. 5, 1976; Lucas Lewis Meredith Jr., born March 3, 1924. Pvt. Lucas Lewis Meredith died May 31, 1927 and is buried between his two wives in Rocky Run Methodist Church Cemetery, DeWitt, VA with a government marker.

PAUL BROWNING PHIPPS, is a member Of the Col. John Sloan Camp #1290 in Greensboro, NC. He has been a member since Jan. 13, 1984. The father of Paul Phipps was Robert Sanders Phipps. He was a Private in Co. C, Freeman's Regiment, Johnson's Division, North Carolina Troops. He served as a guard at the Salisbury Prison in Salisbury. NC. Robert Sanders Phipps was born on Dec. 22, 1845 and died on June 22, 1924. Before and after the War, Robert Sanders Phipps was a farmer. He married Sallie Virginia

Browning, mother of 5: Paul B. Phipps, who was born on Oct. 3, 1874. She died May 4, 1965. Both are buried in Alamance Presbyterian Cemetery in Greensboro, NC.

Robert Sanders Phipps had several children. His children and their spouses are:

Minnie Tidball Phipps, born Feb. 28, 1871, died Jan. 6, 1958, married Daniel West Cochran.

Wallace Gilmer Phipps, born Feb. 21, 1872, died March 30, 1932, married Mary "Mollie" Annie Gannon.

William Eugene Phipps, born Nov. 26,1874, died Dec. 28, 1925, married Jamie C. Carson.

Joseph Sanders Phipps, born Nov. 6, 1880, died Nov. 11, 1961, married Mary S. "Mamie" McKnight.

John Robert Phipps, born Sept. 18, 1887, died Dec. 28, 1953, married Mary Helen Barber.

Avery Phipps, born Dec. 4, 1893, died Dec. 24, 1974, married Cora L. Allred.

Charles Henry Phipps, born April 18, 1884, died March 25, 1955, married Lois Ruth Patterson Lavelle.

Infant Phipps, born July 13, 1908, died July 19. 1908.

Infant Phipps, born July 6, 1909, died July 6, 1909.

Elwood Ross Phipps, born Sept. 11, 1910, married Dortha Viola Coble.

Paul Browning Phipps, born Nov 14, 1913, married Helen Glen Shaw.

Effie Claire Phipps, born Nov. 30, 1918, married Arthur C. Whittle Jr.,

Real Son, Paul Browning Phipps, married Helen Glen Shaw on March 23, 1935 in Danville, VA. She was born Sept.17, 1914 in Guilford County, NC, the daughter of George Kenneth Shaw and Annie Allred. They have two children: (1) Mary Joanne Phipps, born March 2, 1936 and married to James Earl Sharp (2) Helen Paula Phipps, born March 22, 1945 and married to Terry S. White.

Paul Browning Phipps graduated from McLeansville High School in McLeansville, NC. From 1936-38 he worked for Electric Supply Co. Inc.; and from 1940-52 he was employed by Starr Electric Company; and from 1952-84 he was a salesman and store manager for Phipps Hardware Co., Inc. all in Greensboro. He is a member of Mt. Pleasant Methodist Church on Burlington Road in Greensboro, of which he was Treasurer for six years.

CLIFTON PATRIC PIERCE, born June 10, 1912 in Morehead City, NC, the son of John West (d. 1921) and Rosa Lean (Mitchell) Pierce (d. 1954).

Clifton was a streetcar operator in Richmond VA from Sept. 21, 1933 to Sept. 1, 1946 and a bus operator from Sept. 1, 1946 to June 1, 1974. He was a member of the Baptist Church and served in the military during WWII in the 9th Army, Artillery and attained the rank of T-5.

On April 23, 1920 in New Albany, IN, he married Margaret Egnew, born Sept. 22, 1917 in New Albany to William and Edna Egnew. They have one daughter Jean who is married lo Earnest Sheckell. Member of Lee Jackson, Camp #1, New Albany, IN, 1924.

Clifton's father, Pvt. John West Pierce, served in Co. F, 59th Regt. with Commanding Officer Cherry. John was born Nov. 21, 1844, died October 1921 and is buried in a private cemetery in Colerain, NC. He was a farmer in Colerain and married Harriet Ann Perry who was born May 28, 1846, died April 17, 1899 and is buried in a private cemetery in Colerain

John West's children are Helena Ann, Sarah Josephine, John West Jr., Shady Daucy, Flora May, Charley Franklin, Martha Jane, William Edward, Guston Van Buren, Leroy Jennings, Emma Susie, Anna Manteo, John Franklin, Floyd Spicer, Frederick Cook and Clifton Patric.

John was a farmer in Colerain, NC and a storekeeper in Morehead City, NC. He served in the Calvary from September 1862 until June 1863 and in the Infantry from June 1863 until the end of the war. He was captured June 21, 1863 at Upperville, VA and exchanged June 25th at City Point, VA. He served in the infantry at Richmond and Petersburg, VA.

CHARLES GILFORD PINKSTON, born June 4, 1909 in Norfork, AR to Thomas Jefferson and Mel Zelda (Trotter) Pinkston Children of first marriage are Tob Pinkston, buried near Batesville; Ben Pinkston, buried near Culp; and Mandy Pinkston Landrum buried near Oil Trough,

AR. He went through 9th grade and obtained GED equivalent. His last year to attend school was around 1928.

Charles first started out in refrigeration in Topeka, KS. He later moved to Long Beach, CA and worked for Douglas Aircraft in Quality Control and retired after 27 years in 1971.

He belongs to the Republican Party and is a member of the Southern Baptist Church. He became a Master Mason in Blue Lodge in California in 1965 and is Tyler in Blue Lodge in Mtn. Home; joined Scottish Rite and Shrine in 1972. He and his wife are quite active with the Masonic Demolay and Rainbow Girls. Both are members of the Order of Eastern Star, of which he was sentinel. Legion of Honor, Secretary and Treasurer. American Legion, VFW, DAV, and Order of the Purple Heart.

He wrote war articles for the *Baxter County Bulletin* during WWII, concerning "life on the front." He served in the US Army during WWII, serving as a Medical Technician with the 413th Anti-aircraft Battalion He was inducted into Army in October 1942 and saw a lot of action at Normandy Beach and the Battle of the Bulge. Though wounded, he refused to be sent back to the hospitals.

On June 12, 1937 in Levy, Pulaski County, AK he married Faye M. Massengale. born May 19, 1919, Marble City, AR to Dewey and Maude (Jackson) Massengale. They have one son Charles Gary Pinkston, born Oct. 18, 1941. His first wife was Rose and his second wife was Janice.

He first joined SCV Headquarters Camp #584, then transferred to General Jo Shelby Camp #1414, in Harrison, AR on March 4, 1998. Mr. Pinkston is a very energetic 88 year old and loves life. He and his wife are happily married and are each their own "best friends." They lead a very active life in their many fraternal organizations and are known as Dad and Mom to many Demolays and Rainbow Girls.

THOMAS ELMO TATUM, was the son of WBTS veteran James W. Tatum, Pvt. serving in the Confederate Army as a courier for the Navy Yard at Edward's Ferry, Halifax Co. North Carolina. He enlisted at the age of 14 serving as a courier and also working in the CSS Ram Alebmarle. After the war, his father, who was

an inventor, developed many items including a molasses pump, a chair with a fan, window shades, all of which he received a patent on. After working as a merchant-inventor for 75 years, he retired and lived to be 93 years old.

Thomas followed his Dad's footsteps by enlisting in the US Army in 1942. He trained to become a signalman and was shipped to England in 1942 but was later medically discharged for asthma. Returning to Durham, NC, he became a fertilizer merchant and later worked for Duke Power in maintenance until he retired in 1976. Even though he is 87 years old, he looks 60 and is looking forward to attending more SCV meetings.

GEORGE MILHOLLAND WHEATLEY, was born March 21, 1909 in Baltimore, MD to William F. and Theresa (Milholland) Wheatley. He attended Catholic University, Washington, DC; Harvard Medical School, Boston; Columbia School of Public Health, NY and earned BS, MD and MPH degrees. Worked in medical administration and from 1941-74 was the medical director at the Metropolitan Life Ins. Co. and from 1974-96 at Suffolk County, NY Dept. of Social Services Medical Director. President, American Academy of Pediatrics, 1960-61.

Married first to Eleanor Dodge (1933-69); second to Virginia Callan (1970-97) and on Sept. 6, 1997 in London, England, he married Ludy Lorna D. Snow who was born Sept. 2, 1914, in Scotland.

Children: George Jr., married Judith Thompson; Mary Ellen married M. Rausch: and Sarah married, Wm. Bradford.

His father, Cpl. William F. Wheatley, served in Co. 1, 1st Maryland Regt. with Commanding Officer Bradley T. Johnson. He was born March 20, 1844, died in May 1922 and is buried in Cathedral Cemetery, Baltimore. He married to Christine Bowling.

Real Grandsons

Updated February 15, 2004

Alabama
Matthews, Elliott Robertson III
Watkins, William E.

Arkansas
Gladish, Bill F.
Massey, Samuel Alexander, Jr.
Pinkston, Gary

Florida
Caldwell, Daniel D.
Elliott, Robert G.
Hardy, William Nash
Herring, Ronald A.
Howze, William D.

Georgia
Caldwell, Daniel D.
Mccall, Guyton B.
Milford, Charles E.
Scarborough, Earnest H.

Louisiana
Lester, Henry
Lowrey, James Marvin
Mason, Wilbert W.

Maryland
Forbes, William Albert

Minnesota
Fairbanks, George

Missouri
Burkhead, Carl
Hopper, Austin Curtis

North Carolina
Blow, George E.
Willis, Frank

South Carolina
Harrell, Chris (Age 33)
Parker, James

Texas
Delbridge, John Davis
Henley, William Branch, Jr.
Riley, Paul A.

Virginia
Jervey, Willlam Palmer, Jr.
Jones, Catesby Penniman
Lee, George Taylor, Iii
Mccausland, Alexander
Mccracken, Thomas Melvin
Nelms, Turner Shepherd
Rose, Murray F.
Swank, Walbrook D.
Whitmore, Horace Scott

Washington
Scarborough, Earnest H.

Real Great Grandsons

Alabama
Watkins, William E.

Alaska
Crowder, John E.

Arkansas
Hise, Lloyd
Massey, James Troy
Massey, Jeffery Wayne
Massey, John David
Massey, Kevin
Massey, Sammy Joe
Rollins, John

California
King, Rowland R.
White, John O.

Florida
Williams, John D.

Georgia
Schreck, Peter, Jr.
Sullivan, Edward Percival Head

Kentucky
Watkins, Lowry Rush, Jr.

Louisiania
Ed Cailleteau

Maryland
Bach, Joseph F.
Tyler, Benjamin M. Iii

Missouri
Ayres, Gary G.
Hopper, Austin Curtis

Mississippi
Furr, Randle E.
Mccowan, Earl

New Jersey
Maiden, Michael S.

North Carolina
George E. Blow

Mcleod, Waverly T.
Rascoe, J. Peter, Iii
Roberts, Harold Knox, Jr.
Willis, Frank
Jones, Daniel W.

South Carolina
Bailey, Walter M.
Crouch, William T.
Parker, James
Wolfe, Steven L.

Tennessee
Green, Jim

Texas
Block, Granvel J.
Davidson, Bob G.
Freeman, Jack P., Jr.
Hedstrom, Carlos A., Jr.
Loudermilk, Gary
Perry, George
Sandifer, Eric A.
Toal, Glenn W.

Virginia
Lee, Charles Carter
Short, Shelton H., III

SOURCES

Information in this *Sixty-fifth Anniversary Book* was obtained from many sources, especially from the following sources:

Short History of the Order of the Stars & Bars by S. Perrin Toole, Historian General, Order of Stars & Bars, 1965.

Military Order of the Stars & Bars 50th Anniversary Book by Past Commander General, Military Order of Stars and Bars, Lindsey P. Henderson Jr. and other contributors to the *Fiftieth Anniversary Book*, 1988.

Military Order of Stars and Bars Records, Lynn J. Shaw, Adjutant General Military Order of Stars and Bars, 1996.

Military Order of the Stars & Bars 60th Anniversary Book by Past Historian General, Military Order of Stars and Bars Daniel W. Jones and other contributors to the *Sixtieth Anniversary Book*, 1998.

Data bases maintained by MOSB-IHQ, Ben C. Sewell, III, Executive Director.

Museum of Confederacy, Richmond, Virginia.

North Carolina Department of Cultural Resources, Raleigh, North Carolina.

Numerous private collections of photographs and other information.

MOS&B Original Members

1-0 Gen. Homer Atkinson
Petersburg, VA

2-0 Capt. Samuel A. Ashe
Raleigh, NC

3-0 Capt. James Andrew Dowdy
Seagoville, TX

4-0 Lt. Benjamin M. Robinson
Orlando, FL

5-0 Lt. Wyatt T Hill
Lynchburg, VA

6-0 Lt. Peter Keyser
Rileyville, Page Co, VA

7-0 U James A. Lowry
Mount Verde, FL

8-0 Co. James M Stewart
Little Rock, AR

9-0 Cadet William Morison Wood
Old Hickory, TN

10-0 Maj. O. Richard Gellette
Shreveport, LA

11-0 Maj. Stephen Peters Halsey
Lynchburg, VA

12-0 Lt. McKendree Evans
Richmond, VA

13-0 Cadet Carter R. Bishop
Petersburg, FL

14-0 Lt. Noah M. Brock
Darlington, IN

15-0 Capt Holland Middleton Bell
Fayette, AL

MOS&B Membership Roster

Last name	First name	Middle Name	Suffix	MOSB #	City	State
ABEL	JACK	FREDERICK		6920	JONESBORO	GA
ABELL	CHRISTIA	AVEN- LOMBANA		4282	ALEXANDRIA	VA
ABELL	RICHARD	BENDER		541	ALEXANDRIA	VA
ABELL	STEPHEN	GEORGE		6025	CHESTER SPRINGS	PA
ABELL	TILLMAN	JESSE	III	6914	CORDOVA	SC
ABELL	TILLMAN	J.	JR	6913	CORDOVA	SC
ABNEY	LINCOLN	M		3764	MANDEVILLE	LA
ABNEY	LOUIS	O.		3758	AUBURN	AL
ACKER	KELLY	M. K.		2468	MAIL RETURNED	TX
ADAMS	CARL	RAYMOND		7237	TEXAS CITY	TX
ADAMS	DAVID	M.		5228	RALEIGH	NC
ADAMS	FRANK	W.		5832	INDEPENDENCE	MO
ADAMS	MELROSE	B.		6429	FALLS CHURCH	VA
ADAMS	WILLIAM	EUGENIUS	JR	2031	ATHENS	GA
ADDISON	FERGUSON			1165	W. PALM BEACH	FL
ADERHOLDT	FRANK	W.	JR	3437	HATTIESBURG	MS
ADKINSON	MARK	NOLEN		6394	WARRACRES	OK
AIKEN	DR DAVID	WYATT		6054	NEW ORLEANS	LA
AKIN	BILLIE	G.		5526	WACO	TX
ALARID	JOSEPH	VICTOR		6895	SANTA BARBARA	CA
ALBERT	GARY	D.		5077	STOKESDALE	NC
ALDIS	G	RONALD		6425	HOUSTON	TX
ALDIS	JEFFREY	ALLAN		6731	HOUSTON	TX
ALDRIDGE	GEORGE	THOMPSON		6399	JOHNSTON	SC
ALEXANDER	JAMES	GILBERT	JR	6952	MADISON	AL
ALEXANDER	THOMAS	W.	H	3853	RALEIGH	NC
ALFORD	EDWARD	CARROLL		7302	GALAX	VA
ALGEE	HAROLD	DWAYNE		7152	HOT SPRINGS	AR
ALISON	THOMAS	L.	JR	4382	FAUNSDALE	AL
ALLEN	'	GEORGE		6918	ASHEVILLE	NC
ALLEN	WALTER	G.	M D	1866	PONTE VEDRA BEACH	FL
ALLISON	DAVID			5472	ARLINGTON	TX
ALLISON	DAVID	LEE		7079	CUYAHOGA FALLS	OH
ALLRED	THOMAS	R.		5463	ANNISTON	AL
ALMOND	DANIEL	K.		2821	OKLAHOMA CITY	OK
ALSTON	CHARLIE	DUNN		946	SCOTLAND NECK	NC
ALVAREZ	EMIL	DALE		5749	HOUSTON	TX
AMENDOLA	DAVID	WALTER		6541	CARY	IL
AMMONS	JOHN	J		3933	PANAMA CITY	FL
ANDERSON	KENNETH	J.	SR	5119	MEDON	TN
ANDERSON	REV ALIS	C		5297	FREDERICK	MD
ANDERSON	ROGER	KARL		6675	SHREVEPORT	LA
ANDERSON	STEPHEN	U		7323	NORTH ROYALTON	OH
ANDERSON	WADDY	MCFALL	III	6785	GREENVILLE	SC
ANDREWS	BEN	CURTIS		6812	GRAPEVINE	TX
ANDREWS	COL WILL	D		7290	VIRGINIA BEACH	VA
ANDREWS	GENE			4451	NASHVILLE	TN
ANDREWS	HOWARD	PHILIP		6053	MOBILE	AL
ANDREWS	RICHARD	A		6811	GRAPEVINE	TX
ANKERS	MARVIN	THOMAS		6389	BRANDY STATION	VA
ARNOLD	BRUCE	ROBERT		7282	PINEVILLE	MO
ARNOLD	ROBERT	STANLEY		7030	ST. PETERS	MO
ASHLEY	ALLEN	L		7340	HONEA PATH	SC
ASTON	MACDONAL	KING		7040	LOUISVILLE	CO
ATCHLEY	JOE	CHARLES		5244	ENID	OK
ATCHLEY	MARK	C.		5009	LEXINGTON	SC
ATKINS	NORMAN	GENE		6585	GROVER	NC
AUSTIN	KENNETH	H.	JR	3897	SUFFOLK	VA
AVARITT	LARRY	DON		7051	VILONIA	AR

AYRES	GARY	GENE		6473	HUMANSVILLE	MO
AYRES	ROY	EDWIN		6795	HUMANSVILLE	MO
AYRES	WILLILAM	KELLY		6766	FLEMINGTON	MO
AZEVEDO	CHRISTOPHER	DEAN		5664	WARRENSBURG	MO
BACH	JOSEPH	FRANCIS		5627	HAGERSTOWN	MD
BADER	STEVEN	CLEMENT		6469	SAVANNAH	GA
BAGBY	JAMES	M.		6017	INDEPENDENCE	MO
BAGBY	KENNETH	ROY		6954	SHELBY	NC
BAGBY	RICHARD	H		1899	RICHMOND	VA
BAGG	JAMES	ERSKINE	JR	7239	GALVESTON	TX
BAGGETT	JAMES	C	JR	7060	MAGNOLIA SPRINGS	AL
BAILEY	GREGORY	BRIAN		7139	ALABASTER	AL
BAILEY	JEFFARES	RAY		7278	LOGANVILLE	GA
BAILEY	JOHN	PARKER		7221	LIBERTY	TX
BAILEY	KINCHEON	H.	III	2245	RALEIGH	NC
BAILEY	LT COL K	H	JR	1097	RALEIGH	NC
BAILEY	RUSSELL	B.		2374	COVINGTON	TN
BAILEY	STUART	ARMSTRONG		7324	LOXAHATCHEE	FL
BAILEY	WALTER	M	III	7018	SUMMERVILLE	SC
BAKER	ALBERT	JOSH		5252	HOUSTON	TX
BAKER	BERNARD	D.	JR	4228	DANVILLE	VA
BAKER	BRUCE	ADDISON		4017	AUSTIN	TX
BALDWIN	DAVID	MCRACKAN		5404	KINGSLAND	GA
BALDWIN	EUGENE	F.	JR	3341	ATHENS	GA
BALDWIN	JAMES	J	III	6105	GREENVILLE	SC
BALDWIN	RONALD	GLENN		7295	ASHEVILLE	NC
BALKE	ROBERT	CARL		7261	TEXAS CITY	TX
BALLARD	DANIEL	J		5169	ATHENS	GA
BALSLEY	GEORGE	LEE		938	RAYTOWN	MO
BALTZEGAR	PAUL	STEVEN		2306	DAYTONA BEACH	FL
BANE	NED	BARBEE		4454	PULASKI	VA
BANKS	SMITH	CALLAWAY		3968	STATESBORO	GA
BANKSTON	JOHNNY	BRYAN		6229	BILOXI	MS
BARBARE	CHARLES	RICHARD		5176	TRENTON	SC
BARCUS	CYRUS	CARTER		6774	BURNET	TX
BARDIN	JAMES	NELSON		948	GARDEN GROVE	CA
BARICEV	JOSEPH	HUGH		5960	OCEAN SPRINGS	MS
BARKER	CHRISTOP	SYLVANUS	III	5160	DALLAS	TX
BARNES	HENRY	PRESTON		6870	STOCKTON	AL
BARNES	JEFF			6088	FOREST	MS
BARNES	KILEY	PRESTON		7059	STOCKTON	AL
BARNETT	HOWARD	DALE		7177	JONESBORO	AR
BARR	JAMES	FALVY	ABA, ATP	6781	CHICAGO	IL
BARR	WILLIAM	EVANS		6619	ARLINGTON	VA
BARR	WILLIAM	WARREN		6862	CHICAGO	IL
BARRETT	DAVID	WINSTON		2380	TUCKER	GA
BARROW	CHARLES	K		3545	GRIFFIN	GA
BARRY	RAYMOND	JOSEPH	JR	7125	ATLANTA	GA
BARTON	JUDSON	DOYLE	JR	5093	HARTWELL	GA
BASS	JAMES	L		3677	SMITHTON	MO
BASS	JOHN	R		3666	SPRING HOPE	NC
BASSETT	TIMOTHY	FRANK		7211	CUMMING	GA
BATEMAN	JACOB	L.	III	2361	MONTGOMERY	AL
BATEMAN	STEPHEN	MICHAEL		7026	HOUSTON	TX
BAUER	FRED	GRAHAM		6244	HUNTLAND	TN
BAXTER	DAVID	MARK		4116	MACON	GA
BAXTER	DR ROBER	S.		3652	NEW ORLEANS	LA
BAXTER	OSCAR	FITZ-ALAN	V	6912	VIRGINIA BEACH	VA
BAY	JAMES	THOMAS		6528	SIX MILE	SC
BEALS	EUGENE	THOMAS		5184	COLLINVILLE	IL
BEAN	WILLIAM	LEWIS	JR	7263	CULPEPPER	VA
BEARD	JOHN	HARRIS		6254	HOUSTON	TX
BEARD	ROBERT	LARRY		7229	ALVIN	TX
BEARSS	EDWIN	C		711	ARLINGTON	VA

BEASLEY	HORACE	JEFFERSON	III	7291	KNOTTS ISLAND	NC
BEASLEY	THOMAS	TARRY	II	1198	MEMPHIS	TN
BECK	DANIEL	HANSEN		6925	BESSEMER CITY	NC
BECK	DONALD	E		5302	ROCKVILLE	MD
BECKER	RANDALL	WILLIAM		7169	HOT SPRINGS VILLAGE	AR
BEESON	LARRY	E		5473	KING	NC
BELFLOWER	ROBERT	ALAN		6335	DE RIDDER	LA
BELL	DR CHARLES	D.	MD	7078	ROSANKY	TX
BELL	JOHN	CARTWRIGHT	JR	2753	ROSLYN	NY
BELL	JOHN	SAMMONS		3942	AMELIA ISLAND	FL
BELL	KENNETH	C.	JR	4219	AMARILLO	TX
BELL	WILLIAM	F.	JR.	111	SILOAM SPRINGS	AR
BELVIN	THOMAS	GLENN		5199	GARNER	NC
BENNETT	BOBBY	W		5767	GLENDALE	AZ
BENNETT	CHESTER	A		3553	DUBLIN	OH
BENNETT	DAVID	A		3988	BOLIVAR	OH
BENNETT	WILLIAM	J.		6114	NEWNAN	GA
BENTON	THOMAS	H		4487	JEFFERSON	GA
BERKELEY	CHARLES	CARTER	JR	5744	SAN ANTONIO	TX
BERLY	TIMOTHY	WAYNE		7285	CHARLOTTE	SC
BERRYHILL	CASWELL	DRAKE		3904	RALEIGH	NC
BERRYHILL	WILLIAM	I.	JR	653	RALEIGH	NC
BESECKER	KENNETH	HARLEY		5095	MARTINEZ	GA
BEST	WILLIAM	ROGER	II	6721	ASHEVILLE	NC
BETHARD	ALVIN	YOUNG		3208	LAFAYETTE	LA
BETHUNE	EVERETT	P.	JR	1661	LOUISVILLE	KY
BETSILL	DANIEL	JACK		6467	FT. WORH	TX
BETSILL	JERRY	DON		6466	FT. WORTH	TX
BETSILL	JOHN	DAVID		6464	FT WORTH	TX
BIGGS	MURCHISO	B		4176	LUMBERTON	NC
BILLUPS	TRAVIS	ANTHONY		7240	TEXAS CITY	TX
BIRDSONG	DOUGLAS	R		4456	NEW COLUMBIA	PA
BISHOP	AUBREY	A.	JR	5111	MOBILE	AL
BISHOP	LEE	EDWARD	JR	4461	SANTA MONICA	CA
BISHOP	ROBERT	L		6503	COLONIAL HIEGHTS	VA
BLACK	DONALD	B.		5152	ELKMONT	AL
BLACK	SCOTT			3008	KATY	TX
BLACKERBY	B.	J.		6686	AURORA	CO
BLACKERBY	MICHAEL	L		5038	AZLE	TX
BLACKMON	BERT	DANIEL	III	6558	BAY MINETTE	AL
BLACKWELL	TOMMY	SCOTT		7245	MELBOURNE	FL
BLAIN	JERRY	WILLIAM EDWARD		7283	GLADSTONEM	
BLALACK	JOE	RAY		3349	HUMBLE	TX
BLANTON	CURTIS	HUGH	JR	2296	JACKSONVILLE	FL
BLEVINS	BOBBY	RAY		7289	MCKENNEY	VA
BLICK	GEORGE	RUBEN		5259	EMPORIA	VA
BLOCK	CHRISTOP	JAMES		7098	ORANGE	TX
BLOCK	GRANVEL	J		7101	ORANGE	TX
BLOW	GEORGE	E		4051	INDIAN TRAIL	NC
BLYTHE	C.	EARL		5320	SCAFORD	VA
BLYTHE	WILLIAM	J.	JR	1841	HOUSTON	TX
BOARDMAN	REV. COL	ARMISTEAD		6737	MONUMENT	CO
BOATWRIGHT	BENJAMIN	JR		3780	COLUMBIA	SC
BOBIER	GEORGE	F.	JR	4037	SOUTHGATE	MI
BOCKMILLER	STEPHEN	R		2878	MIDDLETOWN	MD
BOLDT	HENRY	CHARLES	JR	6462	FT WORTH	TX
BOLDT	JONATHAN			6800	FT WORTH	TX
BOLDT	KEVIN			6463	FT. WORTH	TX
BOLEN	JACK	C		5573	BRANDON	FL
BOLES	DONALD	LEE		7331	GLOUCESTER PT	VA
BOLICK	ANTHONY	DAI		5579	MAIDEN	NC
BOLTON	JAMES		JR	1925	RICHMOND	VA
BONAR	CHARLES	ALVIN		6975	BURLINGTON	WV
BONAWIT	LLOYD	FRANKLIN	REV	6559	FT LAUDERDALE	FL

BONEY	DONALD	L		1431	CHAMBLEE	GA
BOONE	JEFFREY	MICHAEL		6867	LOXLEY	AL
BOONE	JEFFREY	DANA		6874	LOXLEY	AL
BORIE	EDWARD	TAYLOR LEWIS		6768	BATON ROUGE	LA
BOSWELL	EDDIE	FAIN		6367	CARTERSVILLE	GA
BOSWELL	FREDERIC	N		7154	DESTIN	FL
BOUDREAU	ROBERT	G.		6888	PARKER	CO
BOUDREAUX	DONALD	J		7120	LAFAYETTE	LA
BOWDEN	BILLY	ED		5018	FLORISSANT	MO
BOWEN	JUSTIN	LEE		6441	SAN PEDRO	CA
BOWEN	WILLIAM	FRANKLIN		6770	SAN ANGELO	TX
BOWMAN	L.	LINTON	III	6827	LAKEWAY	TX
BOWMAN	TIMOTHY	DALE		6356	CECILIA	KY
BOYD	GARY	WAYNE		6747	WASHINGTON	NC
BOYD	HARRY	J.		6628	RICHMOND	VA
BOYER	TYRIE	ALVIS		2783	JACKSONVILLE	FL
BRABHAM	JAY	FRANK		6810	JAMESTOWN	NC
BRADEN	LARRY			5225	CHARLESTON	IL
BRADLEY	KENNETH	P		820	DERBY	KS
BRADLEY	ROBERT	WESTON		6850	COATESVILLE	PA
BRADSHAW	RIPLEY	ARIN		6681	CHANDLER	TX
BRADSHAW	ROBERT	BRETT		4328	LITTLE MOUNTAIN	SC
BRADY	BYRON	E		3452	RALEIGH	NC
BRAME	ARDEN	HOWELL	JR, II	6215	ROSEMEAD	CA
BRANHAM	RICHARD	AUSTIN	JR	5317	ST CLOUD	FL
BRASELL	LEWIS	DAVIS		2686	MOBILE	AL
BRASHEAR	DAVID	S		2086	LONG ISLAND CITY	NY
BRASWELL	EDWIN	BENTON	JR	930	HIGH POINT	NC
BRECKINRIDGE	CARY	LUKE		5628	SALEM	VA
BREITHAUPT	RICHARD	H.	JR	4165	VAN NUYS	CA
BRENT	GERALD	PAGE		5085	OLIVE BRANCH	MS
BREWTON	MARSHALL	LAYTON	JR	6404	ORLANDO	FL
BRICE	JAMES	CLOWNEY	JR	5096	EASLEY	SC
BRICKEY	CDR DONALD	W.		5429	COTTONTOWN	TN
BRIDGES	DAVID	POWELL		7063	ALEXANDRIA	VA
BRIDGES	GEORGE	F.	JR	1504	KEYSTONE HEIGHTS	FL
BRIGGS	CHARLES	E		7075	GIBSON CITY	IL
BRIGGS	HOUSTON	W.	II	3759	KISSIMMEE	FL
BRIGHT	BOBBY	BRIGANCE	SR	7038	MEDON	TN
BRIGHT	DWAINE	LEROY	JR	6994	ST. DAVID	AZ
BRIM	DANIEL	H		3234	CATAULA	GA
BRITTON	CHARLES	WAYNE		3063	OKLAHOMA CITY	OK
BRODERICK	SCOTT	M		3927	JACKSON	LA
BRODIE	EDWARD	FULFORD		6400	HOUSTON	TX
BROMBERG	CHARLES	CLAYTON		2677	JACKSONVILLE	FL
BROOKE	GEORGE	MERCER	III	6555	ALEXANDRIA	VA
BROOKS	DR NEWTON	JAMES	JR	7178	CLARKSVILLE	TN
BROOKS	MICHAEL	ANDREW		6809	WINSTON-SALEM	NC
BROTHERTON	RALPH	J.	SR	6090	SPRING HILL	FL
BROWN	DANA	LANE	SR	5170	SAVANNAH	GA
BROWN	DON	E		3471	SALEM	IL
BROWN	H.	BENNETT		1275	LAKE PARK	GA
BROWN	HAROLD	LEE		6621	ALEXANDRIA	VA
BROWN	JOSEPH	E		5330	WAYNESBORO	MS
BROWN	LARRY	ROSS		5293	KENAI	AK
BROWN	LARRY	T		5560	GREENSBORO	NC
BROWN	ROBERT	A		3468	PRAIRIE CREEK	IN
BROWN	ROBERT	G	SR	5528	LEESBURG	VA
BROWN	THOMAS	WALTER		4345	LAKE CITY	FL
BROWN	WESLEY	BALLARD		7074	AKLIE	VA
BRYANT	MARSHALL	D		6814	SAN ANGELO	TX
BUCHANAN	JACE	STUART		7191	MORGANTON	NC
BUCHANAN	PATRICK	J		3785	MCLEAN	VA
BUCKLES	STANLEY	DEE		6941	MT. PULASKI	IL

BUCKNER	WILLIAM	GORDON		2667	MARSHALL	MO
BUFFKIN	WARD	MAURICE		7053	FLORENCE	SC
BULLARD	RAYMOND	LEE		5116	JACKSONVILLE	FL
BULLOCK	HENRY	JERRY		7000	GULFPORT	MS
BULLOCK	STEVEN	JERROD		7002	GULFPORT	MS
BULLOCK	WILLIAM	ROBERT	JR	6030	DARDANELLE	AR
BUNTING	BILLY	L	JR	5790	GREENSBORO	NC
BURCH	ERNEST	W.	JR	2613	GAINESVILLE	FL
BURFORD	ROBERT	DAVID		6015	KIRKWOOD	MO
BURKS	BARNEY	L		5533	VIRGINIA BEACH	VA
BURKS	CHARLES	DERL		5133	ELDON	MO
BURNETT	ARTHUR	H		5814	GILBERT	SC
BURNETTE	CHRISTOP	STEVEN		7206	FANCY GAP	VA
BURNETTE	VAN	T.	DR	4421	WINTER HAVEN	FL
BURNHAM	WILLIAM	HENRY		7071	CHARLOTTE	NC
BURNS	BENJAMIN	W		3848	LAKE CHARLES	LA
BURNS	MARK	ANDREW		6771	TROY	MT
BURRUSS	EDMUND	COLEMAN		6725	POWHATAN	VA
BUSH	DR JAMES	F.		3912	FT. COLLINS	CO
BUSSEY	ANTHONY	L		6901	SAN ANTONIO	TX
BUTLER	CHARLES	VOIERS	JR	1272	PARIS	TN
BUTLER	EDWARD	F.	SR	5995	SAN ANTONIO	TX
BUTLER	GEORGE	REVIS	JR	5776	ATLANTA	GA
BUTLER	J.	CARLTON		5206	EMPORIA	VA
BUTTGEN	JACK	ELLSWORTH		6523	STAFFORD COUNTY	VA
BUTTGEN	LOUIS		JR	6522	STAFFORD COUNTY	VA
BUTTGEN	LOUIS		III	6571	STAFFORD COUNTY	VA
BUTTGEN	PHILIP	NATHAN		6911	STAFFORD	VA
BYRD	D.	HAROLD	III	1590	DALLAS	TX
BYTHER	PAUL	F	JR	6492	TAMPA	FL
CAHOON	HOLLIS	B		3878	GREENSBORO	NC
CAILLETEAU	EDWARD	OVERTON		1763	BATON ROUGE	LA
CAIN	JONATHAN	WALKER		7305	TROY	AL
CAIN	PATRICK	MARTIN		7306	TROY	AL
CAIN	ROY	NELSON		6943	POWHATAN	VA
CALDWELL	CARROLL	WAYNE		6691	SPARTANBURG	SC
CALLICOTT	RICHARD	ROSS		2208	MEMPHIS	TN
CALVIT	GEORGE	A		5352	MINDEN	LA
CAMP	GEORGE	MARK		6175	MINDEN	LA
CAMPBELL	BENJAMIN	CARTER		7011	CHOUDRANT	LA
CAMPBELL	J.A.	BARTON		5213	MIDLOTHIAN	VA
CAMPBELL	JAMES	RANDOLPH		6169	STONEVILLE	NC
CAMPBELL	JOHN	OWEN		3522	SEPULVEDA	CA
CANIPE	MARCUS	JULE		2566	CHESTERFIELD	SC
CANTRELL	JAMES	CAGE	JR	7241	GALVESTON	TX
CANTRELL	MARK	LEA		1654	EL RENO	OK
CAPOROSSI	DALE	T		3928	SHARON	PA
CARAKER	MIKE			6882	ELGIN	IL
CARLETON	DR CHARL	C.		2231	WINTER PARK	FL
CARLTON	GILBERT	WATSON		6563	DENVER	CO
CARPENTER	BOBBY	SCOTT		5224	CHERRYVILLE	NC
CARR	TONY	L.	SR	5857	NORTH AUGUSTA	SC
CARRELL	DOUGLAS	CREED		7106	FT. WORTH	TX
CARROLL	JAMES	L		4256	COLUMBUS	TX
CARROLL	JOHN	E.	III	5265	KISSIMMEE	FL
CARROLL	JOHN	MOORER		6314	HARDEEVILLE	SC
CARROON	ROBERT	G		733	W. HARTFORD	CT
CARSWELL	ROBERT	M.	III	4038	MOBILE	AL
CARTER	ANTHONY	B		3184	NESBIT	MS
CARTER	FRANKIE	LELAND		6638	FRUITVALE	TX
CARTER	JAMES	LEWIS		5485	FITZGERALD	GA
CARTER	JAMES	ANDREW		5648	CHARLES CITY	VA
CARTER	JENNINGS	FAULK		7122	MONROEVILLE	AL
CARTER	LUTHER	FREDRICK		6121	FLORENCE	SC

CARTER	ROBERT	THOMAS		6386	TULLAHOMA	TN
CARTER	WAYNE	M.		5231	EDEN	NC
CASEY	JAMES	ROBERT		6641	KIANA	AK
CASTER	JAMES	G		3064	OKLAHOMA CITY	OK
CASTLE	ROBERT	VADEN		6983	ASHLAND	KY
CATHEY	BOYD	D.	DR	3549	WENDELL	NC
CATLIN	WILLIAM		JR	7123	JACKSONVILLE	FL
CATON	STANLEY	L		3453	RALEIGH	NC
CAUDILL	STEPHEN	ROGERS		6915	CEDAR RAPIDS	IA
CAVAROC	JOHN	PETER		3289	NEW ORLEANS	LA
CHAIN	BOBBY	L		6293	HATTIESBURG	MS
CHAMBERS	CHARLES	E		3320	HOUSTON	TX
CHANDLER	GLENN	EDWIN		2474	JACKSONVILLE	FL
CHANDLER	TROY	GRAYSON		6769	LAFAYETTE	LA
CHARLES	MICHAEL	HARRISON		1999	NEW YORK	NY
CHASTAIN	WILLARD	E		7107	LAWRENCEVILLE	GA
CHAUVIN	GEORGE	FREDERICK		4239	ST. AUGUSTINE	FL
CHESSON	WESLEY	EARLE		2172	NEW CASTLE	DE
CHIESA	ALFRED	JOSEPH		7336	NEWPORT NEWS	VA
CHILDERS	HUMPHREY	H		4086	COLUMBIA	SC
CHISOLM	WILLIAM	DEE	JR	5453	CAYCE	SC
CHOATE	MARK			4287	DICKSON	TN
CLAAR	RICHARD	W.		6237	LEESBURG	VA
CLAGETT	BRICE	MCADOO		1241	FRIENDSHIP	MD
CLARDY	STANLEY	W		6668	STATESVILLE	NC
CLARK	ALLEN	H		3065	PARIS	TN
CLARK	JOSEPH	BURNEY	JR	1365	JACKSONVILLE	FL
CLARK	KENNEDY	HELM	JR	2022	LOUISVILLE	KY
CLARK	ROBERT	MUREL	JR	1492	DALLAS	TX
CLARKE	BOYKIN			5379	WAYCROSS	GA
CLAY	CURTIS	ADAIR		6526	WOODLAWN	VA
CLEMENTS	CHARLES	M.	III	2950	BUENA VISTA	GA
CLEMENTS	FREDERIC	DENNY		6908	WASHINGTON	DC
CLEMMER	GREGG	S		5298	GERMANTOWN	MD
CLEMMONS	RONALD	T		1951	MURFREESBORO	TN
CLONINGER	BRUCE	ALAN		5535	CHERRYVILLE	NC
COBB	SAMUEL	JEFFERSON	JR	6542	HOUSTON	TX
COCKERHAM	NORMAN	LEE		6807	CARLTON	OR
COFER	LESLIE	ALLEN	III	6216	LIVERMORE	CA
COGBILL	JOSEPH	A		3865	MACON	GA
COHOON	THOMAS	WILLIS		6841	SUFFOLK	VA
COLBAUGH	BARRY	LYNN		6381	CARTERSVILLE	GA
COLE	SCOTT	CRAIG		5825	TAZEWELL	VA
COLEMAN	C.	WAYNE		6539	BROKEN ARROW	OK
COLEMAN	COL ROBE	S.		5607	NEWPORT NEWS	VA
COLEMAN	JOHN	WALTON		2763	JACKSONVILLE	FL
COLLIER	COL JOHN	THORNTON		703	ARLINGTON	VA
COLLIER	CURTIS	HARRIS	III	6382	ATHENS	GA
COLLIER	JOHN	ALAN		4348	SAN ANTONIO	TX
COLLINS	GREGORY	THOMAS		5092	KENTS STORE	VA
COLLINS	JAMES	A.		6265	TROUTVILLE	VA
COLLINS	JARED			7112	COVINGTON	TN
COLLINS	RALPH	LEE		4225	MARIETTA	GA
COLLINS	ROY	WAYNE		7050	COVINGTON	TN
COLLY	MAURICE	L		2016	BAY ST LOUIS	MS
COLVIN	DAVID	PAYNE		7339	CARY	NC
CONE	D.	K		5406	ALLENDALE	SC
CONNEL	ALLEN	C.		6632	ORANGE	TX
CONNEL	EDGAR	BUFORD		7049	ORANGE	TX
CONNEL	SHANE	MICHAEL		7100	ORANGE	TX
CONNELL	RANDALL	WAYNE		2703	HOUSTON	TX
CONWELL	GARY			4251	KANSAS CITY	MO
COOK	DANIEL	GULLETT		6154	TIBURON	CA
COOK	JOSEPH	WILLIAM	III	3428	HIXSON	TN

Last	First	Middle	Suffix	Num	City	State
COOK	LOWRY	M		4413	BOONE	NC
COOKE	JAMES	E.	JR	4061	RICHMOND	VA
COONCE	JAMES	W		5460	RAYTOWN	MO
COOPER	BRIAN	H		3778	MARIETTA	GA
COOPER	BRIAN	L		7117	KEY WEST	FL
COOPER	CARL	FREDERIC	III	6679	LITTLE ROCK	AR
COOPER	JERRY	W	SR	7127	FANCY GAP	VA
COOPER	LEE			3515	FT. WALTON BEACH	FL
COOPER	RAY			3514	JACKSONVILLE	FL
COOPER	ROYAL	O		3310	JEFFERSON CITY	MO
COPPOCK	THOMAS	JOHN		6980	RED OAK	TX
CORBETT	H	DANLEIGH		6871	BAY MINETTE	AL
CORLEW	GARY	L		6861	VARNA	IL
CORTNER	CLARENCE	ROBERT		6450	WINCHESTER	TN
CORTNER	JAMES	DUDLEY		6530	MANCHESTER	TN
CORTNER	JAMES	CLARENCE		6451	WINCHESTER	TN
CORTNER	JOHN	ALEXANDER		6453	WINCHESTER	TN
CORTNER	JOHN	DAVID		6452	WINCHESTER	TN
CORTNER	JOHN	MARK		6454	WINCHESTER	TN
COUCH	ARTHUR	A		1820	NASHVILLE	TN
COUCH	ROBERT	LAUGHLIN	JR	2056	TULLAHOMA	TN
COULTER	BENJAMIN	H.		6886	CALHOUN	GA
COURTNEY	DON	R		2351	EL RENO	OK
COWDREY	WILLIAM	ARNOLD		7272	JACKSONVILLE	FL
COX	EDDIE	LEE		7218	MINERAL WELLS	TX
COX	JOHN	EARL		6884	VIRGINIA BEACH	VA
COX	RAYMOND	ROY		5669	DALLAS	TX
COX	WALTER	ROBISON	JR	4452	MONROE	GA
COX	WALTER	R.	SR	4415	MONROE	GA
COXE	PATRICK	C		5270	BENNETTSVILLE	SC
CRAFT	COLUMBUS			6998	ROLLA	MO
CRAGHEAD	WILLIAM	SAM		5200	RICHMOND	VA
CRANE	ROGER	A		5771	TAMPA	FL
CRAWFORD	JAMES	M		2187	DE FUNIAK SPRINGS	FL
CRISLER	CLIFTON	W		4120	ALEXANDER CITY	AL
CRISLER	THOMAS	CLIFTON		6949	ALEXANDER CITY	AL
CROCKER	THOMAS	NORMAN		4118	CRESTON	IA
CROCKETT	THOMAS	H.	JR	5729	RICE	VA
CROOK	ROBERT	W		6057	BATON ROUGE	LA
CROOK	ROBERT	L		697	FLORENCE	MS
CROOK	WARREN	C.	III	3216	LURAY	TN
CROUCH	WILLIAM	THOMAS		7095	AIKEN	SC
CROWDER	DR. ROBE	DOUGLAS		806	DALLAS	TX
CROWDER	JOHN	EDWARD		5572	BIG LAKE	AK
CRUTCHER	JOHN	SIMS	III	6738	ATHENS	AL
CUMMINGS	GEORGE	ELLIOTT		2555	TOWSON	MD
CUMMINGS	JAMES	W		3385	ALEXANDRIA	VA
CUNNINGHAM	DR. JAME	S.	DDS	2890	HOUSTON	TX
CUPPLES	JAMES			2266	WILDERSVILLE	TN
CURRY	BURTON	KING		4096	TUSCALOOSA	AL
DALEEN	KEITH	I		3606	SEDALIA	MO
DAME	JOEL	E		7253	OKLAHOMA CITY	OK
DAMRON	ROBERT	R		6997	NICHOLASVILLE	KY
DANIEL	PAUL	GANTT		5452	DACULA	GA
DANIEL	RICHARD	P		4341	STONE MOUNTAIN	GA
DANIEL	WILLIAM	CECIL	JR	4119	ANNISTON	AL
DARDEN	EDWARD	BOYLE	JR	6745	CASHIERS	NC
DAUGHTRY	TIMOTHY	CARR		6924	GREENSBORO	NC
DAVES	ALFRED	COLE		1789	MOBILE	AL
DAVES	RICHARD	F		6674	MOBILE	AL
DAVIDSON	BOBBY	GENE		6606	TYLER	TX
DAVIS	CHARLES	C		4297	RALEIGH	NC
DAVIS	DONALD	EUGENE		2079	MOSS POINT	MS
DAVIS	FRANKLIN	ROBERT		6684	GREENVILLE	TX

DAVIS	GREGORY	ALBERT		6515	VALE	NC
DAVIS	HAROLD	FRANKLIN	III	2826	MT PLEASANT	SC
DAVIS	JAMES	SELMAN		6548	ST AUGUSTINE	FL
DAVIS	JEFF			6880	GAINESVILLE	GA
DAVIS	JOHN	LYNNWOOD	JR.	7045	ARLINGTON	TX
DAVIS	JONATHAN	SELMAN		7114	ST AUGUSTINE	FL
DAVIS	SAMUEL	L		3768	LAKELAND	FL
DAWSON	SAMUEL	COOPER	JR	177	SALISBURY	VA
DAWSON	SAMUEL	COOPER	III	245	FREDERICKSBURG	VA
DAY	RICHARD	LEE		3397	VINE GROVE	KY
DEAN	JOHN	W		7039	TOWNSEND	GA
DEAN	PURL	GORDON		5846	LADY LAKE	FL
DEARING	REINHARD	J		5482	SLIDELL	LA
DELANO	HUGH	S		4323	CRANFORD	NJ
DELCOURE		RICK		6740	STANWOOD	WA
DELLINGER	DR HUBER	L.	JR	6847	MEMPHIS	TN
DELOACH	JIMMIE	DALE	JR	6805	HOLCOMB	MS
DeLORME	CECIL	BRUX		6095	SAVANNAH	GA
DELORME	HARRY	HAYNESWORTH		6340	SAVANNAH	GA
DELP	JAMES	EDWIN		2909	SAN JOSE	CA
DENARD	ODIAN	DAVID		6945	LAWRENCEVILLE	GA
DENSMORE	THOMAS	ALLEN	SR	5281	KISSIMMEE	FL
DePASS	WILLIAM	BRUNSON	JR	6917	COLUMBIA	SC
DERRYBERRY	WILLIAM	COOPER	JR	5319	PIEDMONT	AL
DERST	D	MORGAN			SAVANNAH	GA
DERST	EDWARD	J.	III	6134	SAVANNAH	GA
DETERDING	ARTHUR	JOSEPH		5694	FLORISSANT	MO
DEWEESE	MICHAEL	W		4475	PLANO	TX
DIAL	MILLER	D. M. F.		4163	BATON ROUGE	LA
DIBRELL	ROBERT	W		3442	HOUSTON	TX
DICKENS	RAYMOND	A.	III	5765	HOUSTON	TX
DICKENS	RAYMOND	A.	JR	5348	HOUSTON	TX
DICKENSON	CHARLES	SAMUEL		5470	NESBIT	MS
DICKEY	DAVID	HERSCHEL		5101	SAVANNAH	GA
DICKEY	DAVID	BRADFORD		5614	SAVANNAH	GA
DICKINSON	ROBERT	LEE	JR	6973	COLUMBIA	SC
DIEKMANN	DR RICHA	T		6495	PORT ST. LUCIE	FL
DIGIUSEPPE	THOMAS	E.		5127	WEST NEWBURY	MA
DILL	RYAN	THORNTON		6678	PINE BLUFF	AR
DILLINGHAM	JOHN	CASKEY		5650	CENTREVILLE	VA
DILLON	WILLIAM	WESLEY	JR	6899	SPRINGFIELD	TN
DINKLE	RAYMOND	C		2627	WEST ALLIS	WI
DINWIDDIE	JAMES	WILLIAM		6525	LINWOOD	NC
DISMUKES	ALAN			2678	BIRMINGHAM	AL
DIXON	CHARLES	EDWARD		4214	NEW PALESTINE	IN
DIXON	DARRYL	EUGENE		4215	INDIANAPOLIS	IN
DIXON	KENNETH	EUGENE		3259	NEW PALESTINE	IN
DIXON	RONALD	DAVID		4213	INDIANAPOLIS	IN
DOAN	HENRY	CLARK			COLLIERVILLE	TN
DOBBS	LARRY	WAYNE		6221	OKLAHOMA CITY	OK
DOCKERY	WALTER	E		6561	TUSCALOOSA	AL
DODD	ROBERT	E		5635	PLANO	TX
DODGE	ROBERT	J		4178	RALEIGH	NC
DODGEN	CARROLL	D		6986	LA PORTE	TX
DONNELLY	JOHN	THOMAS	JR	6527	STAFFORD	VA
DORMAN	WILLIAM	R		4174	BIRMINGHAM	AL
DORSEY	BRANDON	DOUGLAS		6748	LEXINGTON	VA
DRAKE	CHARLES	EDWARD DRAKE		7069	SAVANNAH	GA
DRAUGHON	ELMO	L		3766	VENTURA	CA
DREW	CARLTON	PLATT	SR	5174	PALATKA	FL
DREW	JOHN	JOSEPH	III	3214	FORTSON	GA
Du MONT	JOHN	S.		63	HANCOCK	NH
DUBOSE	JOHN	ALLISON		5856	SAVANNAH	GA
DUBOSE	WILLIAM	E.	JR	4203	NEW ZION	SC

DUDLEY	WILLIAM	E.		6887	JONESBORO	AR
DUGGAR	CHARLES	B		6644	DUNCAN	OK
DUNAVANT	DAVID	MICHAEL		5359	RIPLEY	TN
DUNAVANT	THOMAS	S.	JR	5360	RIPLEY	TN
DUNKLEY	JOHN	D.	JR	6101	SAN ANTONIO	TX
DUNNAVANT	DR. JAME	W	JR	6760	LAS VEGAS	NV
DUPREE	WAYNE	LAWRENCE		7293	VIRGINIA BEACH	VA
DUPRIEST	DENNIS	B.	JR	1415	DALLAS	TX
DURANT	HENRY	L.	LT COL	2414	COLUMBIA	SC
DYE	DONALD	E.	JR	4044	ROANOKE	VA
EADES	JACK	R		4265	SAVANNAH	GA
EANES	JAMES	GREGORY		7031	CREWE	VA
EARGLE	M.	EARL		3595	W. COLUMBIA	SC
EARLY	CURTIS	ALLEN		7052	WILLOWICK	OH
EARLY	JACK	JONES		6419	LOUISVILLE	KY
EARLY	LARRY	ALLAN		6652	RAVENNA	OH
EARNEST	BRITTON	FRANK	SR	4025	VIRGINIA BEACH	VA
EASON	ROBERT	ORVILLE		5529	WOODSTOCK	GA
EASTERLING	KEVIN	WILLIAM		4189	RAPID CITY	SD
EASTERLING	WILLIAM	D		4190	NORMAN	OK
EASTERLY	ERNEST	ST. CLAIR	III, Ph.D.	4414	WATSON	LA
ECHOLS	JOHN	L	SR	876	SOUTHAVEN	MS
EDELEN	CHARLES	JENKINS		5827	ARLINGTON	VA
EDGERTON	NORRIS	ERVIN		4388	CHASE CITY	VA
EDMOND	ROBERT			2629	WAYNESBORO	GA
EDWARDS	DAVID	MICHAEL		7032	WADESBORO	NC
EDWARDS	DOUGLAS	BRADY		7333	WADESBORO	NC
EDWARDS	LUKE	CORY		7334	WADESBORO	NC
EDWARDS	ROBERT	DOUGLAS		767	FT. WALTON BEACH	FL
EDWARDS	ROBERT	DOUGLAS	II	1172	FT. WALTON BEACH	FL
ELDER	LLOYD			5102	OKLAHOMA CITY	OK
ELLER	DALE	JOEY		7085	DEMOREST	GA
ELLER	WILDON	ANDREW		6894	DEMOREST	GA
ELLIOTT	ROBERT	GARRISON		1384	PORT ORANGE	FL
ELLIOTT	WILLIAM	REID		3602	MACON	GA
ELLIS	JOHN	HUNTER		6580	MATTHEWS	NC
ELLIS	WILSON	THOMAS		5286	MATHEWS	VA
ELLISON	SAMUEL	D.	III	3118	COLUMBIA	SC
ELMORE	FLETCHER	L.	JR	1807	LOUISVILLE	KY
ELMORE	J.	W		6372	MAGNOLIA	AR
ELMORE	MARSHALL	DELL		6370	MAGNOLIA	AR
ELMORE	THOMAS	CRAIG		5668	COLUMBIA	SC
ELMORE	WILLIAM	D.		6371	MAGNOLIA	AR
EMANUEL	EDGAR	ALLEN		7244	JACKSONVILLE	FL
EMBREY	BRIAN	MURRAY		7273	STAFFORD	VA
EMBREY	CHARLES	ALARIC	SR	6519	STAFFORD	VA
EMBREY	CHARLES	ALARIC	JR	6520	STAFFORD	VA
EMBREY	JOHN	MURRAY	JR	6521	SPOTSYLVANIA	VA
EMBREY	NICHOLAS	THOMAS		7068	STAFFORD	VA
EMERSON	JOHN	HUDSON		673	CARY	NC
ENGLISH	DANIEL	DAVIS		5414	ATLANTA	GA
ENGLISH	DARRELL	K.		5140	CHARLEMONT	MA
EPES	SAMUEL	C		1919	RICHMOND	VA
EPPERSON	LEROY	VINCENT		6633	NEW ALMADEN	CA
EPPERSON	RANDALL	CRAIG	PhD	6828	MODESTO	CA
ERLICK	RALPH	P.	JR	4432	CINCINNATI	OH
ERWIN	EDDIE			7313	WINNSBORO	LA
ERWIN	GOODLOE	YANCEY		4129	ATHENS	GA
ERWIN	RONNIE	E.		6985	COLUMBIA	TN
ESTES	NEIL	D.		5612	LONG BEACH	CA
EUBANKS	JONATHAN	SLOAN		6631	HOUMA	LA
EVANS	DAVID	SAVAGE	JR	3728	CHARLOTTE	NC
EVANS	JAMES	MICHAEL		6889	FOREST HILL	LA
EWELL	GERALD	L	SR	6396	MANCHESTER	TN

EZELL	THOMAS	EUGENE		6177	SCOTT	AR
FAGGERT	WILLIAM	CLAYTON		4352	OXFORD	MS
FAGGERT	WILLIAM	EARL		4353	HEIDELBERG	MS
FAIRBANKS	GEORGE	F		7046	MINNEAPOLIS	MN
FALLEN	ALLEN	CARL		3876	TULSA	OK
FARGASON	JOHN	THOMAS		4053	JUNCTION	TX
FARR	COL WARNER	D		3749	FAYETTEVILLE	NC
FARR	JOSEPH	MICHAEL		6971	INMAN	SC
FARRAR	JAMES	PENN		7300	EASTLAND	TX
FAST	JERRY	L		6819	OSCEOLA	MO
FAULK	WILLIAM	GARY		6926	PLEASANT GARDEN	NC
FAULKNER	WILLIAM	DAVID		7133	LAUREL	DE
FEDERER	KARL	MORALEE		6864	GLENARM	IL
FERGUSON	DAVID	JOE		7088	CEDARTOWN	GA
FERGUSON	GARNETT	LANE	JR	6576	MARIETTA	GA
FERGUSON	JAMES	L		2945	AMERICUS	GA
FETNER	A.	C.	JR	6064	MOUNT PLEASANT	SC
FIELDS	RICHARD	M		3307	PLEASANT GARDEN	NC
FINKS	JACK	COFFMAN		3556	MUSTANG	OK
FINNEGAN	MARC	K		7028	TINLEY PARK	IL
FISHER	HENRY	FRANCIS		6614	HUDDLESTON	VA
FITZGERALD	EDWARD	R		7010	WOODBRIDGE	VA
FITZGERALD	GEORGE	B		3480	HOUSTON	TX
FITZGERALD	JEFFREY	J		7167	BURLINGTON	NC
FITZHUGH	CLAY			6130	ARLINGTON	TX
FITZHUGH	EDWARD	ALEXANDER		7208	ARLINGTON	TX
FLANARY	RYAN	JOHN		6332	FLAT ROCK	MI
FLANARY	TOMMY	JOE		6331	RIVERVIEW	MI
FLANDERS	MACK	H		7311	GRANBURY	TX
FLATT	CURTIS	ALLEN		6056	FARMERS BRANCH	TX
FLEMING	JIMMY	EDWARD		6773	SAN ANGELO	TX
FLETCHER	ERNEST	E		3880	FRANKLIN	VA
FLETCHER	JOHN	L		3825	28630 Villa del Prado	OC
FLETCHER	MICHAEL	RODNEY		6168	MARCO ISLAND	FL
FLEWELLEN	JACK	EDWARD		7185	FREDERICKSBURG	VA
FLOOD	CLOYD	ANTHONY	JR	6014	BUMPASS	VA
FLORA	SAMUEL	R		3767	LEXINGTON	KY
FLORMAN	STEPHAN	J		4011	ANDOVER	MN
FLOYD	DAVID	LAFAYETTE		6257	LILBURN	GA
FLOYD	LINTON	EUGENE	III	3296	GAINESVILLE	FL
FORBES	LTC WILL	A		4450	CHEVY CHASE	MD
FORBES	PHILIP	A		5016	PURCELLVILLE	VA
FORBES	ROBERT	CLARK		3328	MACCLESFIELD	NC
FORCUM	JAMES	R.	JR	6483	BEAVERCREEK	OH
FORD	CARL	D		1870	LAUREL	MS
FORD	KEITH			7314	WINNSBORO	LA
FORREST	JOHN	T		3467	TERRE HAUTE	IN
FORRESTER	JAMES	WILLIAM		6437	GREENVILLE	SC
FOUCHE	JIM	MORGAN	JR	2899	MARIETTA	GA
FOUNTAIN	KENNETH	H.	JR	6560	WATERTOWN	TN
FOWLER	EDWIN	CHARNER		7042	BOSSIER CITY	LA
FOWLKES	HUGH	DALE		6634	TYLER	TX
FOX	RONALD	CONLEY GLANCE		6472	APACHE JUNCTION	AZ
FRANCIS	DANNY	ALBERT		6401	WARRENVILLE	SC
FRANKLIN	DAVID	W		5394	GRAPELAND	TX
FRANKLIN	KEITH	ALLEN		6504	FALLS MILLS	VA
FRARY	TODD	BARTHOLOMEW		6891	WOODSTOCK	GA
FREEMAN	CLYDE	NEWELL	JR.	1122	ESCONDIDO	CA
FREEMAN	JACK	PHILLIPS	III	4255	MIDLOTHIAN	TX
FREEMAN	JACK	P.	JR	1355	MIDLOTHIAN	TX
FREEMAN	JAMES	ROBERT		6937	NASHVILLE	TN
FREEMAN	JAMES	RICHARD		6935	NASHVILLE	TN
FREEMAN	MICHAEL	EDGAR		6938	NASHVILLE	TN
FREEMAN	WILLIAM	HARVEY	III	6936	NASHVILLE	TN

FRERE	CHARLES	RICHARD	JR	7089	ST. AUGUSTINE	FL
FRISCH	ROBERT	M.	JR	2787	MIDDLESEX	NJ
FRY	FRANK	BARNUM	II	7168	HOPATCONG	NJ
FRYE	ROBERT	ALLEN		7341	LEXINGTON	SC
FUERST	JACK	N		2854	HOUSTON	TX
FULGHUM	DAN	NEEL		6184	CONROE	TX
FULLER	J.	BECKWITH		249	HOPEWELL	VA
FULLER	JEFFERSO	C.	III	5822	COLUMBIA	SC
FUNCHESS	EDWARD	E		3589	MCCOMB	MS
FUNDERBURK	JAMES	A		6695	LINCOLNTON	NC
FUNKHOUSER	KARL	M		2925	ARLINGTON	VA
FURR	RANDLE	ELIAS	JR	6459	WESSON	MS
FURR	RANDLE	E.	SR	4457	LELAND	MS
FURR	RODNEY	EUGENE		6617	ALBEMARLE	NC
GAINES	F.	PENDLETON	III	5611	PHOENIX	AZ
GAINEY	JOSEPH	R		3056	SPARTANBURG	SC
GALLAGHER	A	E		3748	MEXICO	MO
GALLANT	THOMAS	E		6688	OCALA	FL
GARDNER	GERALD	GENE		2615	ALBUQUERQUE	NM
GARDNER	RODNEY	S		6974	W COLUMBIA	SC
GARESCHE	W.	L		3271	MAITLAND	FL
GARLAND	JOSEPH	EGGLESTON	II	6461	CHARLOTTESVILLE	VA
GARRETT	EMZY	STUART		6630	SAN MARCOS	TX
GARRETT	TIMOTHY	LEE		7137	MOKENA	IL
GARRIS	PRESTON	F		1508	LA GRANGE	NC
GARRISON	CHARLES	E		6087	BROWN SUMMIT	NC
GARRISON	DAVID	L.	JR	4092	HOUSTON	TX
GARRISON	JAMES	GARDINER		4363	MONTECITO	CA
GARRISON	MARTY	P		5220	HARRISON	AR
GARRISON	ROBERT	ADAM		4429	HOUSTON	TX
GARTIN	FORREST	LEE		6640	ANCHORAGE	AK
GARTIN	ROBERT	SCOTT		5012	ANCHORAGE	AK
GASQUE	ALLARD	HARRISON		5344	COLUMBIA	SC
GASTON	JAMES	M.	JR	967	AMERICUS	GA
GAY	ASHBY	LEE		2459	RICHMOND	VA
GAY	JOSIAH	BYNUM	III	1826	FRANKLIN	VA
GAYESKI	JOSEPH	M		6322	KINGSPORT	TN
GENTRY	JON	MICHAEL		7170	SPRINGFIELD	IL
GERITY	PATRICK	EDWARD		3161	LITTLETON	CO
GERRY	GEORGE	CHRISTOPHER		3516	SANFORD	NC
GHOLSON	BILL	D	JR	6069	HOOPESTON	IL
GIBBS	JAMES	L.	SR	5154	ROCHELLE	GA
GIBBS	RALEIGH	J		4268	ROCHELLE	GA
GIBSON	JAMES	E		6383	FAYETTEVILLE	AR
GIBSON	ROBERT	MOSS		6505	SAN ANTONIO	TX
GIEGER	GERALD	ALLEN		7047	EVERMAN	TX
GIGGLEMAN	CRAIG	MARTIN		6875	DALLAS	TX
GILBERT	FRANK	CLAY		5559	JEFFERSON	GA
GILBERT	SCOTT	KENDRICK	JR	3985	FAYETTEVILLE	GA
GILBREATH	BYRON	A		2975	STEPHENVILLE	TX
GILL	RAYMOND	WARREN	JR	6364	FREDERICKSBURG	VA
GILLHAM	FRED	H	JR	4370	MT. PLEASANT	TN
GILLHAM	FRED	HIME	SR	3053	COLUMBIA	TN
GILLIAM	NICHOLAS	BARNET	SR	6103	DALLAS	TX
GILLIAM	PRESTON	LEON		5858	TRACY	CA
GILLIS	NORMAN	BURKE	JR	7009	MCCOMB	MS
GINN	JOE	DANIEL	JR	7017	CHERRYVILLE	NC
GIUFFRE'	DENNIS	MICHAEL		5507	HOUSTON	TX
GIUFFRE'	JAMES	DONALD		5506	HOUSTON	TX
GIUFFRE'	RICHARD	ALAN		5513	HOUSTON	TX
GIVENS	ROBERT	MICHAEL		6556	BEAUFORT	SC
GLADNEY	THOMAS	BUEL	JR	7082	BESSEMER	AL
GNUSE	SAM	B		6068	ALTAMONT	IL
GODFREY	ALFRED	REED		5854	VA. BEACH	VA

GODFREY	GEORGE	VERNON	JR	6860	WARRENTON	VA
GODWIN	DAVID	FRANK		6712	LAKEVILLE	MN
GOGGANS	584	ALLEN		4162	PHENIX CITY	AL
GOINGS	ROBERT	JASON		5210	GRANITEVILLE	SC
GOLDWIRE	HENRY	CRAWFORD		6734	IRVING	TX
GOMEZ	THOMAS		JR	6754	CORPUS CHRISTI	TX
GOODLOE	JOHN	MICHAEL		6183	ALEXANDRIA	VA
GOODMAN	DONALD	P		3807	FORT WORTH	TX
GOODRICH	JASON	T		6923	LAWRENCEBURG	TN
GOODRICH	THOMAS	BRANDON		6845	VA BEACH	VA
GOODRICH	THOMAS	H		4322	VIRGINIA BEACH	VA
GOODRICH	WARD	A.		4321	VIRGINIA BEACH	VA
GOODWYN	ROSWELL	ALBERT		6625	FREDERICKSBURG	VA
GOOLSBY	CHARLES			5295	WASHINGTON	DC
GORDON	ARVID	CHARLES		6905	CLAYTON	GA
GORDON	JAMES	W		4275	ATHENS	AL
GORDON	PAUL	WILSON		2018	MEMPHIS	TN
GORDON	PAUL	TULANE	IV	3116	HOUSTON	TX
GORDON	TULANE		III	2769	HOUSTON	TX
GORRELL	L.	R		5636	RALEIGH	NC
GORRELL	ROBERT	GERARD		7180	RALIEGH	NC
GOSS	BARRY	KEITH		6665	COLUMBIA	SC
GRAHAM	JOHN	R.	DR	5001	SPARTANBURG	SC
GRAHAM	ROBERT	VIRGIL	JR	276	SAVANNAH	GA
GRAMMER	RICHARD	ALWYN		7217	ROSSVILLE	GA
GRANT	A.	GORDON		5443	METAIRIE	LA
GREEN	BRIAN	MICHAEL		728	KERNERSVILLE	NC
GREEN	JAMES	EDWARD	JR	6007	MEMPHIS	TN
GREEN	RALPH		JR	1221	ADDISON	TX
GREEN	RALPH			1219	FAIRVIEW	TX
GREENLEAF	HERBERT	MORGAN		7243	ST. AUGUSTINE	FL
GREENLEAF	MICHAEL	CALDWELL		7090	ST. AUGUSTINE	FL
GREENWELL	HARVEY	FRANKLIN		6672	ALTOONA	FL
GREGG	ASBURY	WELLBORN		3268	HOUSTON	TX
GREIF	EDWARD	EARL		7174	WICHITA	KS
GRESSETTE	JAMES	H.	JR	3524	ORANGEBURG	SC
GRIFFETH	DAVID	DWIGHT		4358	COLBERT	GA
GRIFFETH	JOE			4357	DANIELSVILLE	GA
GRIFFIN	LOWELL	M		4109	LOUISVILLE	KY
GRIFFIN	PATRICK	J	III	6851	DARNESTOWN	MD
GRIFFIN	PETER	M		5296	POOLESVILLE	MD
GRIFFIN	WILLIAM	GLEN	JR	6444	BATON ROUGE	LA
GRIFFITH	JOHN	K.	JR, MD	7155	LAKE CHARLES	LA
GRIFFITH	ROBERT	C		318	SHREVEPORT	LA
GRIMES	JAMES	R		3109	PLYMOUTH	NC
GRISSOM	JOE	LYNWOOD		2389	ROANOKE	VA
GRISSOM	JOHN	FARRAR		3348	WASHINGTON	DC
GRISSOM	LARRY	ALLYN		5146	UNIVERSITY PLACE	WA
GROOME	RICHARD	GEORGE		3859	SUWANEE	GA
GROSS	DALE	LYNDON MACKENZIE		6648	ST PETERSBURG	FL
GROVES	ROBERT	WALKER	III	7034	SAVANNAH	GA
GRUBB	JACKSON	ROY	JR	4311	THOMASTON	GA
GRUBB	JAMES	GARNETT		4313	THOMASTON	GA
GULLEY	PHILLIP	W		4258	ORANGEBURG	SC
GWINN	DAVID	ARNOLD		2223	BRIGHTON	TN
GWINNER	MYRON	W		4249	TULSA	OK
HACKNEY	W.	GERY		5996	BIRMINGHAM	AL
HADAWAY	ROBERT	E		1288	SAVANNAH	GA
HAGUE	ERIC	JOSEPH		6680	LAKE GENEVA	FL
HAILEY	WILLIAM	RANDY		3722	SOUTHAVEN	MS
HALBROOK	STEPHEN	PORTER		1713	FAIRFAX	VA
HALE	GORDON	DEAN		6573	BERRYVILLE	AR
HALE	NATHANIA	DEAN		7231	BERRYVILLE	AR
HALE	ROBERT	N.	SR	4100	ATHENS	GA

HALEMEYER	DALE	ROBERT		7138	GOLDEN EAGLE	IL
HALEY	FRANK	JEFFERSON		3136	MCLEAN	TX
HALEY	J	EVETTS	JR	3135	MIDLAND	TX
HALEY	JAMES	E	III	3137	CANADIAN	TX
HALL	GEORGE	W.	JR	5570	DIAMONDHEAD	MS
HALL	HOWARD	RAY	JR	7093	PHILADELPHIA	PA
HALL	JACK	SHELTON	JR	7203	COVINGTON	TN
HALL	MARK	A		2837	LAKELAND	FL
HALL	MARSHALL	L		4036	POWDERLY	TX
HALL	THOMAS	CALDWELL		7326	ST PAULS	NC
HALLE	DAVID	PHILIP	JR	2069	COLLIERVILLE	TN
HALLIGAN	ED	MILTON		2455	SOUTH DAYTONA	FL
HAMBY	DENSON	BALTZELLE		6817	COOSA	GA
HAMBY	DEREK	SEAN		6816	ROME	GA
HAMER	JOHN	ERWIN		1099	ALEXANDRIA	VA
HAMILTON	PHILLIP	RONALD		5828	GREENVILLE	SC
HAMILTON	RENALDO	J.	L/C	3052	ORLANDO	FL
HAMMER	G.	WILLIAM		2240	CENTREVILLE	VA
HAMMOND	ALFRED	L.	JR	7226	ALACHUA	FL
HAMNER	DARRELL	LELAND		6782	SAN ANGELO	TX
HAMPTON	EWING	STEWART	JR	5801	TUSCALOOSA	AL
HANKINS	BILLY	RAY		4387	WAYNESBORO	MS
HANNA	JAMIE	C		7265	BOSSIER CITY	LA
HANNERS	PHILLIP	MICHAEL		5975	LAGRANGE	GA
HANSBARGER	JOHN	E		6021	RICHMOND	VA
HANSON	LT COL J			3225	JACKSON	MS
HARDEMAN	DR FRANK	JR.		1435	SAVANNAH	GA
HARDEMAN	FRANK	III		1434	THUNDERBOLT	GA
HARDING	DOUGLAS	M		4289	NEW YORK	NY
HARDING	EDWARD	LLOYD		7288	WASHINGTON	NC
HARDY	PATRICK	J	MD	3531	CHESTERFIELD	MO
HARDY	WILLIAM	NASH		6756	HOLLYWOOD	FL
HARKE	MICHAEL	R.		6190	NORWALK	CT
HARLAN	CALVIN	W		4405	SUMMERTOWN	TN
HARLEY	DWIGHT	GREGG		6268	LINCOLNTON	GA
HARLEY	ROGER	O		5860	CHAPIN	SC
HARMON	JEROME	BRITE	III	6789	FAYETEVILLE	NC
HARMON	MICHAEL	A		5057	LEXINGTON	SC
HARNESS	DANNY	R.		5145	HARRISON	AR
HARRELL	CHARLES	ZELMUND		3390	WEATHERFORD	OK
HARRELL	MICHAEL	DAVID		7223	WARNER ROBINS	GA
HARRELL	RAYMOND	E		5486	DOERUN	GA
HARRIS	ELMOR	COX		5633	RICHARDSON	TX
HARRIS	JAMES	C.		732	SALTILLO	MS
HARRIS	JOE	PARKER		6604	CARTHAGE	TX
HARRIS	KENNETH	ROBERT		7037	VIRGINIA BEACh	VA
HARRIS	LYTTLETO	T.	IV	3663	HOUSTON	TX
HARRIS	MICHAEL	J.		7008	YAZOO CITY	MS
HARRIS	ROBERT	SANDERSON		3260	MIAMI	FL
HARRIS	WILLIAM	LLOYD		2682	BARTOW	FL
HARRISON	JOHN	TURBEVILLE	JR	5362	NEWPORT NEWS	VA
HARRISON	ROY	JUDSON	JR	6592	POWHATAN	VA
HARRISON	THOMAS			7210	GORMAN	TX
HART	FREDERIC	LEE	III	6045	SUFFOLK	VA
HART	SPENCER	LEE	IV	6840	SUFFOLK	VA
HARTLEY	GEORGE	W		7111	MOBILE	AL
HARVEY	JAN	VORIS		6365	FREDERICKSBURG	VA
HARWOOD	JAMES	GEORGE		4488	OKLAHOMA CITY	OK
HATCHETT	MITCHELL	VINCENT	SR	5848	JACKSON	TN
HATTAN	DEAN	HENRY		5264	CLARKSTON	WA
HAVIRD	KURT	BARVO		3299	LAKE CITY	FL
HAWKINS	BENJAMIN	REED		3911	BILOXI	MS
HAWKINS	ROBERT	L.	JR	3163	JEFFERSON CITY	MO
HAWKINS	ROBERT	L.	IV	3265	OXFORD	MS

HAWKINS	ROBERT	L	III	3162	REDLANDS	CA
HAWKS	CHARLES	T		5582	RALEIGH	NC
HAYES	CHARLES	HOWE		7327	TYLER	TX
HAYES	MICHAEL	DANN		6341	GRINNELL	IA
HAYNES	JOHN	DAVID		6605	TYLER	TX
HAYS	JEREMY	MILLER		6806	POPLAR BLUFF	MO
HAYWARD	J.	D		3339	BRANDON	FL
HAYWARD	JAMES	B		3340	BRANDON	FL
HEAD	JAMES	L.		5659	GENEVA	FL
HEAD	WILLIAM	IVERSON		7153	KINGSPORT	TN
HEBERT	JOHN	A		4149	GONZALES	LA
HEDSTROM	CARLOS	A	JR	1224	DALLAS	TX
HEINRICH	ROGER	LEE		6984	LEBANON	IL
HELBLING	ROGER	MERRILL		6803	ANDERSON	IN
HELLUMS	LAWRENCE	ALAN		6718	OXFORD	MS
HELM	DAVID			4303	NEWNAN	GA
HELMS	RALPH	RICHARD		3347	LAKELAND	FL
HELTON	GARY	S		4316	MCDONOUGH	GA
HEMBREE	CHAPIN	HUNTER		7190	AUBURN	GA
HEMPHILL	GEOFFREY	GUY		6148	VIRGINIA BEACH	VA
HEMPHILL	ROBERT	LAUX		6020	GOULDSBOR	PA
HENDERSON	DAVID	R		3571	WAKE FOREST	NC
HENDERSON	WILLIAM	BAILEY	JR.	6885	OCILLA	GA
HENLEY	JAMES	MILTON	JR	7029	HUNTSVILLE	AL
HENLEY	WILLIAM	B.	JR	841	DALLAS	TX
HENNESSEY	JEB	P		6266	OXFORD	PA
HENRY	JOHN	BURTON		7192	NEWPORT	TN
HERBERT	JOHN	THOMAS		1656	BRENTWOOD	TN
HERNDON	REV. THO	EUGENE		6055	BROKEN ARROW	OK
HERRING	RONALD	A		3772	LAKELAND	FL
HERRON	STEWART	LYNWOOD		4327	SOUTHAVEN	MS
HESTLEY	ALAN	BRYAN		6964	BIRMINGHAM	AL
HESTLEY	BENJAMIN	MADISON		6963	PELL CITY	AL
HIBBERT	ROBERT	R	III	7128	RED OAK	VA
HICKEY	DENNIS	JOHN	IV	2106	SPRINGFIELD	VA
HICKS	BYRON	PENDLETON		5997	FERRUM	VA
HICKS	EVERETT	EDSEL		6897	OLD TOWN	FL
HICKS	HAROLD	LEE		6955	BOLIVAR	MO
HIERN	BARRIE	C	SR	6575	SHANNON	GA
HIGGINBOTHAM	CHARLES	RUFUS	JR	1045	BURKE	VA
HIGH	JAMES	A		7140	STATESBORO	GA
HIGHSMITH	THOMAS	W		3591	EVANS	GA
HILL	CHARLES	GILBERT		6932	UPPER MARLBORO	MD
HILL	DAVID	WAYNE		6927	MANAKIN SABOT	VA
HILL	JAMES	A.	JR	3517	RALEIGH	NC
HILL	JAMES	MAYFIELD		6946	KNOXVILLE	TN
HILL	WILLIAM	O	JR	1451	CULPEPER	VA
HILLHOUSE	BILLY	K		5400	ALBANY	GA
HILLIS	BRUCE	R		6058	DEXTER	MO
HINDS	BEN	DAVID		6543	FORNEY	TX
HISE	LLOYD	VANCE		6822	HOT SPRINGS VILLAGE	AR
HODGE	ROBERT	LEE		6752	ALEXANDRIA	VA
HODGES	ALVA	GLENN		5399	NASHVILLE	GA
HODGES	CHARLES	ANTHONY	DDS	2965	CHATTANOOGA	TN
HOGAN	RICHARD	ALLEN		6818	NORTH AUGUSTA	SC
HOLBROOK	JAMES (J	HARGROVE		6727	ARDEN	NC
HOLCOMBE	DAVID	G.		6443	HARVEY	LA
HOLDER	A	DOYLE		7020	DENTON	TX
HOLLAND	R.	KURT		7119	MISSOURI CITY	MO
HOLLEY	JOSEPH	L.	JR	7257	AUGUSTA	GA
HOLLINGSWORTH	MARC			6775	COLORADO SPRINGS	CO
HOLMAN	WAYNE	JAMES	III	6052	GLEN ELLYN	IL
HOLMES	JAMES	STEVENS	JR	2656	KENNESAW	GA
HOLMES	ROGERS	B.	SR	1363	ORANGE PARK	FL

HOLT	WILLIAM	ANDREW	IV	7097	CHERRYVILLE	NC
HONAN	JAMES	TERRY		6892	EUFAULA	AL
HONNOLL	WILLIAM	DANNY		2136	JONESBORO	AR
HOOVER	JOHN	EDWARD		7024	HOUSTON	TX
HOPKINS	WALTER	CRAIG	SR	6361	OWENSBORO	KY
HOPPER	CURTIS			5679	JEFFERSON CITY	MO
HORNE	HERBERT	LILES	SR	6551	MIDWEST CITY	OK
HORTON	FRANKLIN	NELSON		6044	FAYETTEVILLE	NC
HORTON	PERCY	WEBSTER		6599	DURHAM	NC
HOTZE	BRUCE	R		5449	HOUSTON	TX
HOTZE	DR STEVE	F.		3147	KATY	TX
HOUCHINS	JOHN	F		5512	HOUSTON	TX
HOUSEKNECHT	BYRON	W		3763	CHANDLER	AZ
HOUSTON	TOM	H		7043	HOUSTON	TX
HOVIS	THOMAS	E		6477	FAIRFAX	VA
HOWARD	RICKY	PAUL		7215	SPRINGFIELD	MO
HOWELL	BRUCE	I		5144	CARY	NC
HOWLETT	ROBERT	YATES		5986	ROANOKE	VA
HOWZE	WILLIAM	DOUGLAS	SR	6276	BRANDON	FL
HUBBARD	JAMES	NORMENT		7080	OKLAHOMA CITY	OK
HUBBARD	TERRY	JAMES		7081	OKLAHOMA CITY	OK
HUBERT	JAMES	H.	III	5117	GREENSBORO	GA
HUDDLESTON	JEFFREY	VANCE		3723	COLLIERVILLE	TN
HUDGINS	THOMAS	PARKER		6805	VA BEACH	VA
HUDSON	AVERY	ALAN		5179	ARDMORE	TN
HUGGHINS	WILLIAM	ROWE		5347	HOUSTON	TX
HUGHES	HOWARD			4360	WEST COLUMBIA	SC
HUGHES	J.	CLIFF		4416	CORINTH	MS
HUGHES	JERRY	GORDON	SR	6802	OLD HICKORY	TN
HUIET	BEN		III	4310	TYRONE	GA
HULL	LONGSTREET	MURROW		7146	TULLAHOMA	TN
HURST	FREDERIC	M		3814	MICHIGAN CITY	IN
HUSS	JOHN	EMMET		5011	RALEIGH	NC
HUTCHESON	JOHN	M		3043	TROY	AL
HUTTO	WILLIAM	CHAD		6996	BECKVILLE	TX
HUTTO	WILLIAM	T	III	6995	COLORADO SPRINGS	CO
HUX	BRANDON	WILLIAM		3906	LOUISBURG	NC
ICE	MONTE	DAVID		4331	FT. WAYNE	IN
ILER	WILLIAM	B.	JR	3404	LUTZ	FL
INGRAM	DONALD	M		2292	HOLLY SPRINGS	MS
IRBY	HENCE	WOODFIN		6958	BERTRAM	TX
IRBY	MARK	JOSEPH		6960	LIBERTY HILL	TX
ISAAC	DALE	E		6226	THAMES	OC
ISETT	PHILIP	EDWARD		6308	EDMOND	OK
IZARD	EDWARD	DRUMMOND		6859	CHARLESTON	SC
JACKS	THOMAS	EDWARD		6217	ABITA SPRINGS	LA
JACKSON	ANDREW	S		4046	LAUREL FORK	VA
JACKSON	BILLY	J		7200	HOHENWALD	TN
JACKSON	BOBBY	WARD		7262	LEAGUE CITY	TX
JACKSON	BOYD	W		1954	MANCHESTER	TN
JACKSON	CECIL	RAY		4350	MELVILLE	LA
JACKSON	JOEL	EARLY MATHEWS		6398	ST JOSEPH	LA
JACKSON	MILES			5687	LULA	GA
JACKSON	MORRIS	KENT	DR	6957	NACOGDOCHES	TX
JACKSON	STEPHEN	THOMAS		7321	ANDERSON	IN
JAMISON	ALBERT	L		3914	BOERNE	TX
JANKOWSKI	REGINALD	B		3367	JEFFERSON CITY	MO
JARRETT	D.	F.		5585	RALEIGH	NC
JARRETT	JEFFREY	D.		5586	RALEIGH	NC
JARRETT	WILLIAM	GUY	JR	1697	RALEIGH	NC
JARVIS	JAMES	GERALD		6741	SPRINGFIELD	MO
JEFFERIES	ROY		JR	6977	GAFFNEY	SC
JEFFERSON	CHARLES	T		5991	ST CHARLES	MO
JENKINS	HUGH	MALCOM	JR	5381	WOODBINE	GA

JENKINS	THOMAS	J		5263	PALM BAY	FL
JENNINGS	CHARLES	A		3842	ALEXANDRIA	VA
JENNINGS	WILLIAM	R		6823	HARRISON	AR
JERVEY	WILLIAM	P	JR	6586	POWHATAN	VA
JETER	MANNING	THOMAS	III	6050	SALUDA	NC
JOHNSON	ALBERT	SYDNEY	III	7019	BISHOP	GA
JOHNSON	CHARLES	OWEN		769	ARLINGTON	VA
JOHNSON	CLARKE	WRIGHT		5398	LYONS	GA
JOHNSON	ELLIS	RANDAL		3730	MIDDLETOWN	OH
JOHNSON	GEORGE	HERBERT		5239	WINCHESTER	TN
JOHNSON	ISHMAEL	HERMAN	JR	6470	DES MOINES	IA
JOHNSON	KEITH	ANDREW		7279	SOUTHLAKE	TX
JOHNSON	STEVEN	L		7188	HOOVER	AL
JOHNSON	THOMAS	EARL	JR	5484	COVINGTON	TN
JOINER	GARY	DILLARD		6286	SHREVEPORT	LA
JONES	ALBERT	DEAN	JR	4237	PLYMOUTH	NC
JONES	CALVIN	ODELL		6233	FERRUM	VA
JONES	CATESBY	PENNIMAN	DCS	1294	SPRINGFIELD	VA
JONES	DANIEL	W		4359	CARY	NC
JONES	DAVID	H.		5113	RALEIGH	NC
JONES	DERRELL			5269	JACKSON	AL
JONES	GILBERT	F		6726	RUFFIN	NC
JONES	GLENN			6357	LOWELL	AR
JONES	GORDON	W		3368	JEFFERSON CITY	MO
JONES	JOHN	HALLBERG		2862	MINNEAPOLIS	MN
JONES	LTC RICH	BOWDEN		5322	WILMINGTON	NC
JONES	MARK	PERRIN	III	2871	LITTLE ROCK	AR
JONES	MARVYNE	RAY	III	7176	JONESBORO	AR
JONES	MICHAEL	DAN		5027	IOWA	LA
JONES	RANDALL	BRACKIN		7298	EUUIS	TX
JONES	ROBERT	HOLMES		7087	MACON	GA
JONES	ROBERT	N	JR	6978	CHATFIELD	TX
JONES	STEVEN			6988	LEXINGTON	SC
JONES	THOMAS	GLENN		6076	CLEBURNE	TX
JONES	WAYNE			6655	FLINT	TX
JONES	WEBSTER	STANLEY		6313	GREENVILLE	SC
JONES	WILLIAM	NOLAN	JR	7156	STOKESDALE	NC
JONES	WILLIAM	WELLINGTON		6839	SUFFOLK	VA
JORDAN	ROBERT	PORCH		7062	JACKSONVILLE	AL
JORNLIN	R.	MICHAEL		3948	ROANOKE	VA
JOWELL	WILLIAM	HOLT		3141	MIDLAND	TX
KAREL	JOHN	A		3686	ST, GENEVIEVE	MO
KASTEN	LAWRENCE	CANNON		6612	CAPE GIRARDEAU	MO
KEA	JAMES	ANDREW		6645	UVALDA	GA
KEATHLEY	DR GILBE	H		5695	MCKINNEY	TX
KEATHLEY	JERRELL	G		5972	LEESBURG	VA
KEEVER	ROBERT	LAMAR		6878	ENNIS	TX
KEHOE	CORNELIU	J		5376	HOUSTON	TX
KEISTER	WALDO	WILLIAMS		6857	FREDERICKSBURG	VA
KELLEY	WILLIAM	TIMOTHY		6596	NORTON	VA
KELLEY	WILLIAM	FRANKLIN		6601	NORTON	VA
KELLUM	CHARLES	D.	MD	3806	MACON	GA
KELLY	JULIAN	DANTZLER	JR	5148	SAVANNAH	GA
KELLY	MICHAEL	GENE		3820	WEST COLUMBIA	SC
KEMP	ARTHUR	W		7129	MAX MEADOWS	VA
KEMP	HARRY	TALTON	JR	6972	ROSWELL	GA
KENNEDY	BURLEY	RUFF		5467	LEXINGTON	SC
KENNEDY	REMBERT	JERVEY		6402	SUMTER	SC
KEOWN	JAMES	M		3164	COLUMBIA	MO
KERLIN	JAMES	R		5677	OCALA	FL
KERLIN	WILEY	C		6387	OCALA	FL
KERR	HAROLD	WINFIELD	SR	6865	DELAND	FL
KERR	HAROLD	WINFIELD	JR	6866	EUSTIS	FL
KESLER	DANIEL	DODSON		5336	CHAMBERSBURG	PA

KILLGORE	WILLIAM	E		4284	ALEXANDRIA	AL
KILLIAN	REV JOHN	H		3668	MAYTOWN	AL
KING	DR ROWLA	RUTHERFORD		6550	QUARTZ HILL	CA
KING	KENNETH	DAYTON		2719	O'BRIEN	FL
KIRCH	PETER			6981	MT. HOME	AR
KIRK	CHRISTOP	TODD		6961	GEORGETOWN	TX
KIRK	DUSTIN	WAYNE		6962	GEORGETOWN	TX
KITCHEN	GARY	DENNIE		6643	DEXTER	MO
KLAGES	JEFFREY	WILLIAM		7284	RENO	NV
KLAR	ROLAND	EMIL	JR	6990	SAN ANTONIO	TX
KNECHTMANN	JAMES	ALLEN		7148	ALMEDA	CA
KNIGHT	NATHAN	ALAN		6969	COTTONTOWN	TN
KNIGHT	RICHARD	H.	JR	591	NASHVILLE	TN
KNIGHTON	CHRISTOP	MICHAEL		7144	STAUNTON	VA
KNOWLES	DR WILLI	R.	SR	1674	HOUSTON	TX
KNOWLES	JAMES	A		4229	MERIDIAN	MS
KOMAN	ALAN	JAMES		6192	EAST POINT	GA
KRANICHFIELD	ANDREW	M		5981	SEDALIA	MO
KRANTZ	AL			6831	BREAUX BRIDGE	LA
KRISCH	RUDOLPH	C.	III	4281	SAN ANTONIO	TX
KUNDAHL	GEORGE	GUSTAVUS		6554	ALEXANDRIA	VA
KURIGER	RICHARD	CHARLES	IV	5158	HOUSTON	TX
KURLANDER	JOHN	THOMAS		5987	APPOMATTOX	VA
KUYKENDALL	ARTHUR	R.	JR	2490	EDGEWATER	FL
KYZER	EMERSON	RANDOLPH	JR	5261	MIMS	FL
LABORDE	DR SANFO	J	MD	7222	ABBEVILLE	LA
LAFFERTY	ROY	ALLEN		6779	LAWRENCE	KS
LAIRD	JAMES	D		2113	MESA	AZ
LAMBERT	DOBBIE	EDWARD		6231	STAFFORD	VA
LANCASTER	CARROLL	T.	JR	5350	ZEPHYR	TX
LANCASTER	DR RICHA	M		3784	MELBOURNE	FL
LANDRUM	EVAN	PRICE	III	2141	OCALA	FL
LANE	MARTIN	STAKES		5841	RICHMOND	VA
LANE	THOMAS	B		2855	HOUSTON	TX
LANG	DAVID	F		4060	LONG BOAT KEY	FL
LANGDALE	ANDERSON	SIDNEY		5862	DORCHESTER	SC
LANGFORD	LOUIS	SHERWIN	JR	6896	ANDERSON	SC
LANGLEY	JAMES	ALLEN		7175	JONESBORO	AR
LANHAM	EDWARD	JORDAN		6113	BROOKS	GA
LANIER	STEVE	TRAVIS		2085	LAKE CHARLES	LA
LANKFORD	WILLIAM	JOSEPH		7166	HOLLYWOOD	FL
LAPSLEY	BRADFORD	NOYES		4095	PLANO	TX
LARKIN	HAYWOOD	BARNETT	JR	4378	WARR ACRES	OK
LASTER	EDWARD	CARROLL	JR	6369	SHREVEPORT	LA
LATHAM	LARRY	WAYNE		5455	BRUNSWICK	GA
LATIMER	ALLEN	B		3104	HORN LAKE	MS
LATTA	EVERETTE	MICHAEL		6598	RALEIGH	NC
LATTA	STANLEY	MICHAEL		6697	CARY	NC
LATTURE	SAMUEL	GAYDEN		2275	GREENSBORO	AL
LAW	PHILIP	HERBERT		6562	FAIRHOPE	AL
LAWRENCE	HOWARD	RAY		7318	MOKELUMNE HILL	CA
LEACH	HOWARD	OWEN		2218	JACKSON	MS
LEAK	SIDNEY	LEON	III	7269	MANCHESTER	TN
LEE	CHARLES	CARTER		6595	POWHATAN	VA
LEE	DONALD	E		4071	HOUSTON	TX
LEE	GEORGE	T.	III	6594	POWHATAN	VA
LEE	RICHARD	WILLIAM		6967	SATSUMA	FL
LEE	ROBERT	E.	M D	5311	HAINES CITY	FL
LENZINI	RUSSELL	RAYMOND		6792	MACON	MO
LEONARD	ALAN	CARROLL		6744	TRYON	NC
LERCH	BOBBY	R		4340	ATLANTA	GA
LESLEY	CURTIS	D		6713	COMANCHE	TX
LESLEY	JOHN	T.	JR	3725	TAMPA	FL
LESLEY	ROYCE			6714	COMANCHE	TX

LESLIE	THOMAS	S		3097	HARRISON	AR
LESTER	HENRY	L		5411	MINDEN	LA
LESTER	JAN	H.		5754	LAKELAND	FL
LEVERETT	LT COL C	O.		5299	HAGERSTOWN	MD
LEWIS	DANNY	LAYNE		5673	LAVON	TX
LEWIS	TOOMBS	DUBOSE	JR	3313	WATKINSVILLE	GA
LIGON	JAMES	H.	SR	6919	RICHMOND	VA
LINDSEY	ROBERT	KIRK		6618	ALEXANDRIA	VA
LINTECUM	JOHN	ARCHA		7141	HILSVILLE	VA
LINTECUM	MARK	ANTHONY		7145	HILLSVILLE	VA
LINTHICUM	GEORGE	EMORY	III	6234	OWINGS MILLS	MD
LIPSCOMB	JAMES	HORACE	III	899	ATLANTIC BEACH	FL
LITTLE	ROBERT	LEE	JR	7132	ROANOKE	VA
LLOYD	CHRISTOP	M		4411	VIRGINIA BEACH	VA
LONGMIRE	ROBERT	JACKSON		7131	JACKSONVILLE	FL
LOONEY	ROBERT	W.		6227	WYLIE	TX
LORTON	DONALD	EDWARD	JR	5992	PENHOOK	VA
LOTT	DAVID	LEE		6220	LONGVIEW	WA
LOUDERMILK	EWELL	LEE		6715	SAN ANGELO	TX
LOUDERMILK	GARY	LLOYD		6716	HASKELL	TX
LOUDERMILK	GARY	M		6139	BROWNWOOD	TX
LOUM	MICHAEL	ROY		7232	NO. LITTLE ROCK	AR
LOVE	JOSEPH	BLAND	III	3035	JACKSONVILLE	FL
LOVELACE	CREIGHTO	L		7286	FOREST CITY	NC
LOWE	JEFFREY	CARTER		6710	FAYETTEVILLE	GA
LOWMAN	JOHN	D.	SR	5990	RADFORD	VA
LOWRANCE	EUGENE	S.		5149	ENNIS	TX
LOWRANCE	ROBERT	S		6876	RICHARDSON	TX
LOWREY	JAMES	M		4014	SULPHUR	LA
LUCAS	STEPHEN	J		4206	DENTON	TX
LUFFMAN	ELDEN	H.	SR	2658	OCALA	FL
LUFFMAN	JERRY	LANE		6567	CHATSWORTH	GA
LUMSDEN	JOHN	R		6430	ALEXANDRIA	VA
LUNDY	LOREN			6656	MISSION	KS
LUNDY	SHERMAN	PERRY		6514	BURLINGTON	IA
LUNGER	WILLIAM	PLESS		6098	ARLINGTON	VA
LUNSFORD	PERRY	CHARLES		2560	MANSFIELD	GA
LUPFER	MICHAEL	SIMS		1649	LEESBURG	VA
LUPTON	WILLIAM	CLYDE	SR	6288	KEITHVILLE	LA
LUSK	MICHAEL			4444	TEXARKANA	TX
LYDAY	TRAVIS	QUINTON		6480	MANASSAS	VA
LYKINS	ROBERT	CLYDE		1351	NASHVILLE	TN
LYNCH	JOHN	WARREN		6565	SENOIA	GA
LYON	GENE	FLEMING		6310	RICHMOND	VA
LYON	WILLIAM	M	JR	7252	MOBILE	AL
LYONS	ROBERT	E		3170	BALTIMORE	MD
MACGREGOR	ALARIC	RIDOUT	III	7274	STAFFORD	VA
MACMAHON	WILLIAM	OTIS	III	7329	BIRMINGHAM	AL
MADDOX	JERRYM. JERRY	AVEN		6143	DUNWOODY	GA
MADER	DAVID	CHARLES		6720	MOBILE	AL
MAGRUDER	A.	CLARKE	SR	5067	ALEXANDRIA	VA
MAHARREY	JACKIE	EARL		6970	BRIGHTON	TN
MAHAVIER	DAVID	HENRY		5403	SPRING	TX
MAIDEN	MICHAEL	SAYRE		6309	WEST ALLENHURST	NJ
MAJORS	CHARLES	READ	JR	4338	LEBANON	TN
MAJORS	MARVIN	DON		6635	HAWKINS	TX
MALLORY	JOHN	M		4483	SAVANNAH	GA
MALLORY	MARSHALL	PHILLIPS		7189	GADSDEN	AL
MANESS	CHARLES	KENNETH		5222	WASHINGTON	NC
MANGUM	JOHN	WILLIAM		5728	SONOITA	AZ
MANN	HORACE		III	3790	CHESTER	VA
MANN	WILFRED	E		3789	PETERSBURG	VA
MANNING	TIMOTHY	DAVID	SR	5321	STOKESDALE	NC
MANNING	TIMOTHY	DAVID	JR	5361	COLUMBIA	SC

MAPLES	DARRELL	L		5171	JEFFERSON CITY	MO
MARKS	CLIFFORD	K		1769	ALBANY	NY
MARKS	DR. HERBERT	W.		3619	METAIRIE	LA
MARSH	LAWRENCE			3034	NEW ORLEANS	LA
MARSHALL	MARVIN	JOSEPH		6707	VALKARIA	FL
MARSTON	WILLIAM	WESLEY		7248	ALACHUA	FL
MARTIN	EDWIN	AYDLETT		5426	GREENSBORO	NC
MARTIN	KNOX			6330	MEMPHIS	TN
MARTIN	STEPHEN	GERALD		7077	INDEPENDENCE	KY
MARTIN	STEPHEN	D.		6930	PENNINGTON GAP	VA
MARTIN	WILLIAM	HOWARD		6524	GREENSBORO	NC
MASON	JAMES	DEMERE		3934	JACKSONVILLE	FL
MASON	JAMES	WALTER	II	6564	MANDERVILLE	LA
MASON	JOHN	THOMAS		2103	COVINGTON	TN
MASON	WILBERT	W.		6289	SHREVEPORT	LA
MASSEY	JAMES	TROY		2441	HARRISON	AR
MASSEY	JEFFERY	WAYNE		2483	EDMOND	OK
MASSEY	JOHN	DAVID		2527	YUKON	OK
MASSEY	SAMMY	JOE		2538	DAMASCUS	AR
MASTERS	COL JOHN	J.	SR	3857	ST AUGUSTINE	FL
MASTERS	LTC BURT	LEWIS		3866	ST AUGUSTINE	FL
MASTERS	LTC JOHN	J.	JR	3863	ST AUGUSTINE	FL
MASTERSON	ROBERT	BENJAMIN	JR	4462	MT. HOPE	AL
MATHEWS	WILLIAM	LEE		7113	VICKSBURG	MS
MATTHEW	WILLIAM	M		1002	CHARLESTON	SC
MATTHEWS	MONTGOME			7204	PLANO	TX
MATTISON	WILLIAM	HARVEY		3975	AMORY	MS
MAUCK	BEVERLY	S.	JR	6478	RICHMOND	VA
MAUPIN	ARMISTEA	J		4278	RALEIGH	NC
MAXWELL	ALVAN	DWIGHT		2124	JACKSONVILLE	FL
MAXWELL	FRANK	F		2654	JACKSONVILLE	FL
MAXWELL	ROBERT	C		3690	WATER VALLEY	MS
MAY	MICHAEL	L		5323	JACKSONVILLE	FL
MAY	ROBERT	E		7179	OLD TOWN	FL
MAYES	JAMES	RANDOLPH		6316	BLYTHE	GA
MAYO	FRANK	E.		6133	BREVARD	NC
MAYO	JEFFREY	KING		5331	FOREST	MS
MCBEE	STANLEY			3321	HOUSTON	TX
MCBURNEY	ANDREW	SLOAN		5421	DORSET	VT
MCCALL	GUYTON			6683	ATLANTA	GA
McCALL	THOMAS	SCREVEN		1622	BULLARD	TX
MCCAMPBELL	JAMES	E		4177	RAMSEY	IN
McCANN	JAMES	RICHARD		7199	MORMON LAKE	AZ
MCCARTNEY	N.	WRIGHT	JR	5181	KENT	WA
MCCAUSLAND	DR ALEXANDER			5988	ROANOKE	VA
McCLELLAN	WAYMON	LARRY		6636	TYLER	TX
MCCLOUD	MICHAEL	ELIOT		5736	EL SEGUNDO	CA
MCCOWN	EARL	M.	JR	5073	CLEVELAND	MS
MCCOWN	EARL	MITCHELL	III	6420	CLEVELAND	MS
MCCOWN	JOHN	WESLEY		6421	TUPELO	MS
MCCOWN	LEONARD	JOE		2291	IRVING	TX
MCCRACKEN	THOMAS	MELVIN		6620	MIDLOTHIAN	VA
McCULLAH	ARLIS	MICHAEL		5784	RUSSELLVILLE	AR
MCCULLOUGH	JOSEPH	A	III	6162	HONEA PATH	SC
McDANIEL	BARRY	ALLEN		6258	HULL	GA
MCDANIEL	DANNY	R		6535	BASTROP	LA
McDANIEL	STANLEY	ALLEN		6081	GAINESVILLE	GA
McDONALD	JOHN	EDMONDSON		2196	SMYRNA	TN
MCENTIRE	JAMES	F		3779	ATHENS	GA
McFALL	F.	LAWRENCE	JR	2694	DANVILLE	VA
MCGAVOCK	JAMES	P.	III	3017	EL RENO	OK
MCGEE	PATRICK	J		7061	NAPERVILLE	IL
MCGEHEE	JACKIE	F		5219	OMAHA	AR
MCGHEE	JAMES	E		5676	JEFFERSON CITX	MO

McGLOTHLIN	CHRISTOPHER	LEE		6145	DANVILLE	VA
MCGRADY	JOSEPH	HARRY		7142	HILLSVILLE	VA
MCGUIRE	CHARLES	DAN		3472	RESTON	VA
MCKEE	KENNETH	BRIAN		7149	MCCONNELSVILLE	OH
MCKENZIE	JERRY	DALE		6696	BESSEMER CITY	NC
MCLENDON	ROBERT	GARRETT	JR	2372	GAINESVILLE	FL
MCLENDON	ROBERT	GARRETT	III	2815	ONEONTA	AL
MCLEOD	MICHAEL	DAVID		5183	KELLER	TX
MCLEOD	WAVERLY	T.	SR	951	FAYETTEVILLE	NC
McMATH	GEORGE	A		7083	GAINESVILLE	GA
McMICHAEL	CHARLES	E		5110	SHREVEPORT	LA
MCMILLAN	MARK	BURRIS		6959	CEDAR PARK	TX
MCMILLAN	ROBERT	MALCOLM	JR	6906	STOCKTON	AL
MCMORDIE	WILLIAM	D		6921	LAPORTE	TX
MCNARY	DR C	FRED		2077	HOLLY HILL	FL
MCNEESE	BENJAMIN	P.	JR	3273	SUMTER	SC
MCNEILLY	ROGER	MARVIN		5187	LAWNDALE	NC
MCNUTT	BRUCE	EVAN		7048	COMANCHE	TX
MCSWINE	STERLING	B.		6102	HOUSTON	TX
MCVAY	PAUL	FRANK		5060	SAVANAH	GA
MCWILLIAMS	LORENZO	DOW	III	7173	WHITEHOUSE	TX
MEADOWS	CHARLES	EDWARD	JR	7110	CARLSBAD	CA
MEADOWS	JOHN	BUFORD	JR	5840	AUSTIN	TX
MEADOWS	JOHN	B		5314	AUSTIN	TX
MEADOWS	JOSHUA	STEWART		6033	ELGIN	TX
MEADOWS	KARL	CLIFFORD	SR	6650	POWHATAN	VA
MEADOWS	RUSSELL	FLOYD		5069	ADEL	GA
MEARS	PAUL	A.	SR	6753	TUCSON	AZ
MEDCALF	JOSEPH	ALFRED	JR	7022	BARNESVILLE	GA
MEDCALF	JOSEPH	ALFRED		7023	BARNESVILLE	GA
MENEFEE	RICHARD	REID		7187	SUN CITY CENTER	FL
MERK	JOHN	LAMAR		6498	CORAL GABLES	FL
MERKEL	CRAIG	PLOWMAN		3706	GARLAND	TX
MERRITT	CHARLES	G.		5715	HUNTINGDON	TN
MERRITT	KENNETH	L.		5717	HUNTINGDON	TN
MERRITT	KEVIN	L.		5716	PHOENIX	AZ
MERSHON	ROBERT	C		7309	ELK RIVER	MN
METZ	CRAIG	HUSEMAN		3228	VIENNA	VA
MEWBORN	ALBERT	BENNETT		6115	MARION	NC
MILLER	ARTHUR	W.	JR	2633	BURLINGTON	NC
MILLER	CHARLES	M.		6755	CAMPBELL	MO
MILLER	EDWARD	BURKE	III	6693	TAYLORS	SC
MILLER	FLOYD	CEBURN		5059	DALLAS	TX
MILLER	FRANK	L.	III COL	70	CASHIERS	NC
MILLER	JEFFORDS		JR	5603	ST. CLOUD	FL
MILLER	JEFFORDS	D		5602	KISSSIMMEE	FL
MILLER	RONALD	H.		6041	MARIETTA	GA
MILLER	RONALD	WILLIAM		4185	COALGATE	OK
MILLS	JAMES	W.	JR	3196	METAIRIE	LA
MILLS	ROBERT	L		6834	WEST PLAINS	MO
MIMS	ROBERT	FORREST		6922	PORTLAND	OR
MINNIECE	JOHN	GRESHAM	IV	3229	HOUSTON	TX
MINSON	FRED	HARRISON	III	6992	CHESTER	VA
MINTER	LEONARD	DIGGS	JR	7247	MATHEWS	VA
MINTER	STEPHEN	ALAN		7303	BEAVERLETT	VA
MITCHAM	MICHAEL	WAYNE		6717	TAMPA	FL
MITCHELL	BOBBY	JOE		2024	HOLLY SPRINGS	MS
MITCHELL	DAVID	BENJAMIN		6660	CORAL GABLES	FL
MITCHELL	DAVID	PATRICK		7312	ANDERSON	AL
MITCHELL	MICHAEL	JOSEPH		6440	MIAMI	FL
MITCHELL	TERRY	E		5407	SHREVEPORT	LA
MITCHELL	WALTER	B		2386	MESQUITE	TX
MIXSON	LAWRENCE	HARRY	III	6724	MT PLEASANT	SC
MOCK	WALTER	ALLEN		2669	RICHMOND	VA

MOLLERE	PHILLIP	DAVID		3755	NEW ORLEANS	LA
MONCURE	CONWAY	BAGWELL		6593	RICHMOND	VA
MONCURE	JOHN	LEWIS		6546	HOUSTON	TX
MONIN	CARL	A		3145	TULLAHOMA	TN
MONTGOMERY	LTC VICT	M.		6161	GREER	SC
MOON	BENNIE	LEE		5497	OXFORD	GA
MOONEYHAM	OSCAR	JETER	III	6491	COLORADO SPRINGS	CO
MOORE	CHARLES	W		1033	SHREVEPORT	LA
MOORE	DAVID	WINSTON		6778	VIRGINIA BEACH	VA
MOORE	DONALD	WAYNE		6666	VA BEACH	VA
MOORE	DOUGLAS	NEWLIN		5196	TITUSVILLE	NJ
MOORE	HARRISON	GERALD	IV	7033	HOUSTON	TX
MOORE	HOWARD	WARE	JR	6344	TULSA	OK
MOORE	LTC WILL	WORSHAM	JR	7130	PANAMA CITY	FL
MOORE	MATT	P		6657	STILLWATER	OK
MOORE	MATTHEW	GLEN		7067	WAVELAND	MS
MOORE	MUNSEY	A		6777	CHASE CITY	VA
MOORE	ROBERT	HENRY	JR	6151	EASTON	MD
MOORE	ROBERT	MARK		7066	LAKE CORORANT	MS
MOORE	ROBERT	GLEN		7065	LAKE CORMORANT	MS
MOORE	THOMAS	LEE		6776	WINCHESTER	TN
MOOREHEAD	WILLIAM	F.		6326	WEIRSDALE	FL
MOORHEAD	RICHARD	DOYLE		7307	WINTER PARK	FL
MOOSE	JAMES	ROBERT		6066	MASCOUTAH	IL
MORDECAI	WILLIAM	G.	JR	5157	RALEIGH	NC
MOREHEAD	DAVID	W.		3308	DUNKIRK	MD
MORGAN	DAVID	G		7109	COOKEVILLE	TN
MORGAN	DR JAMES	F	PHD	4067	RENTON	WA
MORGAN	HERSCHEL	BRYAN		7227	SYLACAUGA	AL
MORGAN	KENNETH	DERRELL		6249	SENECA	SC
MORING	RONALD	CRAIG		3792	CARSON	VA
MORRIS	HAROLD	J.		6877	GAINESVILLE	GA
MORRIS	JACOB	MICHAEL		7330	FORT WORTH	TX
MORRIS	M	KEITH	JR	6881	SUFFOLK	VA
MORRIS	PERRY	CRAIG		6240	JOHNSTON	SC
MORRIS	PHILIP	L		4261	ROCKY MOUNT	NC
MORRIS	RICHARD	MICHAEL		7184	FORT WORTH	TX
MORRIS	WILLIAM	BOBBY		6253	TUCSON	AZ
MORRIS	WILLIAM	RICHARD		5745	FORT WORTH	TX
MORRISON	GEORGE	TIMOTHY		6263	FAYETTEVILLE	TN
MORROW	LAWRENCE	BUREN		6873	BAY MINETTE	AL
MOSCOE	JOHN	SHEPHERD		7171	VIRGINIA BEACH	VA
MOSCOE	MARK	ROBERT		7292	CORPUS CHRISTI	TX
MOTES	JAMES	VIRLYN MICHAEL		6629	MARIETTA	GA
MOTLEY	CHARLES	G		115	RICHMOND	VA
MOTZ	CHARLES			6569	NEW BRAUNFELS	TX
MOULDEN	BURT	MICHAEL		7280	ALVIN	TX
MOUTON	PATRICK	E.	JR	1408	EUNICE	LA
MOYE	WILLIAM	JENNINGS		7104	BRIDGE CITY	TX
MUELLER	MARK	CHRISTOPHER		3529	DALLAS	TX
MULLER	WESLEY	STEPHEN		2510	HARRISON	AR
MULLINS	TEDDY	PATTON		6856	WISE	VA
MURRAY	ROBERT	R		4435	MIMS	FL
MURREY	JOSEPH	H.	JR	3102	JONESBORO	AR
MYATT	JODY	LYNN		6639	MARTINEZ	GA
MYERS	MATT	J.		5831	KANSAS CITY	MO
MYERS	STANLEY	ALAN		6358	LINN	MO
MYERS	THOMAS	LOREN		3669	HOPE MILLS	NC
NALLS	CHARLES	T		3535	HUNTSVILLE	AL
NALLS	JOSEPH	B		3534	HUNTSVILLE	AL
NANCE	ANDREW	WARREN		7162	SUNRISE	FL
NANCE	MATTHEW	CHRISTOPHER		7161	SUNRISE	FL
NASS	WALTER	P.	JR	3231	HOUSTON	TX
NEAL	HAMILTON	M.	JR	5155	KENTWOOD	LA

NELMS	TURNER	SHEPHERD		6624	POWHATAN	VA
NELMS	WALTER	CHAPMAN		6623	MECHANICSVILLE	VA
NEWTON	JACK	W		3802	CHAMBLEE	GA
NOBLE	CLYDE	E		1298	ATHENS	GA
NOEGEL	RICHARD	A		7086	GREENSBORO	GA
NORMAN	TRACY	ALAN		5010	LEXINGTON	GA
NORTH	RONALD	EARL		6123	SHARPSBURG	GA
NORTHCUTT	MAX			6435	MANCHESTER	TN
NUGENT	CHARLES	THOMAS	IV	7058	SAN DIEGO	CA
NUNN	ROY	ROBERT		7310	LOS GATOS	CA
ODEN	JOHN	EARNHARDT		3909	GREENSBORO	NC
ODEN	WILLIAM	KELLAM	IV	7317	WILMINGTON	NC
ODEN	WILLIAM	K.	JR	1005	GREENSBORO	NC
ODEN	WILLIAM	KELLAM	III	3910	WILMINGTON	NC
ODNEAL	CLAYTON	J	JR	7021	VANZANT	MO
O'HERN	FRED	H.	JR	3154	OCALA	FL
O'NEIL	CALVIN	P		3631	EUNICE	LA
ORCUTT	HOMER	A.	JR	6609	ANDALUSIA	AL
O'REILLY	CRAIG	BURRUS		6373	PICKENS	MS
O'REILLY	JOHN	CASNER		6374	PICKENS	MS
ORLEBEKE	PETER	WILLIAM		2176	DALLAS	TX
ORR	RODNEY	G.		6384	ARLINGTON	TX
O'STEEN	THOMAS	C		5583	APEX	NC
OUTLAW	PERRY	JAMES		2297	FAIRHOPE	AL
OWEN	RALPH			6509	TULSA	OK
OWENS	ROBERT	L.	SR	6518	BAKERSVILLE	NC
PACE	PAUL	C.	III	3596	GAINESVILLE	FL
PAGE	MICHEL	DOUGLAS		6893	BRASELTON	GA
PAGE	WILLIAM	EUGENE	IV	6291	MICANOPY	FL
PALMER	ALAN	RAY		6460	DREW	MS
PALMER	CECIL	RAY		6407	WARNER ROBINS	GA
PARK	DR LELAN	M.		2722	DAVIDSON	NC
PARKER	REV JAME			566	CHARLESTON	SC
PARKER	ROM	BRAGG		6723	EMERALD ISLE	NC
PARKIN	GARY			6060	POPLAR BLUFF	MO
PARKS	URIE	EDWARD	JR	1959	JACKSONVILLE	FL
PARKS	WILLIAM	HAMILTON	II	2622	TRIMBLE	TN
PARRISH	JAMES	L.	III	3544	GAINESVILLE	FL
PARSONS	GEORGE	HUGH	JR	6709	DOUGLASVILLE	GA
PARSONS	JERRY	R.		6297	PENNINGTON GAP	VA
PASCHAL	WILLIAM	E		3662	APPLING	GA
PASLEY	JAMES	M		3311	LAKE OZARK	MO
PATERSON	WILLIAM	DANIEL	JR	6260	CENTREVILLE	VA
PATRICK	JAMES	C		4477	DECATUR	IL
PATTERSON	JAMES	G		6243	MURFREESBORO	TN
PATTERSON	KENNETH	RAY		4326	EDEN	NC
PATTERSON	KENNETH	RAY			EDEN	NC
PATTON	EDWARD	LEE		5844	PELHAM	TN
PATTON	JAMES	LEWIS		5023	MELBOURNE	FL
PAULK	WILLIAM	ESTON	JR	6942	CULLOWHEE	NC
PAYNE	JAMES	T		5978	SPOTSYLVANIA	VA
PAYNE	JOSEPH	LIGON	III	7158	CLEVELAND	SC
PEACOCK	GEORGE	RANDALL		6968	HELENA	AL
PEARCE	ANTHONY	CHARLES		6788	POWHATAN	VA
PEARCE	JEFFREY	W		7186	HOMESTED	FL
PEARCE	JOHNNIE	L.	SR	6334	LEAD HILL	AR
PEARSON	GEORGE	R.	JR	1453	RALEIGH	NC
PEDRICK	CHARLES	W		3062	LARGO	FL
PEELER	SCOTT	LOOMIS	JR	7225	VALRICO	FL
PEEPLES	KENNETH	W		4392	AYNOR	SC
PEGRAM	LARRY	L		4376	MONTGOMERY	IL
PENNEBAKER	FLETCHER	A		4431	BONNEVILLE	AR
PENNEBAKER	ROBERT	D		4430	BONNEVILLE	AR
PERDUE	HERBERT	EDWARD		7344	ROANOKE RAPIDS	NC

PERKINSON	W.	BAXTER	SR	3316	MATOACA	VA
PERRY	GEORGE	ANDREW		5289	OVERTON	TX
PERRY	MICHAEL	ROBERT		6987	MECHANICSVILLE	VA
PERRY	RICHARD	J		5817	SPRINGFIELD	MO
PERRYMAN	FRANK	LEE		7115	ALEXANDRIA	VA
PERRYMAN	JEFF	DAVID		5793	WEDDINGTON	NC
PETERMANN	EDWARD	ROSS		6944	LAGRANGE	GA
PETERSON	DAVID	STANLEY		6355	TULLAHOMA	TN
PETERSON	MICHAEL	BLAINE		6034	GRANGEVILLE	ID
PHEBUS	CHARLES	EDWARD		5185	SAN ANTONIO	TX
PHILLIPS	EARLE	WARDON		6677	PINE BLUFF	AR
PHILLIPS	JAMES	GORDON		7233	NORTH SALT LAKE	UT
PHILLIPS	LEE	ASHLEY		6730	SUGAR LAND	TX
PHILLIPS	PHILIP			2714	PADUCAH	KY
PHILLIPS	ROBERT	STANLEY		5007	CACHE	OK
PICKENS	RICHARD	LYNN		6572	HORN LAKE	MS
PICKETT	HENRY	CLAY	III	6277	CHESAPEAKE	VA
PICKETT	RAYMOND	J		6698	BELLEROSE	NY
PIERCE	JOHN			7057	ALPHARETTA	GA
PINSON	JAMES	W		3057	HONEA PATH	SC
PIPPIN	HENRY	C.	JR	2337	GULFPORT	MS
PISTON	WILLIAM	G		6176	SPRINGFIELD	MO
PITTS	ALVIN	L		1786	MARKSVILLE	LA
PITTS	DR NEAL	CHASE		3218	BLUFFTON	IN
PITTS	GORDON	A		3691	FORISTELL	MO
PITTS	GORDON	A.	II	3692	WRIGHT CITY	MO
PITTS	ROBERT	HILL	IV	6904	LAKE CITY	FL
PITTS	ROBERT	HILL	III	6903	WELLBORN	FL
PIXLER	H.	RICHARD		6456	SANDY	UT
PLASTER	HUBERT	T.	JR	6481	WINCHESTER	VA
POE	WILLIAM	EARL		6189	NEWNAN	GA
POHL	CLIFFORD	H.	JR	3014	CINCINNATI	OH
POLK	GEORGE	J.	JR	1502	WALLER	TX
POLLARD	JAMES	L		4306	MCDONOUGH	GA
POLLITT	PAUL	CHRISTOPHER		7236	KANEOHE	HI
POMAR	PAUL	M		6950	ST. AUGUSTINE	FL
POOLE	BENNIE	P		5626	SPRING HILL	TN
POPE	EDWARD	L	JR	6388	DALZELL	SC
POPE	JAMES	E.		6837	SUFFOLK	VA
POPE	JOE	DELWIN		2699	SAN ANTONIO	TX
POPE	LEROY		III	6838	SUFFOLK	VA
POPE	ROBERT	HARRIS	JR	5436	RALEIGH	NC
PORTER	HOMER	PATRICK		6207	CARTHAGE	TX
PORTER	ROBERT	EUGENE		6385	NATCHEZ	LA
POULTON	MAJ WILL	S.	JR	6339	HENRIETTA	NY
POUSSON	STEVEN	L		4028	ANGLETON	TX
POWELL	ERNEST	GRAVES		7164	COVINGTON	TN
POWELL	FRANK	B	III	3738	WAKE FOREST	NC
POWELL	LARRY	JAMES		7163	W. PALM BEACH	FL
POWELL	ROBERT	DYLAN		7165	WEST PALM BEACH	FL
POWELL	RONALD	L		2409	CINCINNATI	OH
POWELL	WILLIAM	S		4010	CHAPEL HILL	NC
POYNER	MATTHEW	PACE		7055	LILBURN	GA
PRATHER	MICHAEL	WAYNE		4365	CLANTON	AL
PRATHER	NORMAN	W		4364	CLANTON	AL
PRESLEY	PAUL	DUANE		6735	BRANDON	FL
PRESSLER	HERMAN	PAUL	III	7260	HOUSTON	TX
PRESTON	JOHN	DAVID		3996	PAINTSVILLE	KY
PRICE	COL DAVI	H.		5292	NORTHPORT	AL
PRICE	RICHARD	DANIEL	M.D.	5272	HINESVILLE	GA
PRICE	STEPHEN	C.		6321	GARLAND	TX
PRINCE	LESTER	GLENN		6077	PLANO	TX
PRINE	MARION	RANDOLPH	JR	5015	SAN DIEGO	CA
PRYOR	DAVID	WAYNE		2248	OXFORD	MS

PRYOR	EDWARD	G.		5313	SAN ANTONIO	TX
PRYOR	MICHAEL	TY		5042	HERMITAGE	TN
PRYTHERCH	HERBERT	F.		6855	ORIENTAL	NC
PUCKETT	ROGER			4217	COLONIAL HEIGHTS	VA
PULLEY	COLLIN	G.	JR	3903	COURTLAND	VA
PURCELL	JAMES	HOPPLE SOUTH	JR	6325	ST CLOUD	FL
PURKINS	RICHARD	THOMAS		3386	MANASSAS	VA
QUIMBY	CHARLES	BATEY		6742	FERRIDAY	LA
QUINNELLY	ROBERT	ALLISON		6610	BILOXI	MS
QUINNELLY	WILLIAM	HIRAM	JR	6611	PURVIS	MS
RACHELS	MARK	EDWARD		6979	WAXAHACHIE	TX
RAGLAND	LEE	F		4142	CAPE GIRARDEAU	MO
RAIFORD	WILLIAM	KENNETH		6758	FREDERICKSBURG	VA
RAILSBACK	GLENN	ALBERT	IV	6676	PINE BLUFF	AR
RAILSBACK	GLENN	ALBERT	III	6029	PINE BLUFF	AR
RALEY	TOMMY	MARTIN		6146	FORT WORTH	TX
RAMSAY	ANDREW	KNOX	III	6700	ASHBURN	VA
RAND	CHARLES	L.	III	4325	MONROE	LA
RAND	HENRY	ASHLEY		6150	TUSCUMBIA	AL
RASCOE	JOHN	PETER	III	6516	EDENTON	NC
RATHER	JOHN	MARK		5378	MOBILE	AL
RAWLS	S.	WAITE	III	7287	CHICAGO	IL
RAXSDALE	VICTOR	ROCHE		6602	ROBERT	LA
RAY	WILLIAM	CARROLL		6976	LEESBURG	VA
RAYFIELD	THOMAS	F		2902	LEXINGTON	NC
REA	CHARLES	NEAL		6397	HARRISON	AR
REA	RICHARD	EUGENE		1806	EL RENO	OK
REAMES	JOHN	NEELY		2214	GAINESVILLE	FL
REAMES	ROBERT	CLARK		6403	BIRMINGHAM	AL
REASOR	STEPHEN	M.		6353	DRYDEN	VA
REAUX	ALVIN	CECIL		7041	LOCKPORT	LA
REAVES	ROBERT	J.	JR	6966	HUNTSVILLE	AL
REAVES	STEVEN	F		6965	TALLADEGA	AL
REAVES	WILMER	PATRICK		5386	MUNFORD	AL
RECTOR	JEFF	FREDRICK		5081	COLUMBIA	TN
RED	GALE	FRANKLIN		6863	0' FALLON	IL
REDWINE	THOMAS	EMMETT	SR	6566	NEWNAN	GA
REECE	DANIEL	DAVIS		5629	NORTH AUGUSTA	SC
REED	THOMAS	C		7224	FLINTVILLE	TN
REID	DR BYRON	LYNN		4299	WESTMORELAND	TN
REID	JOHN	S	JR	7150	SEVIERVILLE	TN
REID	SAMUEL	FRASER	JR	3036	ORANGEBURG	SC
REINAUER	B.	FRANKLIN	III	3920	NEW YORK	NY
RENOUF	STEPHEN	R		6185	SAN LORENZO	CA
REXROAD	RANDALL	E		5413	MOUNDSVILLE	WV
RHEA	GEORGE	DARRELL		6392	MIDLAND	TX
RHEUDASIL	JAMES	E.		6682	TYLER	TX
RHODES	THOMAS	B	III	6872	SUMMERDALE	AL
RICE	JOHN	WALTER	JR	1010	JACKSONVILLE	FL
RICE	MARION	JENNINGS		6049	ATHENS	GA
RICE	STEPHEN	M		4207	YUKON	OK
RICHARDSON	HENRY	BURLEY		6692	FAIRPLAY	SC
RICHARDSON	OLIVER	VASSAR	JR	6658	OKLAHOMA CITY	OK
RICHARDSON	WILLIAM	M		3317	SUFFOLK	VA
RIFE	RALPH	JAMES		6703	GRUNDY	VA
RILEY	DR THOMAS	L		2435	HOPKINSVILLE	KY
RILEY	PAUL	A		5510	HOUSTON	TX
RINGHOFFER	JOSEPH	E.		6311	MOBILE	AL
RITCHIE	STEPHEN	L		7328	MUNCIE	IN
RITTENBERRY	ELMER	LEE	JR	4288	COLUMBIA	TN
RIVERS	WALTER	EUGENE		6163	BIG STONE GAP	VA
ROACH	RONNIE	SMITH		2824	MEBANE	NC
ROBERSON	RICHARD	W.		6909	WASHINGTON	DC
ROBERTS	EUGENE	STEP		5329	WAYNESBORO	MS

ROBERTS	HAROLD	KNOX	JR	7035	SALISBURY	NC
ROBERTS	JIMMIE			4248	EAGLE POINT	OR
ROBERTS	LARRY	OWEN		3099	WARSAW	KY
ROBERTS	MARK	A		4186	GREER	SC
ROBERTS	SURRY	P		3905	RALEIGH	NC
ROBERTS	WAYNE	D		3410	LEXINGTON	SC
ROBERTSON	JAMES	C		514	GAINESVILLE	FL
ROBERTSON	PRESTON	TAYLOR		3900	TALLAHASSEE	FL
ROBINETTE	KEVIN	RAY		6832	COUSHATTA	LA
ROBINSON	ALFRED	BOWNE	JR	5689	SENECA	SC
ROBINSON	IVAN	R.		6096	WOODLAWN	VA
ROCKWELL	WILLIAM	S.	JR	4267	ATHENS	GA
RODERICK	JOHN	THOMAS		6118	ANGIER	NC
RODGERS	THOMAS	MALIN	JR.	7212	ATLANTA	GA
ROGERS	DAVID	LEE		7281	WOODWARD	OK
ROGERS	JAMES	HENRY	III	6667	STATESVILLE	NC
ROGERS	LOYD	LEANDER		7319	WOODWARD	OK
ROGERS	MARK	K		4474	KISSIMMEE	FL
ROGERS	MURRAY	L.		4424	KISSIMMEE	FL
ROLAND	CHRISTOP	HEATH		6780	KANSAS CITY	KS
ROLEN	WILLIAM	A.	III	3926		
ROLLINS	JOHN			6329	DESARC	AR
ROMIG	EDWARD	FRANKLIN	II	5300	RIDGEFIELD	CT
ROOKS	RAYMOND	MICHAEL		6849	BALTIMORE	MD
ROSE	MURRAY	FONTAINE		2445	PAEONIAN SPRINGS	VA
ROSE	WILLIAM	GUY		6423	LAKE MARY	FL
ROSEMAN	ERNEST	DARWIN		6587	CARY	NC
ROSEMAN	GARY	HARLAN		7213	LINDALE	GA
ROUTH	DAVID	KYLE		7228	ROCKWALL	TX
ROWE	JAMES	EDWARD	JR	4436	TITUSVILLE	FL
ROWE	KEVIN	S		7304	MATHEWS	VA
ROWELL	TERRY			6011	HEIDELBERG	MS
ROZIER	CHRISTOP	NEIL		7193	CLAYTON	NC
ROZIER	NEIL	LARRY		7192	RALEIGH	NC
RUDULPH	NAT	GOODWIN	JR	5139	SELMA	AL
RUSSELL	CHRISTOP	LOUIS		5424	MILLERSVILLE	MD
RUTLEDGE	WILLIAM	O.	IV	6347	ASPEN	CO
RUXTON	MARSHALL	H.		1014	KANSAS CITY	MO
RYAN	DARRELL	E		7147	MT JULIET	TN
RYAN	JOSEPH	ROBERT		6415	SUFFOLK	VA
RYAN	RAYMOND	WHITING	JR	6597	POWHATAN	VA
RYBIKOWSKY	MICHAEL	J.		2933	CHARLOTTE HALL	MD
SABLE	CHARLES	MARTIN		7198	UNICOI	TN
SAMMONS	HARRY	C	M D	6799	HERMANN	MO
SANDERS	CHARLES	LARRY		4332	DEXTER	MO
SANDIFER	ERIC	ALTON		7102	BAYTOWN	TX
SANFORD	JAMES	ROBERT		7121	BIRMINGHAM	AL
SAPPINGTON	OLIVER	E.		4007	OAKVILLE	MO
SATCHER	DAVID	SANFORD		6517	EDGEFIELD	SC
SAUCIER	ROBERT	L		7134	SPANISH FORT	AL
SAUNDERS	EVERETT	LEWIS	JR	5833	INDEPENDENCE	MO
SAUNDERS	JAMES	ALLEN		5837	INDEPENDENCE	MO
SAWYER	WILSON	T	III	6844	CHESAPEAKE	VA
SCARBOROUGH	EARNEST	HOYT	JR	6603	OKANOGAN	WA
SCHAEFFER	KARL	F		6312	MASSILLON	OH
SCHALLER	MARTIN	N		5575	BURKE	VA
SCHEER	DAVID	PHILIP		7238	DEER PARK	TX
SCHERMERHORN	WILLIAM	STERLING		6458	MOUNTAIN REST	SC
SCHOOLING	MICHAEL	ANDREW		6455	SAN DIEGO	CA
SCHRECK	PETER	REILLY	JR.	6826	SAVANNAH	GA
SCHROEDER	DON	A		5380	LOWAKE	TX
SCHROEDER	RONALD	EUGENE		5290	BEAUMONT	TX
SCOTT	LELAND	PATRICK		6739	MERRITT ISLAND	FL
SCOTT	RUSSELL	CECIL		6783	RICHMOND	VA

SCOTT	WILLIAM	CASWELL	JR	1838	FLORENCE	AL
SCOTT	WILLIAM	VERNON		6255	SAN ANTONIO	TX
SCOUTEN	ROBERT	EDWARD LEE		7296	CHARLOTTESVILLE	VA
SCRUGGS	JAMES	MARSHALL		5564	COCOA BEACH	FL
SCRUGGS	ROBERT	G		2702	HORSE SHOE	NC
SCRUGGS	ROBERT	T		3166	JEFFERSON CITY	MO
SEALE	HENRY	B		7249	TEXAS CITY	TX
SECHRIST	KIRBY	DALE		5580	LINCLNTON	NC
SEESE	DALE			3574	ELLENBORO	WV
SEIBERT	JOHN	RIX	II	4391	AKRON	OH
SELLERS	MELVIN	L		4218	LAKELAND	FL
SELPH	ELLIS	L.	JR	4224	MORRISVILLE	NC
SEMMES	DR FRANK	W.		6377	TULLAHOMA	TN
SEWELL	MICHAEL			6956	FORT WORTH	TX
SHACKLEFORD	WILLIAM	RUSSELL		6261	CHATTANOOGA	TN
SHAFFER	DR LAWRENCE	B.		3655	OMAHA	NE
SHANNON	JOSEPH	DAN		7195	HAMPSHIRE	TN
SHAVER	RON			2484	COMPTON	AR
SHELTON	ARCH	P		3812	SARASOTA	FL
SHEPERD	JOHNATHAN	DERREK		7342	EDGEMOOR	SC
SHEPPERD	DAVID	ALAN		7259	CARROLLTON	TX
SHERAM	BENJAMIN	STAN		4102	ATHENS	GA
SHERBURNE	EUGENE	EDMOND		6982	FLIPPIN	AR
SHERRILL	SIDNEY	LEE	JR	7322	MEMPHIS	TN
SHIPLER	MICHAEL	DON		6868	BAY MINETTE	AL
SHIPMAN	JOHN	DERRICK		7159	CANTON	NC
SHORT	DR SHELT	H.	III	560	CLARKSVILLE	VA
SHRADER	GEORGE	R		5739	AKRON	OH
SIKES	THOMAS	EDGAR	JR	6000	GREENSBORO	NC
SIMMONS	GORDON	D		5026	LAKE CHARLES	LA
SIMONDS	WARREN	OSSIAN		1112	ARLINGTON	VA
SIMPSON	DAVID	E		3989	LEBANON	TN
SIMPSON	DR KENNE	R.		3951	MILLEDGEVILLE	GA
SIMS	REV JOHN	S		3836	CHATTANOOGA	TN
SINGELTARY	GEORGE	RICHARD		3555	LEESBURG	FL
SINGLETON	DR J.	WHITT	DVM	6166	TULLAHOMA	TN
SIZEMORE	JEFFREY	LEE		5558	KISSIMMEE	FL
SKINNER	TALMADGE	S		1535	ST AUGUSTINE	FL
SLAUGHTER	JOHN	A	III	6502	NEW BERN	NC
SLEMP	LETCHER	BASCOM		6298	BIG STONE GAP	VA
SLOAN	JOHN	G.	JR	3704	ALBERDEEN	NC
SLOAN	RUDY	LEE		4048	LAKE MARY	FL
SMALL	LTC ALVI	L.		814	BEAUMONT	MS
SMITH	ANTHONY	P		1515	RICHMOND	VA
SMITH	CARL	E		3688	MELBOURNE	FL
SMITH	CHARLES	MICHAEL		3359	YUKON	OK
SMITH	CHARLES	H		1671	YUKON	OK
SMITH	DAVIS	REMMELE		1339	HUNTINGTON	wv
SMITH	GORDON	BURNS		1371	SAVANNAH	GA
SMITH	HOWARD	WOODSON		6869	BAY MINETTE	AL
SMITH	JAMES	JACKSON		7196	MT. PLEASANT	TN
SMITH	JAY	COLLIER		7266	MALAKOFF	TX
SMITH	JOHN	MICHAEL		2383	EDGEWATER	CO
SMITH	JONATHAN	MARK		7343	ASHEVILLE	NC
SMITH	JOSEPH	ADRIAN		6787	BEAUFORT	NC
SMITH	KARL	HOMER		6141	LUCEDALE	MS
SMITH	KEN	W		6815	HAZLEHURST	GA
SMITH	LEONARD	ELLIS	III	6198	SOUTH HILL	VA
SMITH	MARVIN	MACLEOD	JR	5349	CYPRESS	TX
SMITH	MICHAEL	A		6158	GREENCASTLE	PA
SMITH	MYRON	CRENSHAW		6711	GREELEY	CO
SMITH	THOMAS	M.	JR	5062	RALEIGH	NC
SMITH	TOMMY	V		7084	ROME	GA
SMITH	WALTER	B		6574	CLAXTON	GA

SNEAD	ROBERT	H		3660	FT MEADE	FL
SNELLGROVE	CHARLES	BRYANT		7270	TUSCALOOSA	AL
SNOWDEN	WILLIAM	K		5388	JACKSONVILLE	AL
SNYDER	PETER	F.	III	4393	RINGGOLD	GA
SNYDER	RICHARD	LESTER		2697	DANVILLE	VA
SOHRWIDE	DAYTON	PATRICK		6395	SAN ANTONIO	TX
SOHRWIDE	KERRY	PATRICK		3875	STILLWATER	OK
SOULE	ROBERT	MURRAY	III	5704	SODDY DAISY	TN
SPARGUR	KEVIN			7091	JACKSONVILLE	FL
SPEARS	DOYLE	C.	SR	3895	WAUCHULA	FL
SPEARS	DOYLE	C.	JR	3895	ATLANTA	GA
SPINDLE	FOREST	G		1149	SUGARLAND	TX
SPINKS	CHRISTOP	MICHAEL		6947	LILBURN	GA
SPIVEY	LT. COL.	B		2228	KODAK	TN
SPOONER	JOHN	EARL		3684	TECUMSEH	MI
SPRINGER	ROBERT	G.	COL	1821	SAN ANTONIO	TX
STACY	RONALD	LEON		6661	RALEIGH	NC
STARK	MIKE	P		5746	FT. WORTH	TX
STARKE	J	BRYANT		4112	ARLINGTON	VA
STARKE	ROBERT	BURWELL	JR	5667	BOULDER	CO
STARNES	DARRYL	FELTON		5713	MECHANICSVILLE	VA
STEARNS	EMORY	WARD		7092	CARY	NC
STEED	JAMES	M		1348	LEXINGTON	KY
STEGER	WILLIAM	E		4151	SAN DIEGO	CA
STELL	RODNEY			5355	MCKINNEY	TX
STERN	DUKE	NORDLINGER		3548	SAINT PETERSBURG	FL
STEVENS	MICHAEL	K		2058	FT WORTH	TX
STEWART	JOHN	NELSON	III	4397	DIAMONDHEAD	MS
STEWART	MURRAY	BAKER		5733	BROKEN ARROW	OK
STEWART	STANLEY	GARDINER		6319	GAINESVILLE	GA
STILLWELL	JOHN	WILLIAM		7136	DOWNERS GROVE	IL
STINSON	JOHN	C		5615	MIDLOTHIAN	VA
STOBER	JOHN	BERNARD	JR	5166	CALIFORNIA	MD
STOHLMAN	ROBERT	ANDREW		7335	SMITHFIELD	VA
STOKLEY	ROBERT	EDWARD		5709	ELIZABETH CITY	NC
STONE	DAVID	LOCKE		6794	PORTALES	NM
STONE	ROBERT	MELVIN		7301	ZEPHYR	TX
STORMS	JOHN	KEMPER	JR	7108	BAY SAINT LOUIS	MS
STORY	SAM		JR	3846	SIKESTON	MO
STOVALL	FRED	D.	JR	4039	PULASKI	TN
STOVALL	GEORGE	A		4199	HOUSTON	TX
STOVALL	JOHN	ALEX		6993	DUBLAN	TX
STOWE	RICHARD	ALLEN	JR	6762	BAKERSVILLE	NC
STRAHL	CHARLES	A		6529	ZANESVILLE	OH
STRATTON	JOHN	LAWTON		6804	FT. WAYNE	IN
STRAUT	RICHARD	KEVIN		7056	ATLANTA	GA
STRICKLAND	MICHAEL	BENNETT		6600	WILSONS MILLS	NC
STROUPE	TONY	THAMER		7332	BESSEMER CITY	NC
STRYBOS	ANDREW	JAMES		7267	ANGLETON	TX
STRYBOS	RONALD	R.	JR	7268	ANGLETON	TX
STUART	J.E.B.		IV	3831	RICHMOND	VA
SULLINS	LTC BARR	E.		4158	LAKEWOOD	CO
SULLIVAN	ALLAN	R		7264	WICHITA	KS
SULLIVAN	EDWARD	PERCIVAL HEAD		6214	MIDLAND	GA
SURLES	DR. JOH	WILLIAM		5466	MACCLESFIELD	NC
SUTPHIN	RANDALL	E		7126	WILLIS	VA
SUTTON	JOHN	CHARLES		7258	ROLLA	MO
SWAN	LAWTON	III		3932	ST. PETERSBURG	FL
SWANK	COL. WAL	DAVIS		1356	MINERAL	VA
SWARINGEN	KENNETH	PORTER		7103	DURHAM	NC
SWEENEY	DAVID	FONTAINE		6991	SAN ANTONIO	TX
SWERTFEGER	L.	JACK	JR	6821	ATLANTA	GA
SWIFT	LEE	W.	JR	1128	ORLEAN	VA
SWISHER	MICHAEL	S		3247	STILLWATER	MN

SYMINGTON	JAMES	MCKIM	JR	6852	MCLEAN	VA
SYPHER	FRANCIS	J	JR	6669	NEW YORK	NY
TALLEY	MELVIN	W		6501	CASTLE ROCK	CO
TALLEY	WILLIAM	H.	IV	6438	PETERSBURG	VA
TALLEY	WILLIAM	HENRY	III	6500	PETERSBURG	VA
TALLMAN	CHARLES	PATTEN		6719	MOBILE	AL
TANKERSLEY	CHRISTOP	R		5634	PLANO	TX
TARRY	SAMUEL	LEWIS	SR	3796	RICHMOND	VA
TATE	BARTON	M		6035	GALVESTON	TX
TATE	CHARLES	D		4312	THOMASTON	GA
TATUM	ROBERT	W.		6299	NORTH GARDEN	VA
TAYLOR	ARTHUR	H.	III	6106	BEAVER DAM	VA
TAYLOR	HERMAN	BANKS	JR	5851	MORRISON	TN
TAYLOR	JACK		II	7201	COLUMBIA	TN
TAYLOR	JAMES	WILLIAMSON		7135	NWEPORT NEWS	VA
TAYLOR	JOHN	M		5553	WETUMPKA	AL
TAYLOR	JOHN	HENRY		7064	RICHMOND	VA
TAYLOR	KURT	M		2357	FAYETTEVILLE	GA
TAYLOR	TERRY	CARSON		7054	OKATIE	SC
TAYLOR	WILLIAM	B		4098	ALEXANDRIA	VA
TEEM	PAUL	LLOYD	JR	2952	GASTONIA	NC
TEMPLIN	JIM			6654	ENNIS	TX
TENNEY	R.	PAUL		5821	WASHINGTON	VT
TERRY	R.	GORDON	JR	2760	JACKSONVILLE	FL
TETRICK	DWIGHT			6345	LUTZ	FL
THIGPEN	ALLAN	D		4204	SUMTER	SC
THOMAS	JASON	BRETT		4034	ATHENS	AL
THOMAS	T.	N.	JR	5208	AIKEN	SC
THOMAS	WILLIAM	HENRY	III	7160	CORAL SPRINGS	FL
THOMPSON	ALAN	GENE		7157	STOKESDALE	NC
THOMPSON	DAVID	CARREL	SR	6061	BLAND	VA
THOMPSON	DAVID	GLENN		5999	LINCOLNTON	NC
THOMPSON	HARRY	L		3459	WINDSOR	NC
THOMPSON	JAMES	C	II	6622	ALEXANDRIA	VA
THOMPSON	JOHN			6274	LINCOLNTON	NC
THOMPSON	WILLIAM	W		5125	SPRINGFIELD	MA
THOMPSON	WILLIAM	HENRY		3760	MARIETTA	OK
THOMPSON	WOODROW	WAYNE		5688	SPRINGFIELD	MA
THORN	AVERY	ODA		7242	TEXAS CITY	TX
THORNHILL	WILLIAM	R		5105	WINTER HAVEN	FL
THORPE	MANER	LAWTON		3886	SANTA BARBARA	CA
THURMAN	DR WILLI	A.	JR	1694	MIDLOTHIAN	VA
THURMOND	WILLIAM	J.	JR	4153	GREENSBORO	GA
TILLINGHAST	JOHN	R		4241	BURLESON	TX
TILLISON	LARRY	KENNETH		4241	JACKSONVILLE	AL
TINSLEY	JAMES	JENNINGS		7315	ALPHARETTA	GA
TINSLEY	WILLIAM	CHARLES		7316	ALPHARETTA	GA
TIPTON	CURTIS	E		3603	SIERRA VISTA	AZ
TIPTON	DOUGLAS	BLAKE		6651	FLORISSANT	MO
TISDALE	ROBERT	EDWARD		7099	BRIDGE CITY	TX
TOAL	GLENN	WAYNE		6743	FERRIS	TX
TODD	DENNIS			5670	RICHARDSON	TX
TODD	JASON	CHARLES		7277	NEWNAN	GA
TODD	JOHN	CHARLES		7216	NEWNAN	GA
TOFFLEMEYER	CAPT. TR	MICHAEL		6613	WOODLAND PARK	CO
TOLBERT	TIMOTHY	JOSEPH		7143	HILLSVILLE	VA
TOMA	RAYMOND	D.	JR	7234	APO	AE
TOMLINSON	COL WILL	HOLMES		1562	JACKSONVILLE	FL
TOOTLE	JAMES	DERWOOD	JR	5397	BELLVILLE	GA
TOULMIN	LLEWELLY	MORGAN		6848	SILVER SPRING	MD
TOWBERMAN	FRANK	K.		5159	CLAREMONT	VA
TRAVIS	JACK	M		3479	RALEIGH	NC
TRAVIS	LIONEL	MAX	III	5516	RICHMOND	VA
TRAVIS	LIONEL	MAX	II	5517	POWHATAN	VA

TREADAWAY	RALPH	FRANKLIN		7214	ADAIRSVILLE	GA
TRESCA	JAMES	T		2911	JACKSONVILLE	FL
TREVISON	JOHN	ALLEN		1068	SYLVANIA	OH
TREXLER	EDWARD	COLEMAN	JR	6337	FAIRFAX	VA
TRIGG	JAMES	KNOX		2937	NASHVILLE	TN
TRIMBLE	WILLIAM	CATTELL	JR	5743	OWINGS MILLS	MD
TUCKER	HILLARY	ALBERT		6824	HOUSTON	TX
TUCKER	ROBERT	BOYD		6278	LAKE BUTLER	FL
TUCKER	SAMUEL	T.	III	6144	PIEDMONT	SC
TUCKER	STEPHEN	FISHER		7197	DICKSON	TN
TUCKER	WALTER	D		5285	RICHMOND	VA
TUDOR	R.	KEITH		3012	DUNWOODY	GA
TURBIVILLE	GRAHAM	HALL	JR	6736	DRIPPING SPRINGS	TX
TURBYFILL	ROBERT	R.	JR	2308	AUGUSTA	GA
TURNER	JAMES	KENNETH		4286	NASHVILLE	TN
TURNER	KENNETH	BRACKMAN		5064	GRANVILLE	TN
TURNER	LLOYD	HASKELL	JR	6694	GREENVILLE	SC
TURNLEY	EDMUND	W.	JR	747	NASHVILLE	TN
TURPIN	CAPT THOMAS	JEFFERSON	USN (ret)	5682	EAST BERLIN	PA
TYLER	BENJAMIN	MAURY	III	7205	CENTREVILLE	MD
TYLER	CALVIN	ZANE	III	6910	STAFFORD	VA
TYLER	GERALD	BAILEY		7044	FERRIS	TX
TYNER	KENNETH	BLAKE		5780	PEMBROKE	NC
TYSON	MICHAEL	H		5014	MOULTRIE	GA
VADEN	NORMAN	C.	JR	3585	BYHALIA	MS
VALSAME	GEORGE	THOMAS		6445	GARNER	NC
VAN DENBURG	JAMES	H.		5045	BIGFORK	MT
VANGILDER	SIDNEY	A		4253	GLEN ALLEN	VA
VAUGHN	GEORGE	GREGORY		5791	HIGH POINT	NC
VAUGHN	JOHN	M.	III	6439	BOCA RATON	FL
VAUGHN	MICHAEL	JEFFERY		5680	FLINT	TX
VEAL	DAVID	LEE		6224	LUBBOCK	TX
VENABLE	JAMES	W.	DR	6170	ADAIRSVILLE	GA
VERNON	FREDERIC	FOSTER		7294	GREENSBORO	NC
VERNON	THOMAS	CARR		6853	LEICESTER	NC
VIA	JOHN	WILLIAM	III	7230	FORT WORTH	TX
VINCENT	JOHN	R.	D	3143	DES MOINES	NM
VINCENT	ROBERT	CARR		718	AMARILLO	TX
VOYLES	DARREN			5523	SMYRNA	GA
WADE	WILLIAM	STEVENSON		2944	WINTERVILLE	GA
WAKEFIELD	CHARLES	EDWARD		6211	KATY	TX
WALKER	CHARLES	CARSON	III	6662	MARTINSBURG	WV
WALKER	DR CHARL	R.		684	BEAUMONT	TX
WALKER	GARY	C		5989	ROANOKE	VA
WALKER	HAROLD			6108	WARRENVILLE	IL
WALKER	PAUL			5333	BAY SPRINGS	MS
WALKER	PAUL	H		1462	AUBURNDALE	MA
WALKER	WILLIAM	DAN		7276	WHITE HALL	AR
WALLS	JOSEPH	NIXON		6879	MARIETTA	GA
WALTERS	JOE	T	JR	6428	WINNSBORO	LA
WARD	DAVID	H		7251	SHELBYVILLE	KY
WARD	NICHOLAS	DONNELL		1088	WASHINGTON	DC
WARE	DAVID	WARREN	JR	7338	NEWPORT NEWS	VA
WARE	JOSEPH	M		3915	SAN ANTONIO	TX
WARING	ROGER	HATCHER		6182	ROANOKE	VA
WARREN	JAMES	OTTO	JR	3638	ORANGEBURG	SC
WARREN	KENNETH	NORMAN	JR	6493	OLIN	IA
WARREN	ROBERT	HOSKINS		7036	REDART	VA
WARREN	TERRY	R		7076	BRIDGEPORT	IL
WATERS	RUSSELL	D		3931	MONTROSE	CA
WATKINS	ARTHUR	WARREN		6750	ROANOKE	VA
WATKINS	JACOB	ZEDEKIAH		6749	ROANOKE	VA
WATKINS	LOWRY		JR	1901	LOUISVILLE	KY
WATKINS	MATTHEW	ALLEN		7320	GARLAND	TX

WATKINS	WILLIAM	ERBY		6931	BIRMINGHAM	AL
WATTS	DR DAVID	R.		5047	NASHVILLE	TN
WEATHERLY	ALVIS	MORRISON	III	5498	MARIETTA	GA
WEATHERLY	ALVIS	MORRISON	JR	5499	ATLANTA	GA
WEATHERLY	JOHN	ROBERT		3324	HOUSTON	TX
WEAVER	SAMUEL	EUGENE	JR	7235	DE LEON	TX
WEBB	JAMES	LINDSAY	JR	3182	LEXINGTON	SC
WEBB	JAMES	DOWARD	SR	6729	SEMMES	AL
WEBB	JOHN	J		2730	BOGART	GA
WEBB	ROY	STANLEY		4103	NEWNAN	GA
WEBSTER	HAROLD	WARREN	JR	7250	JACKSON	MS
WEDDINGTON	GEORGE	LEE	JR	2743	WARRENTON	NC
WEEDEN	DR KENNE	CARL	MD	6178	HOUSTON	TX
WEH	ALLEN	E		2781	ALBUQUERQUE	NM
WEHR	DONALD	LEE		1721	ALTAMONTE SPRINGS	FL
WEIDNER	THOMAS	M		5338	TAYLORS	SC
WELKER	GARY	A		3616	HUNTSVILLE	AL
WELLS	DOUGLAS	J		3955	VALPARAISO	IN
WESSON	DOC	S.JR		5066	LAKELAND	FL
WEST	IRA	LEONARD	JR	156	MOUNTAIN BROOK	AL
WEST	WARREN	W		6701	POWHATAN	VA
WESTBROOK	JACK	K		2139	KNOXVILLE	TN
WESTBROOK	MAITLAND	OLLIE	III	6292	COLUMBIA	TN
WETZEL	DAVID			5522	PLANO	TX
WHEATLEY	ROGER	NEAL		6476	LAGRANGE	GA
WHEELER	THOMAS	JOSEPH		5847	TERRE HAUTE	IN
WHITE	DAVID	NEWTON	SR	7299	PALESTINE	TX
WHITE	JOHN	O		7072	FULLERTON	CA
WHITE	JOHN	BENJAMIN	JR	6269	DECATUR	GA
WHITE	NATHAN	EMMETT	JR	3221	MCKINNEY	TX
WHITE	REV ELIJ	B.	III	6670	HAMILTON	VA
WHITE	ROBERT	EMMETT		5457	DALLAS	TX
WHITE	WENDELL	N.		5020	ALEXANDER CITY	AL
WHITE	WILLIAM	K		6836	ST. GEORGE	UT
WHITEHURST	T.	BAYARD		5118	MERCER ISLAND	WA
WHITESCARVER	ROY	SURFACE		2340	ROANOKE	VA
WHITESIDE	LESLIE	L		4172	ARCHIE	MO
WHITFIELD	GARY	PAGE		6465	FT WORTH	TX
WHITFIELD	JEFFREY	JACK		6468	LUFKIN	TX
WHITLEY	PHILIP	D		7025	HOUSTON	TX
WHITLOCK	PAUL	A.	JR	3507	STATESBORO	GA
WHITMAN	C.	WAYNE		5859	SALISBURY	NC
WHITMORE	HORACE	SCOTT		6791	COLONIAL HEIGHTS	VA
WHITNER	GEORGE	CRABTREE		2154	JACKSONVILLE	FL
WIDENER	DR RALPH	W.	JR	118	FAIRVIEW	TX
WILCOX	ROBERT	A		6590	POWHATAN	VA
WILFLEY	FRANK	PINDALL	JR	2276	MEXICO	MO
WILKERSON	GARY		SR	5071	FT WORTH	TX
WILKERSON	PAUL	RALPH	JR	5985	GREENSBORO	NC
WILKES	DR JERRY	WAYNE		7073	HOBE SOUND	FL
WILKES	DR LESLIE	L		6167	SAVANNAH	GA
WILKES	JEFF			4373	SAVANNAH	TN
WILKINSON	OSCAR	B.	JR	5238	TULLAHOMA	TN
WILKINSON	ROBERT	A		6496	BELVIDERE	TN
WILKINSON	RONALD	LESLIE		5569	WAXAHACHIE	TX
WILKS	KENNETH			5114	JEFFERSON CITY	MO
WILLIAMS	BRADFORD	EUGENE		7118	BATES CITY	MO
WILLIAMS	CALEB	ANDREW		7220	PASS CHRISTIAN	MS
WILLIAMS	CHARLES	L	JR	6902	JASPER	FL
WILLIAMS	CHARLES	L		6009	SAVANNAH	GA
WILLIAMS	CRANSTON		JR	4330	ROANOKE	VA
WILLIAMS	DOUGLAS	WAYNE		7219	FORT WORTH	TX
WILLIAMS	JACK		III	6251	WAYCROSS	GA
WILLIAMS	JOHN	DUNCAN		6883	TITUSVILLE	FL

WILLIAMS	JOHN	MICHAEL		6348	MIDLAND	TX
WILLIAMS	LARRY	G		4463	CLINTON	TN
WILLIAMS	MICHAEL	KENT		3018	BALTIMORE	MD
WILLIAMS	PAUL	HENDERSON BANKS		6536	OWENSBORO	KY
WILLIAMS	REIDY			5203	ST CLOUD	FL
WILLIAMS	ROBERT	D		5402	CAMDEN	AL
WILLIAMS	ROBERT	FRANKLIN		3632	BOWERSVILLE	GA
WILLIAMS	RODNEY	PATRICK		6235	REIDSVILLE	NC
WILLIAMS	SCOTT	K		6032	FLORISSANT	MO
WILLIAMS	STEVE	A.		2581	HUNTINGDON	TN
WILLIAMS	STEVEN	CARL		7207	HILLSVILLE	VA
WILLIAMS	THOMAS	B	SR	7027	GERMANTOWN	TN
WILLIAMSON	BENJAMIN	ROBERT		6379	RALEIGH	NC
WILLIAMSON	GILBERT	EUGENE		6511	FRANKLINVILLE	NC
WILLIAMSON	JOHN	BRADFORD		6659	COCONUT GROVE	FL
WILLIFORD	JAMES	ANDERSON	III	7209	ENNIS	TX
WILLINGHAM	ROBERT	WESLEY		7337	DURHAM	NC
WILLIS	EDWARD	C		6642	EAGLE RIVER	AK
WILLIS	FRANK	A.		6699	LEXINGTON PARK	MD
WILLIS	JOSEPH	WYATT		6304	PRATTVILLE	AL
WILLS	ARTHUR	E.		6447	RALEIGH	NC
WILMETH	JOHN	ROBERT		5640	SAN ANTONIO	TX
WILSON	DARRELL	KEITH		6722	REIDSVILLE	NC
WILSON	DONALD	MALTON		6482	BUMPASS	VA
WILSON	EROS	WAYNE		5056	COLUMBIA	SC
WILSON	HOWARD			6434	PORTAGE	IN
WILSON	JAMES	A	JR.	6989	DES PLAINES	IL
WILSON	KEVIN	J		6813	BROWNWOOD	TX
WILSON	KYLE	ANTHONY		7070	DES PLAINES	IL
WILSON	ROBERT	G.		5098	FAYETTEVILLE	NC
WILT	KENNETH	C		2666	BOYCE	VA
WINTER	EDWARD	JOHN	JR	3870	PINECREST	FL
WISE	REV ROBE	K		6273	VALE	NC
WISE	ROBERT	A		6272	VALE	NC
WISEMAN	DALE	O		6208	ST. PETERS	MO
WITCHER	RICHARD	L		2036	LAKE ALFRED	FL
WITHERSPOON	WILLIAM	L		2868	GALLATIN	TN
WOLF	ROBERT	H.		5161	SAN ANTONIO	TX
WOLFE	HUDSON	G.	III	4396	OCEAN SPRINGS	MS
WOLFE	JOHN	FREDRICK		5819	SPRINGFIELD	MO
WOLFE	STEVEN			6626	COLUMBIA	SC
WOOD	CHARLES	L.		6218	GALENA	MO
WOODFALL	STEVEN	ALAN		7271	PROPHETSTOWN	IL
WOODLOCK	JAMES	Q.		7297	WACO	TX
WOODS	JIMMY	DEE	II	1553	FLORISSANT	MO
WOOLVERTON	DALTON	LEO		2880	NEW ORLEANS	LA
WOOTEN	DAVID	GIBSON		7006	GEISMAR	LA
WOOTEN	JEFFREY			7004	SAUCIER	MS
WOOTEN	JOHNNIE	RALPH		6999	BOGUE CHITTO	MS
WOOTEN	MATTHEW	JARED		7005	BOGUE CHITTO	MS
WOOTEN	MICHAEL	LYNN		7003	SAUCIER	MS
WOOTEN	ZACHARY	GARRETT		7007	GEISMAR	LA
WORSHAM	RALEIGH	ELROY		7124	APOPKA	FL
WRAY	DANIEL	J	SR	2322	OCALA	FL
WRIGHT	JOHN	WINFRED		6156	SAVANNAH	GA
WRIGHT	RICHARD	MORGAN	JR	6119	OAKTON	VA
WRIGHT	WALTER	G.		5075	SAVANNAH	GA
YARBROUGH	HENRY	L		3276	PFAFFTOWN	NC
YATES	JAMES	ALEXANDER		6424	DAYTONA BEACH	FL
YEATMAN	JEFFREY	ALLEN		7181	KANSAS CITY	MO
YEATMAN	LARRY	TODD		7183	KANSAS CITY	MO
YEATMAN	MAJ JOHN	P		7182	CHICAGO	IL
YODER	REV THOM	M.		3561	WEST PADUCAH	KY
YORK	GERRY	D.		5643	DALLAS	TX

140

YORK	JAMES	ROBERT	SR	7013	CORNELIA	GA
YOUNG	SCOTT	R		5477	ATLANTA	GA
ZAPFFE	PAUL			2835	CLINTON	OK
ZEIGLER	EDWARD	T		656	NORTH AUGUSTA	SC
ZIHLMAN	JOE	RALPH		2171	DE SOTO	TX
ZOCH	JOHN	JACOB	SR	6916	SEAFORD	DE

Index

Prather 62
Pratt 90
Preacher 101
Pres. La. Succession Conv. 68
President Jefferson Davis Chapter 72
President Library 16
Price 80, 88
Prince George County 36
Prince John 56
Princess Anne Camp 59
Princess Anne County 60
Private Henry Lawson Wyatt Camp 48
Pruitt 70
Prushankin 50
Pryor 65
Pt. Point 55
Pulaski County 106
Pulley 8, 9, 36, 54, 58
Pursue 89
Puss 104
Pvt. Lorenzo Dow Williams Camp
  #1456 45
Pvt. Wallace Bowling SCV Camp
  1400 39

Q

Quantico 24
Quantrill 14, 80
Quantrill's Raiders 80
Quinn 104
Quysenberry 89

R

R.A. Sneed Camp No.1417 17
Rainocheck 18
Rainoshek 27, 88
Rains 51
Raleigh 22, 23, 26, 28, 41, 42, 46,
  47, 48, 49, 59, 60, 97, 109
Ramsay 55
Ramseur 44, 45
Ramsey 89
Randolph 14, 30, 63, 66
Rankin 71
Raphael Semmes Camp II 13
Rascoe 108
Ratlif 23
Rausch 106
Rea 82
Read 12, 30, 92
Real Daughter 58
Real Son 3, 5, 51, 58, 89, 101, 102,
  104, 105
Rebel Club 12, 30, 74
Rebel Yell 14
Red 67, 68, 88
Redmond 78
Reed 47
Reenacting Unit 12
Reese 72
Renton 101
Requiescat in Pace 89
Resaca 85
Reseda 77
Reynolds 66
Rhea 48, 52
Rhodes 61
Rich 101
Richard Hubbard chapter 92
Richard Kirkland Chapter #174 50
Richmond 11, 21, 22, 23, 26, 28, 44,
  46, 47, 55, 57, 58, 59, 60,
  75, 91, 98, 100, 104, 105,
  109
Richmond Professional Institute 11
Richton 101
Rickerson 70, 71
Riggs 15
Riley 107
Rileyville 22, 109
Rivers 54
Rivers Bridge 52, 54
Riverside 77

Roanoke 14, 30, 58, 63, 66, 101,
  102, 103
Roberdeau 91
Robert E. Lee 10, 13, 14, 17, 30, 47,
  49, 71, 85, 103
Roberts 8, 51, 52, 53, 54, 60, 72,
  107, 108
Robinson 22, 25, 57, 58, 109
Rockingham 45
Rockingham County Chapter #586
  45
Rockwell 31, 44
Rocky Run Methodist Church 104
Roderick 42
Rogers 41, 43, 63, 82
Roland 48
Roll 82
Rollins 107
Rome 85
Romig 39
Rookie Chapter of the Year 44
Rose 107
Rosehill Cemetery 67
Roseman 5, 42
Ross 43, 92
Roswell 17, 82, 83
Rotary Club 89
Rountree 64, 65
Rowe 64
Rudulph 62
Rural Retreat 101
Russell 37, 38
Russellville 12, 75
Rutledge 53
Ryan 72, 79

S

S&W Hosiery Co 103
S.C.V. Executive Council 17
Sabetha 14
Sabine Pass Medal 88
Sagers 101
Salem 41, 49, 103
Salisbury 104
Salvation Army 46
Samuel 68
San Antonio 23, 84, 92
Sanders 44, 104
Sanderson 42
Sandifer 108
Sanford 47
Santa Anna 86
Sappington 81
SAR 11, 12, 63, 94, 102
Savannah 23, 26, 27, 52, 63, 65
Saye 88
Saylors Creek 64
Scales 30, 44
Scarborough 107
Scarce 101
Schooling 83
Schreck 108
Schweppe 88
Scimitar Shrine Temple 12
Scotland 106
Scott 57, 61, 62, 79, 104
Scottish Rite 11, 12, 106
Scroggins 101
Scruggs 81
Seabolt 101
Seagoville 22, 109
Seale 84, 85
Searcy 76
Sechrist 45
Sedalia 80
Selma 62, 100, 101
Semmes 13
Senter 18, 27
Sessions 101
Sessoms 103
Sewell 5, 87
Sexton 101
Seymour 91

Shannon 88, 89
Sharp 72, 105
Shaver 12, 76, 77
Shaver Camp 77
Shaw 9, 73, 105
Shaw-Battle Chapter 73
Sheckell 105
Shelby 12, 16, 68, 80, 106
Shenandoah 47, 75
Shepherd 74, 107
Sherman 52
Shipler 61
Shipman 43
Shipp 60
Short 108
Shoup 69, 70, 71
Shreve 22, 64, 65, 78, 79, 99, 109
Shreve-Rountree 64, 65
Shreveport 22, 78, 79, 99, 109
Siegner 44
Siler City 41
Simmons 24
Simms 68
Simpson 86, 88, 89, 103
Sims 73
Sinclair 11, 101
Singleton 15, 76
Skinner 37, 88
Siaton 76
Slep 23
Sloan 43, 103, 104
Smith 8, 9, 14, 18, 23, 28, 30, 40,
  42, 44, 49, 50, 54, 58, 61,
  64, 66, 68, 78, 82, 83, 84,
  86, 89, 101
Smith's Bend 86
Smyrna 101
Snead 63
Sneed 17, 100
Snow 106
Snyder 44, 73
Society of Colonial Wars 15
Society of the Cincinnati 15
Society of the Order of the Southern
  Cross 14
Society of the Sons and Daughters
  of the Founders 15
Society of the War of 1812 15
Sohrwide 8, 9, 75, 82, 84
Sons of Confederate Veterans 16,
  21, 26, 27, 29, 37, 38, 39,
  40, 41, 43, 45, 46, 47, 48,
  49, 50, 55, 58, 59, 61, 62,
  63, 65, 69, 70, 71, 74, 75,
  76, 77, 81, 86, 87, 89, 91
Sons of the American Revolution 11,
  15
Sons of Union Veterans 40
South Carolina Society 36, 50, 51, 52
South Mountain 104
Southampton Historical Society 11
Southaven 16, 27
Southaven High School 16
Southern Baptist Church 106
Southern Cross of Military Service 21
Southern Historical Collection 48
Spangler 103
Spanish/American War 86
Spooner 64
Sprigg 78
Spring Hope 49
Springfield 68, 80
Springwood Cemetery 54
Squires 23
St. Augustine 26, 40, 63, 64, 65, 101
St. Clair 78, 79, 82
St. James City 101
St. Johns County 64
St. Louis 23, 24, 26, 28, 75, 80, 100
St. Petersburg 63
Stacy 46
Staford 101
Stanford 103

Stanton 73
State Capitol Foundation 48
Statesville 101
Statuary Hall 55
Staunton 23
Stephens 24, 55, 65, 66, 100
Stepp 41, 44
Stevens 64, 65, 80
Stewart 22, 63, 72, 83, 109
Stillwater 75
Stillwell 68
Stinson 54
Stober 37, 39
Stockton 80, 81
Stone 101
Stone Mountain 66
Stonewall 44, 49, 56
Stoney Creek Battery 52
Stowe 43
Strange 59
Stratford 23
Strickland 46
Strohl 21
Stroud 76
Strybos 85
Stuart 30, 50, 55, 57
Stuart Mosby Society 11, 55
Stubbs 86
Suffolk 58, 106
Sul Ross Chapter 92
Sullivan 49, 108
Summers 43
Sumter 51, 52, 101
Surratt 37
Sutcliffe 43
Sutherlin 74, 78
Swank 107

T

T.J. Fakes Award 30
Tabor 23
Tallahassee 40
Tallow Hill 102
Tampa 23, 24, 98
Tankersley 91
Tar Heel Junior Historians 44
Tarltons Command 74
Tarrant 101
Tate 85
Tatum 88, 101
Taylor 23, 30, 40, 41, 61, 69, 107
Tebo 88, 89
Templin 87
Tennehill State Park 61
Tennessee Society 16, 72
Tew 41
Texas 67, 84, 87, 88, 89, 90, 91
Texas Rangers 22
Texas Revolutionary Army 86
Thigpen 52
Thomas 39, 51, 89, 100
Thomas C. Hindman Award 12
Thomas Jonathan Jackson-Patrick
  Ronayne Cleburne C 62
Thomaston 66
Thompson 45, 58, 80, 106
Thomson 74
Thorn 79
Thorpe 77
Thrasher's Brig 68
Thurman 58
Tidball 105
Tilghman 24
Tillman 101
Timrod 33
Tippens 74
Toal 87, 108
Todd 18, 27, 91, 92
Tofflemeyer 78
Tomotley Battery 52
Topeka 106
Trans-Mississippi 12, 14, 15, 17, 30,
  34, 36, 74, 75, 78

Printed in the USA
CPSIA information can be obtained
at www.ICGtesting.com
JSHW082351140824
68134JS00020B/2015

9 781596 520332